The Holy Bible is Provably and Verifiably Divinely Inspired

Introduction   *Page 5*

Chapter 1 My Brief Testimony   Page 8

Chapter 2 The Holy Bible is VERIFIABLY Divinely Inspired Page 43

Chapter 3 The Holy Bible is Provably Divinely Inspired   Page 65

Divine Prophecies that Accurately come to pass throughout history to this day are one of those most obvious proofs that the contents of the Holy Bible come to us from the One True God.

The contents of the Holy Bible not only correspond to the most important facts of history; telling us the future accurately before it even happens, but to observable reality, even the stars above. This is another proof of Divine Inspiration in that the Divine Prophecies have been accurate about past, present and future history AND past, present and future REALITY. God Almighty declaring Himself to us not just with His Words, but with His Creation.

Supernatural Miracles that correspond to the God of the Holy Bible, Jesus Christ, are also proof of the Divine Inspiration of the Holy Bible, because the same God who declares Himself therein has been performing miracles throughout history to this very day. Page 87

Common Questions   Page 184

The Contents of the Holy Bible Explains the Why Things Are Made the Way They Are   Page 192

God is Ruling the Nations According to His Words   Page 219

The Holy Bible is the Most Thoroughly Researched Book on Earth   Page 274

It Contains Well Verified Facts of History from Genesis to Revelation

Introduction

The title of this book means that the contents of the Holy Bible are provably and verifiably from our Eternal Creator, Lord and Savior, JESUS, the Christ, the One True God.

The Holy Bible is unlike any other book in all the world. When I make a statement like that, I'm not saying the same God that spoke to the Prophets who came in the flesh before us living on earth today, is no longer speaking to mankind. Instead, I am saying that the One True God, Jesus Christ, has laid the literary foundation of Truth, such that if anyone has a contrary opinion to that of God Almighty's declared Words of Truth in the Holy Bible, it should be dismissed as an errant opinion.

There are many stones upon the earth but when we examine them closely, we can tell how the stones differ and we even value certain stones above others based on our findings. Likewise, there are many books in this world, but let me explain how we know the Holy Bible comes from the One True God, like no other book in all the world. I am not saying that God hasn't inspired other books, I'm only saying that any other Divinely Inspired Books in all the world stand upon the Literary Foundation of Truth Laid by God Almighty Himself and made known worldwide, the contents of the Holy Bible. If any book contradicts the Foundation of Truth given us by God in the Holy Bible, then it fails and should be ignored as a lie or deception.

The unique aspects of the Holy Bible that prove Divine Inspiration means that those contents are more important than all other opinions spoken or written from anyone, past, present and future; especially if those opinions are contrary to the Words of God Almighty, our Eternal Creator, who does not lie and who is Truth itself.

The Holy Bible is written as recorded facts of history, the most important facts of history; how God Almighty Created the Heavens and earth, spoke with mankind throughout our generations and came in the flesh and showed Himself to us, declaring Himself plainly to us. When Jesus Christ came into this world He Created and Made, He but spoke and changed reality instantly just by doing so: healing all manner of ailments, stopping storms, transforming water into wine, feeding thousands, raising the dead and as the last proof of His Divinity and claim of Eternal Life, He publicly died and then raised His Body from the Grave, transfigured it; making it Immortal and Glorious and then Ascended back into Heaven in front of eyewitnesses. Those eyewitnesses were so convinced they had seen and heard God Almighty firsthand that they began telling everyone and is how the New Testament and Christianity came into existence.

But it wasn't just their experiences of hearing and seeing God in the flesh, it was the fact He gave them His Own Holy Spirit, just as He had promised, so that God was with them empowering them to do miracles in His Name, empowering them to go on preaching the Truth even when facing torture and death. No other facts of history are sealed in the blood of those tortured to death for speaking and writing those facts down. The contents of the Holy Bible deserve to be read, studied, respected and revered due to the fact that they are indeed Divinely Inspired, containing the most important information on earth (how to KNOW and learn from the Living God, PERSONALLY) and come to us through the Holy Blood of God Almighty Himself and many of His Prophets and Disciples.

You might think there are no more eyewitnesses of Jesus Christ the One True God apart from His Chosen Apostles and those early Disciples who witnessed Him when He walked in the flesh some two thousand years ago, but there have been eyewitnesses of the Risen Lord Jesus Christ ever since, and many living on earth today; I am one of them.

Chapter 1 My Brief Testimony

That's right, you read the introduction correctly. I have seen the Risen Lord Jesus Christ personally and testify that you can also. Read John 14:20-21. To be sure He isn't residing here on earth, at least after the manner of the flesh but He is here Spiritually in all true believers. Rather He has done exactly what He said He was going to do, leaving this world to prepare a place for those who love and obey Him. (John 14:1-9) WHAT A PLACE! Heaven is so Great and Glorious that words in all languages fail to describe just how Wonderful it really is! Yes, one of the times I was Blessed to see our Lord Jesus Christ, I saw Him shining brighter than the sun and the stars in Heaven. His Power had me suspended above the ground and His Virtues blasted away any impurities in me like the Refiner's Fire purging away the dross, until He had purified me and made me holy. He dimmed Himself just so I could see His features. As His Power drew me over the grass there in Paradise, I floated until I was so close to His Radiant Face that I could look into the pupils of His Eyes and when I did so, I saw the galaxies. The Holy Bible is telling us all the Truth, Jesus Christ is LORD, the One True God.

I don't want this book to be about me and my relationship with our Eternal Creator, Lord and Savior, I just want the reader to understand that it's possible for them to know God Almighty personally (Jer 31:33,34): to see Him, to hear Him, to learn from Him here and now and forever (John 14:20-26) and since I do, I desire that EVERYONE would know Him also. Knowing our Lord and Savior, JESUS, the Christ, will not only make each individual life better, but as a result, the entire world would become more like Heaven. (everyone would benefit by knowing the One who knows everything, is Good, and doesn't lie)

Now I'm not saying that in my own case, knowing God and seeing our Risen Lord Jesus Christ the first time was something that came easy; rather, it felt like some kind of epic struggle, even a very great battle until He Graciously showed Himself to me on the morning of September 29, 1988. I believe it doesn't have to be so difficult, if you will only grasp what He is telling us in the Holy Bible and earnestly seek to know Him and in knowing Him, to love Him and in loving Him, to obey Him.

It was difficult for me, because in all my early years I can't remember anyone telling me that I could KNOW God beyond all doubt, or HOW to Know Him beyond all doubt, so I went about it all the wrong way! Running into figurative walls, trying this and that and all manner of things, searching for meaning, purpose, fulfillment and any job that paid enough to pay the bills. One failure after another and one frustration after another.

Like far too many young people I even tried drinking, drugging, "partying" only to be extremely disappointed. As a young teenager, I saw people killing themselves and calling it a "party", drinking so much they vomited and excreted all over themselves, doing so many drugs that some ended up dying in overdoses! I wish I could forget the time I walked in a room with a group of junkies; one addict was so messed up they were shaking to the point where they couldn't stick themselves with their fix and so was asking the other addicts to help, but they were all so intoxicated none of them could. Finally, the person who was shaking kept sticking themselves over and over until they found a vein and as they were pushing the plunger down blood started squirting out of one of the other holes in their arm. It was such a horrible, nightmarish sight to see that I've hated even the idea of needles and "shooting up" ever since. Talk about "scared straight!"

I don't want to tell the world all the horrific things I've seen in my lifetime, I just want people to understand that I saw and experienced enough to make me a very depressed young man. If you don't know the Good Lord, who do you turn to when overwhelmed by the evil in this world?

Our schools have done a terrible thing by removing the Holy Bible and prayer, telling innocent children they're descended from pond scum and monkeys through "evolution" (evil-u-shun). Even before the age of twenty, I had seen enough evil in this world to make me suicidally depressed. It wasn't that I hadn't seen any good, I had, it's just that the evil I had seen was overwhelming. Crushing poverty, alcoholism, drug addiction, prostitution, and so on. People so messed up that they poisoned themselves to the point of unconsciousness or even death and called that "partying".

I had been taught to believe in evolution and that religion was the "opiate of the masses" and a "crutch for the weak", that there was no God, and that people only used religion because they couldn't face reality. (our schools are doing children very great harm instead of giving them a proper education BASED ON THE WORD OF GOD IN THE HOLY BIBLE). These LIES should not be taught in our schools.

So, after seeing what this world had to offer, I really didn't want any part of it. Others may have been drinking and doing drugs because they somehow were tricked into thinking that was a good time, but after seeing people abuse themselves and hearing of others who overdosed, I thought that if this was all there was to life, here and gone, so much suffering, then I wanted to be gone. So, I found I could escape the horrors of this life temporarily through hallucinogens, like mushrooms and LSD. (NEVER DO STREET DRUGS and, in my opinion, avoid even prescriptions if at all possible. DO YOUR BEST TO STAY HEALTHY LIFELONG). The problem with drugs on the streets, is you have no way of knowing the strength, how much those substances have been cut, or even what those substances really are. Street drugs are even more dangerous than prescriptions because of that. So, you, like many who have overdosed and died, might be used to thinking a certain amount of a certain drug available on the street is your usual fix, when in fact, you might be getting some kind of dangerous substance that can kill you or a higher concentration or purity than you've ever encountered and so can easily overdose. Such was the case when I found someone who claimed to be a college chemist making their own LSD. I thought, same old story, everyone always boasting how great their stuff is compared to everyone else's, just to make sales. Anyway, I was wrong, the guy was telling the truth and I ended up in the hospital as a result. I certainly never did LSD after that. (much of the products on the street are watered downed or cut counterfeits with very little of the claimed intoxicant, even so-called trusted dealers, every now and then get a supply that isn't their usual, so when someone claims their product is pure and uncut, you should be very careful; frankly, I wish everyone would never buy drugs off the street; it's far too dangerous). My life experience has made me extremely cautious even about prescriptions.

Sadly, there isn't alot of expertise in many hospitals with how to deal with someone hallucinating, so they did something they shouldn't have and injected me with depressants to put me to sleep. Someone who is hallucinating doesn't NEED any more drugs! They need someone who will guide them through their hallucinations in a good way. Someone who realizes that all the bright lights are overactive stimuli to someone hallucinating, and so puts them in a dark room with a single candle light. And lets them focus on it dancing all while talking gently to them, making them feel loved, safe and secure. Use quiet words, make them feel comforted, and perhaps introduce chimes gently as they meditate. Talk them down, until they are feeling completely safe and the hallucinations wear off. A comfortable couch or bed, to just relax in as the candle dances for them. Use a calm soothing voice telling them they are safe and secure with nothing to be afraid of, and not too much stimuli (dark room), to bring them down from a "bad trip", telling them they are loved and accepted and feel the safety of their couch, bed and the candle dancing for them. But don't do as the hospital did and use even more drugs. When their initial injections failed, they increased the dosage and unfortunately for me, the depressants stopped my heart and I died there in the hospital. I still remember the experience because it's rather shocking when you die as someone who believes this life is all there is and instead find out you have a spirit the hard way. Yes, I died; no, it wasn't a hallucination.

I saw the monitor flat line and heard the code alarm. I saw the doctors and nurses panicking over my then dead body. I took my right finger and passed it through my left forearm; I looked like my body but was without substance. I knew my spirit had come out of my body. I knew my ghost was called a spirit because I had attended a few Sunday school classes and church meetings when I was younger. During one of those church services, I had said a repeat after me prayer, that went something like, "God? I don't know if You exist or not and Jesus? I don't know if You died to save my soul or not. I also don't know if there is a real Heaven to be gained and a real hell to be shunned but if all that is true, then Lord Jesus, make sure I go to Heaven; Save me and my loved ones."

But when I died as a teenager, I was by then someone believing in evolution and that there was no God. So, it might surprise you that my spirit went upward through the ceiling and next floor of the hospital until I ascended right through the roof. It was night, so I watched the lights of the city, state and then the world fade from view as my spirit continued to move upward through the stars and galaxies all around me. Faster and faster I went, the galaxies and stars were just streaks of light, until I ended up in a place I later read in the Holy Bible was called "outer darkness".

There in the void, God spoke to my spirit, not audibly, but Divine Thoughts entered my spiritual existence and communicated with me, "Alright (in the tone of - 'wiseguy'), if I don't exist can YOU make the sun, moon and stars? Can you make ANYTHING (even an atom or a quark by implication) from this void of nothing? from nothing but your own spirit?"

In less than a nanosecond I realized that even if I tried for all eternity, I could not create anything from nothing but my own spirit, no substance, nothing but my own vain imaginations. The One True God taught me two very important things in that moment: 1) THERE IS A VERY REAL ETERNAL CREATOR and 2) I am not Him!

When I came to that realization, I awoke back on the gurney in the hospital, the staff had succeeded in resuscitating me. You might have thought that I would have asked for a preacher and to have become a Christian, but even though God had let me know He existed, I still didn't know His Identity, He had only conveyed Divine Thoughts to me, I hadn't seen Him. In addition, because of my education, I was trying to dismiss the experience, lying to myself; telling myself it must have been all the drugs, but some things a person just can't dismiss... it happened; it really happened.

So again, without telling you every difficult detail of my life and how I came to know the One True God, I'll bring you to my next crisis.

Due to the lack of adequate paying jobs (I later found out the entire world is being handled, a form of social engineering such that reality in this world is very much of their planning as a way to control/govern the masses).

Young people are faced with the following choices by design: 1) life or death 2) live in civilization or try to survive outside of it 3) If you choose to live within civilization then these are the choices those who imagine they rule the world present to young people in general:

a) continuing education - If the general population chooses continuing education, whether it's college or a trade school, it's with the end goal of working in a profession to become a member of this civilization.

So honorable endeavors on earth is a life spent working in some form or fashion. Some volunteer, some work for money, others work for causes, but the honorable choice involves providing goods and services for others.

b) work - far too many jobs today do not pay adequate wages and are not keeping up with the cost of living. The wealthy rulers of the world have implemented methods of population management and poverty is one of their methods of controlling population growth. (the poor die sooner on average (according to statistics as much as 20 years sooner than those of means) and at least where birth control is made available choose to have less children) This will always be the case as long as greed for profits is the end goal of corporations, especially excessive greed. It's why the global distribution of wealth is so outrageous with less than 1% controlling 50% percent of the world's wealth while all the rest of us are struggling to survive. And about 80% of the world's population survives on less than 10%, with the bottom 1/3 of the population on earth living in growing poverty. There really needs to be a redistribution of wealth, where the profits are not so out of control for the wealthy. I suggest

EVERYONE has the right to be a homeowner as one of those methods of making sure everyone has enough wealth to live. And that affordable housing be made a right by law for everyone.
https://www.youtube.com/watch?v=QPKKQnijnsM and https://www.youtube.com/watch?v=uWSxzjyMNpU

c) military - another method of population management, the wealthy use to manipulate the masses to go to wars of their making. Occasionally, there is genuine infighting among the wealthy, but by and large the poor masses are being manipulated and controlled by the wealthy so called ruling elite

d) crime/imprisonment - if you are unwilling to accept their slave wages, you will be put to forced labor or die prematurely with other people who simply do not like the limited options presented them in this so-called civilization. Very few get careers that are their dream ambitions, with a fulfilling life purpose and adequate pay. According to the statistics cited above, 10-20 percent of the world are relatively well off, the rest are struggling to pay their bills, with about one third of the population struggling just to survive.

I want to say all honorable work is praiseworthy (so don't resort to crime), so you can hold your head up if you do what you can to pay your bills no matter what job you find to do to provide goods and services to others. When we serve Christ, He will guide you in your life's purpose. Remember the Apostle Paul whom we all know due to his calling and writing so much of the New Testament, was a tentmaker. Do what you can in this life and do it well as unto the Lord, knowing you are not defined by what work you do to pay your bills, but whether or not you are a witness for our Lord Jesus Christ. God is watching us always and He tells us a Book of Remembrance is written for all who serve Him. It is what we do for Him that matters most in this life.

e) beg - poverty and homelessness is not necessarily the fault of those suffering from it. Instead, as stated far too many wealthy people living in palaces have great disdain for the poor masses and leave us to fight for the few careers that pay enough to be financially solvent. Many are suffering from depression, simply because if a person is forced into servile work due to the very real lack of careers that pay respectably and keep up with the cost of living, they are paid so pitifully, that they can end up homeless or living in their cars regardless. In America and all over this world the gap between the haves and the have-nots is reaching dangerous levels. Levels that threaten to cause the collapse of law and order and civilization as a whole if it isn't corrected. The arrogance and greed of the few, is leading to widespread corruption and looming crises in which many could suffer and die, simply because too many of the poor masses become that desperate and also due to ungodliness, due to removal of the Holy Bible and prayer from our public schools.

As a young person I considered option a, without a scholarship to pay not only for education but living expenses, it meant years of indentured service to pay off loans for college or trade schools. And working while I continued my education, was daunting to say the least. Few and far between are paid apprenticeship programs. I had already been working for pitiful wages since I was very young; so, I knew I didn't want a life of servile work and slave wages. That left the military with the GI Bill so I could go to college later. Those in power know very few that enter that method of control (military and police powers) ever goes on to higher education for the career they dreamed of when they were younger.

This is another area that needs to change so that MORE PEOPLE are able to go into their desired profession. Scholarships SHOULD BE AVAIBLE TO EVERYONE WHO SHOWS APTITUDE AND ATTITUDE, with only a minimal amount of investment on behalf of those students as long as their grades show they are learning and becoming skillful, instead of going into debt with their lives, sometimes the student loans take many years to pay off! YES, the one percent, need to fund the world! rather than just get richer! (Money is made out of thin air, so mankind needs to decide on investing in each subsequent generation to make the world a better place!)

The military uses overt brainwashing tactics on recruits; I know I went through both the Army and the Navy Basic Training. My problem was that I easily recognized these institutions were using overt brainwashing tactics and that made me distrustful. Even though I wanted to do well, get promoted, I fundamentally could not blindly obey men, who in my own opinion were someone nobody should listen to. Yes, there were great men who had seen combat and who actually cared about recruits to train them seriously about matters of life and death, but there were others that were little more than sadists who pleased themselves by abusing others. My personality was one that just didn't fit with obeying orders from such persons. On the one hand, I could wish all superior officers deserved their rank but on the other knew that wasn't the case at all. Hopefully, your superior officers are people you can respect and follow orders from.

Other matters, such as a personal relationship gone bad, factored into why I was court-martialed, not just my inability to follow orders from certain individuals. Anyway, somehow instead of just dismissing people, the military tries to crush those who aren't a good fit with harmful discharges.

Regan had just come out with the zero tolerance for drugs in the military, and my failed relationship meant that I tried to cope with it any way I knew how. I popped a urine test for THC and that was enough. I hadn't committed any crimes that would have sent me to prison in civilian life, but in the military violations of the UCMJ can put you in the military brig for years even if you didn't commit any kind of serious crime by civilian standards. Regardless, I was being told I was looking at a few years in Leavenworth as a young man. So there in the brig I prayed to the Biblical God, asking Him to deliver me, because going to military prison not only seemed excessive to me, but even life threatening. My life experiences had taught me that more than likely there was a very real God and more than likely He was the God of the Holy Bible, but I still didn't KNOW Him. So, I prayed to Him and asked Him to have mercy on me and not send me to Leavenworth. I also prayed that He would do whatever was necessary for me to go to Heaven and never let me go to hell, even if it meant "whopping me upside my head."

On the day I went to court, it was record rainfall in the state of Illinois; 23 inches of rain fell in a 24-hour period. It was the judge's last case of his career. I had both a JAG and a civilian attorney representing me, but the judge asked them to sit down saying he only wanted to hear from me. He told me he had reviewed my military years of service, including meritorious promotions, nominations to both West Point and Annapolis Military Academies and just wanted to know what had happened in my own words. I don't remember exactly what I said, I just remember what he said afterward. He said that the military wasn't right for me and so he had to give me a discharge that would ensure I wouldn't be allowed to continue in it or to ever even be drafted into it, because "God had something else for me." And when He said those words and brought the gavel down, I saw the clouds in the sky above part in a small circle such that the sunlight that beamed through them formed a spotlight from heaven above that shone right through the window right onto the judge in that moment when he sentenced me essentially to time served. Despite my promotions, commendations and nominations, he also gave me a Bad Conduct Discharge, but I believed it was answer to prayer and that God did indeed have something else for me to do in life. I'm grateful to all the brave men and women who have served and are still serving in our armed forces, as long as we the American people stay true to our Eternal Creator and fight for the liberty established in our US Constitution, our American Christian heritage will keep us all free, because Jesus Christ is the Truth that sets and keeps us all free. I am very thankful for all who serve honorably and very ashamed that I wasn't one of those persons.

I watched a television program recently, in which one of the actors was comforting a child, by saying if he had been paid a dollar for all the mistakes he had made in his life, he'd be a rich man; as his way of telling the child we all make mistakes, just try to learn from them. I could only smile, thinking I'd have been a whole lot richer! :)

Thank the Good Lord, I had a grandmother that had been praying for her children and grandchildren for many years as a faithful Christian. She was good enough to help me get back on my feet after my discharge from the military. I never witnessed anyone who prayed as earnestly as she did virtually every day. She belonged to a "prayer chain" where people got on a conference call and prayed for each other, their families, anything that came to mind regularly. Sometimes she was on her knees for hours! praying humbly non-stop. Even as a young man, I didn't have that kind of stamina! I miss her so much! (she's gone on to Heaven).

She took me with her to church, and I almost wanted to say something to her, but I just couldn't. I couldn't understand how such a godly woman could endure such godless sermons. The preacher didn't even read out of the Holy Bible, but instead lectured about modern psychology. I don't know maybe he might have read a verse or two in the services I attended with my grandmother, but I personally was getting nothing from his sermons. Instead of looking forward to going to church, I found myself wondering if I could endure going. Instead of feeling some kind of joy, it felt like a trial of patience to sit through what seemed to me to be a complete lack of righteous preaching. I much rather preferred listening to my grandmother make simple, meaningful statements like, "God doesn't make junk!" referring even to sinners and unbelievers (that to her everyone should be loved and appreciated and that there's hope for all souls).

    So, I STILL didn't KNOW God, instead I was being inoculated against religion. Even my ever-praying grandmother, hadn't told me I could KNOW God, she had just been a godly good example in righteous living to me. Perhaps she had told me over the early years of my life, but maybe the devil snatched those words and memories away. I really can't remember anyone, not a preacher, not a friend, not a relative, not even a door knocker, who ever said it was possible to KNOW GOD PERSONALLY and learn from Him personally.   So, after I came to know Him, that's been my focus. It's one thing to believe in God, it's another to KNOW Him.

I want to mention one other thing about that church and my grandmother. One day the pastor asked for volunteers from the congregation to go visit one of the parishioners who had had a stroke and let him know that we cared and were praying for him. I looked around and didn't see anyone jumping at the opportunity and thought to myself that it was something I could do so I volunteered. I was not prepared for walking through hospice at all. As a little boy I had visited my great grandmother but when I had done so everyone was in their own rooms, doors shut, very quiet. My parents introduced me to her, and she smiled at me and seemed so loving and good and gave me some coins out of a can she had been saving them in and told me to go get some candy or something sweet that I would like. I was too little to realize she was dying, but years later I realized she gave me what she had, her love and a few coins; so, I remember her fondly.

But walking into this hospice in a much bigger city was very different. The elderly were in wheel chairs in the huge hallways and as I walked by, they were looking as if they were longing for a son, a daughter, a grandchild, a friend, ANYONE who would spend some time with them in their dying moments, to say they care, to let them know they'll be missed until we're all together with them in Heaven. What I thought I could do; I found I could not do at all. We cannot give what we do not have and I didn't have the love, the words, the strength to be around the dying to comfort them. I felt as if the life force was being sucked right out of me with every step. When I walked through the door of the man I was supposed to visit and tried to explain to him why I was there, all he could say over and over in barely intelligible words was, "I don' understan', I don' understan' I don' un'erstan'". Stroke affects everyone differently; it could have been he really didn't understand or it could have been that was all he could say. I needed to have EXPERIENCE when I talked with him but I just didn't. When I got back in my car, the tears came long and strong, it was so sad to see all those lonely souls dying, wishing any of their friends and family were there to comfort them, wishing ANYONE was there to spend some moments of their final moments with them.

I just didn't realize that I NEEDED GOD's LOVE to have that kind of LOVE to give to others! LOVE THAT NEVER RUNS DRY!

It was one of the reasons, that I think "Wisdom of the Elders" should be part of educational settings, where secondary students can go during a semester and speak with people who are dying and ask them what's the most important things they learned in life, what would they like to see continue, what do they hope for the future, and so on with important questions. Put their answers in a searchable database, for anyone who is interested.

Sometimes, they can't speak, sometimes they just need to know someone cares, says hello, maybe reads them the Words of Jesus Christ from the Holy Bible. Maybe it should be on a collegiate level but I thought young people might find direction for their own life by speaking with elders, so I think it should be sophomores, juniors or seniors in high school. And not a field trip, send them in 2 to 3 at a time for each interview. Maybe make it a semester where they give the questions in the first interview and let the elders think about their responses and come back week after week until the semester ends or until the elder goes on to be with the Lord. Important questions that deserve well thought out answers.

It's the many things in this life that are greater a task, greater a trial, greater a test than we can endure on our own, that's the reason EVERYONE NEEDS THE ONE TRUE AND VERY REAL GOOD LORD to be with them THROUGH IT ALL!   (Andrae Crouch - https://www.youtube.com/watch?v=Cvlxwc90BEI "Through It All" great song from an even greater testimony!)

But for someone like myself failing over and over and over again, only to see people dying all alone, feeling unloved, was just another reason that this life just didn't seem anything I really wanted. I came to a point where I had moved out of my grandmother's apartment, I was on my own, working another job, when I had an apartment fire and a couple car fires, lost my job and was once again, wondering WHY was I trying so hard?! to what end? for what purpose? I thought to myself what if I could actually have everything I thought I wanted, a loving wife and children, a prosperous, respected career, home with a happy family, no more failures, no more hardship, everything good. Even then it all seemed empty and meaningless to me if we were just here a matter of decades and then existed no more. When I tried my HARDEST to THINK, REALLY THINK, if I could have all my dreams no matter how realistically impossible they seemed, if I could be happy, here and gone, I not only considered it foolish to go on dreaming when all my dreams had only been crushed over and over with the harsh reality of this world, but I thought even if I actually achieved them, it was all meaningless if we're only vapors in the wind of time, here and gone, soon forgotten. I had been suicidal because most of my life all I wanted was to make friends and found it nearly impossible for me to do and whereas I tended to think other people were so gifted and talented, that I felt it would be an honor to be their friend, it just seemed other people didn't feel that way towards me. (I suppose who wants to befriend someone who seems to make so many mistakes just trying to learn, is what I thought all my younger years.) Anyway, I came to the conclusion, no one would really miss me if I was gone and frankly after so many jobs including two branches of the service, just didn't think I was right for the world or the world was right for me. So, at the point of being homeless, I just wanted to die, I really had had enough of never having any success in life and thought even if I did, by some miracle, that it wouldn't make any real difference if this life was really all there was.

    Back in the military when the sunlight had shown through the dark clouds that day of my court martial, I had prayed, "God, I believe You exist, so make sure I go to Heaven; never let me go to hell; but if I'm about to go, do whatever it takes to get my attention; even if it means whoppin' me upside my head." (I learned to never pray the "but ifs" instead just place yourself in His Hands and ask Him to hold onto you forever! never let you and your loved ones go!)

    But there I was in the not-too-distant future, thinking my life had been so miserable that I just wanted it to be over and thinking that even if heaven and hell were real, I didn't want to go to either one. I just couldn't even imagine a place of endless good times because this world is so far from that. (it's not that I had never experienced really happy, meaningful moments with friends and family, it's just that to me if those life experiences are only fleeting and far too few, then life just didn't seem worth living; when so much of it was full of suffering) I suppose I was so overwhelmed with adversity, failings, and the evil in this world that any good to me seemed insignificant, if not unattainable by my own best efforts. So, my mind was focused on just dying, feeling crushed and stepped on over and over and over again, rejected, unrecognized, unappreciated to the point of feeling unloved, even hated. In my mind good people like the folks who adopted me, even my adoptive grandmother, were only loving and kind to me out of a sense of duty or obligation; not because they really valued me. I couldn't blame them, after all my many mistakes and failures, I found it extremely difficult to value myself. So, part of me thought I would just be doing everyone a favor by leaving in a permanent way.

    Part of the reason I couldn't perceive Love in others, and couldn't really give it in return was because I didn't KNOW GOD! God is LOVE and when He is in your life, you finally have LOVE to give! Sure, it means you hurt, when others are critical, but you GO ON LOVING THEM, because LOVE (GOD) is the answer!

    But right then I was just crushed, no love, no happiness, just misery.

So, I remembered ways I had seen people die, and at least from this side of things, those who had overdosed on depressants like heroin seemed as if they just painlessly went to sleep, while virtually all other methods I could think of involved pain of some kind prior to death. Sedation unto the long and final rest just seemed by far the most preferable method, but I was broke and couldn't even afford to put myself down like an unwanted dog. So not wanting to hurt anyone, I'm ashamed to admit I committed armed robbery for which I am very sorry and apologetic to all persons involved. Just the act of having a weapon pointed at you, whether or not it's loaded, is a traumatizing event and why that's a serious felony offense by law. I didn't get enough money for which I had risked lives for, but the crime had been committed and the police had been alerted. Yes, I have made really bad decisions before I met the Lord and I apologize and accept responsibility for them all. Asking people to forgive me, if I ever offended them in anyway. I try my hardest to live a righteous life, based on loving everyone now, since Jesus Christ saved me.

The police department posted vehicles at all major intersections and shined their spotlights into passing vehicles until they spotted me, and soon I was surrounded by police officers with weapons drawn telling me to get out of my car with hands up. It all just seemed like distant echoes because in my mind this was the moment of my death. I reached over and grabbed my single-shot shot gun that had a round of bird shot in it, but aimed directly into my brain it would have done as intended. I placed the end of the shotgun under my chin aimed up into my head and the thought went to my thumb to pull the trigger. A loud noise like an explosion rang out, and an extremely bright flash of light, such that for a moment I thought I had shot myself but then thought if I had, I wouldn't be thinking. I felt blood running down the side of my head and the nerves in my neck felt like shards of glass cutting me. Then I became angry because I realized one of the cops had shot me and I was still alive. I was angry I was still alive, not that I had been shot in the head, but that he had interfered such that I couldn't even kill myself! I was a failure at that too! I was furious, but was stunned and in a state of shock, such that I couldn't move even though I tried to finish what I had started. Within seconds it seemed the cops had broken the window and dragged me out onto the asphalt where they were discussing taking me into the desert to finish me off and dispose of my body. I was just bummed and angry, that I was still alive. Anyway, while they were discussing what to do with me, paramedics arrived and so they were forced to let me live and I was taken to the hospital where the bullet that had embedded itself and crushed part of my skull was removed.

It was there that I met a specialist who thought I had a genetic trait called Wilson's Disease and who told me to remember I had to reject O negative blood, because I had antibodies to the negative Rh factor and it could kill me. She said that it was extremely important to remember to tell any future medical practitioners not to administer O negative blood, not only because it could kill me, but also if I survived, I could die in one of the slowest most painful ways known to man. (That leads to an entirely different part of my testimony many years later, but I just want to reveal this part to get people to understand how I came to know God Almighty personally.)

So, at the moment I was going to put bird shot in my brain forcefully, was the moment a cop shot me in the side of the head and prevented it at the very instant I would have died. Now some people might imagine they would have become a believer for sure after that, but me, I was just very sad and very angry I was still alive; especially when they told me I was looking at 25 years in prison. (poor people typically do much more time in prison than those who have means to procure legal defense). I hadn't shot anyone, I hadn't even physically touched anyone, the only person who was seriously injured was me! I knew the crimes were serious, but I knew even murderers didn't have such sentences as they were trying to put on me, with perhaps the exception of serial killers or ones that had more than one serious felony in addition to homicide. Anyway, being told in my early twenties that people were trying to lock me up for life, just made me all the more depressed and suicidal, but I was thinking about what had happened. What are the chances that at the exact moment I was going to kill myself, I was spared in the only way possible at the time? and furthermore that part of my earlier prayer about "...never let me go to hell... even if it means whoppin' me upside my head..." kept coming back in my thoughts every day I was in recovery. I was surrounded by the police with drawn weapons and could have been shot anywhere, but I was shot in the side of my head at the moment I would have died if I hadn't been.

So, on the morning of September 29, 1988, I was prostrate on the floor of my jail cell weeping and praying, asking God, if there really was a God, to have mercy upon me. He knew the way He had made me that I just couldn't serve something or someone I only believed in and that I was very sorry, because if the things that had happened to me had happened to others, they probably would have been serving Him long ago. BUT FOR ME, if He was there, He could hear me praying and knew that the way He had made me was that I had to KNOW! I had to be CERTAIN! I couldn't worship or serve anyone or anything I only BELIEVED in; I HAD TO KNOW! So prostrate and weeping, I prayed, "God, You know, that if You remove all doubt from me, I will serve You now and forever." Now God isn't looking for everlasting servants, but I had approached Him as He tells us to in the Holy Bible without even knowing I was doing so.

I was SEEKING TO KNOW HIM! God looks upon mankind for such souls! (I didn't know that until I read it in the Holy Bible after He revealed Himself to me that wonderful morning - Psalm 14:2) Plus I was truly as humble as one can get, prostrate before Him. (Psalm 51:17; 147:3; Isaiah 66:2)

So, on the morning of September 29, 1988, I heard the Voice of God interrupt my silent prayers and thoughts and tell me, "My son, get up off the floor and look out the window." Some might ask, "How did you know it was the Voice of God?" God answered me when I was at my lowest and I have read and listened to many testimonies from other people who said the exact same thing. Perhaps it's only when we're at our lowest that some of us hard heads, hard hearts and troubled souls finally have the sense to EARNESTLY seek Him. Just as I had tried to rationalize my NDE as a teenager and my experience of outer darkness, part of me was thinking I had gone nuts, but His Voice, the Voice of His Holy Spirit, was so Loving, so Gentle, so Masculine, so Wonderful that it was compelling; so, I got up off the floor and looked out the window. There outside the window floating about 40 feet above the ground below, I saw a ball of light. As I was thinking that there was probably some kind of scientific explanation, the Voice of God told me to continue to watch and as I did, the sphere of light expanded to about 12 feet in diameter and our Lord Jesus Christ appeared within the sphere as if He was standing in a Realm of Light and inserting Himself into this dark world.

The next moment I found myself back on the floor worshipping Him, every cell in my body knew I was in the presence of the One True God who had just removed all doubt from me. I wasn't expecting God to speak to me, I certainly wasn't expecting Him to show Himself to me, I was just praying that if He would remove all doubt, I would serve Him now and forever. He did so. (I later realized we can't do anything, even with our best intentions unless God Himself gives us life, breath, every good thing, so we all NEED Him whether or not we understand that Truth.)

Anyway, in that moment I was upset that my entire education was mostly a waste and had taught me lies in the name of science and to deny our Eternal Creator. But I was also REJOICING! GOD IS REAL! HE LET ME KNOW HIM! He even called me one of His sons! So, a mixture of emotions and thoughts were running through me. LIES IN OUR SCHOOLS! Except for reading, writing and arithmetic, much of history and science I had been taught was nonsense. Leaving out the mention of God from history, means that the most important facts of history are omitted in our schools or worse that history has been rewritten. Likewise, leaving out the Truth of our Eternal Creator, from science, means that errant beliefs are being wrongly taught in the name of science. (brainwashing with the lies of evolution and cultic beliefs about how our universe came to be) **The Holy Bible is telling us all the truth, any opinions, scientific or otherwise, contrary to the plain language of its contents are wrong.**

So, God, Jesus Christ, showed Himself to me over 35 years ago, and He revealed Himself to me thereafter as well. We get to know God better; the same way we get to know anyone better - by spending time together. I know God personally and you can too. You don't have to go through what I went through, you just have to obey His Commandment to Repent of thinking you know better than Him (be willing to listen to Him and obey Him) and of every evil thought, word, way and deed (be willing to live righteously by His Grace and Power) and Get Baptized in His Name (Matt 28:18-20; Acts 2:38,39; 4:12) and pray to receive His Holy Spirit of Truth (Luke 11:13; John 14:20-26; 16:13)

For my part I could wish and hope that knowing Him makes us instantly perfect, but instead He is crafting us, molding and making us, transforming us, perfecting us as a Divine Process; so just because I know God didn't mean I ceased making mistakes or was instantly some kind of saint, but it did mean I was telling people ever since that we all need to know God personally for our own good and the good of His Creation.

I spent the rest of my incarceration studying the Holy Bible, learning to apply the Divine Commandments therein, and learning from the Holy Spirit of our Lord Jesus Christ in dreams and visions or by following His leading. God created our mouths; He most definitely speaks to all who have ears to hear. Get quiet in your prayers and ask Him to open your spiritual ears to Hear the Voice of His Holy Spirit speaking to you.

So, I have been studying for decades now, learning what we all should be taught in our public schools how that not only is the Holy Bible accurate and true, historically and scientifically, but that it is provably and verifiably Divinely Inspired, the literary foundation of all Truth given us by our Eternal Creator, Lord and Savior, JESUS, the Christ. Simply put, there is nothing more important to know than the One True God and His Words in the Holy Bible; not just the quality of our present existence, but our everlasting destiny depends on our relationship with Him, knowing Truth and Living Righteously.

EVERYONE should be studying the Words of the One True God, Jesus Christ, in the Holy Bible lifelong. He ABSOLUTELY made the Way for us to KNOW HIM! He tells us to Repent and Be Baptized in His Name, and He will give you His Holy Spirit! So, the scriptures are VERIFIABLY TRUE, anyone and everyone SHOULD OBEY GOD!

Matthew 28:18-20

English Standard Version

[18] And Jesus came and said to them, "All authority in heaven and on earth has been given to me. [19] Go therefore and make disciples of all nations, baptizing them in[a] the name of the Father and of the Son and of the Holy Spirit, [20] teaching them to observe all that I have commanded you. And behold, I am with you always, to the end of the age."

Mark 16:15-16

English Standard Version

[15] And he said to them, "Go into all the world and proclaim the gospel to the whole creation. [16] Whoever believes and

is baptized will be saved, but whoever does not believe will be condemned.

Acts 2:38-39

English Standard Version

38 And Peter said to them, "Repent and be baptized every one of you in the name of Jesus Christ for the forgiveness of your sins, and you will receive the gift of the Holy Spirit. **39** For the promise is for you and for your children and for all who are far off, everyone whom the Lord our God calls to himself."

John 14:20-26

English Standard Version

20 In that day you will know that I am in my Father, and you in me, and I in you. **21** Whoever has my commandments and keeps them, he it is who loves me. And he who loves me will be loved by my Father, and I will love him and manifest myself to him." **22** Judas (not Iscariot) said to him, "Lord, how is it that you will manifest yourself to us, and not to the world?" **23** Jesus answered him, "If anyone loves me, he will keep my word, and my Father will love him, and we will come to him and make our home with him. **24** Whoever does not love me does not keep my words. And the word that you hear is not mine but the Father's who sent me.

²⁵ "These things I have spoken to you while I am still with you. ²⁶ But the Helper, the Holy Spirit, whom the Father will send in my name, he will teach you all things and bring to your remembrance all that I have said to you.

Notice that the Lord Jesus Christ PROMISES to reveal Himself to those who love and obey Him! (verse 21) and that He promises His Holy Spirit will teach us all things! (verse 26) So YOU MUST REPENT AND BE BAPTIZED IN HIS NAME TO RECEIVE THE GIFT OF HIS HOLY SPIRIT! Acts 2:38-39

It why I teach that the Holy Bible is VERIFIABLY TRUE! He has given me His Holy Spirit and He lets me know that I will be learning from Him forever! Jesus Christ DID reveal Himself to me and is continuing in the Revelation the more I get to know Him! I want everyone to know the One True God; He Really is SO AWESOME! By far the greatest thing that has ever happened to me!

I have learned very important things while walking with the Almighty, things I am "sounding the trumpet" about; so, I encourage you to read my other books in addition to this one.

Chapter 2 The Holy Bible is VERIFIABLY Divinely Inspired

Some might wonder why I led off with a brief synopsis of how I came to know our Eternal Creator personally and it's due to the fact that rather than write a long book that fewer people might read, I'm trying to get to the most important facts as concisely as possible. Too many are failing to comprehend just how important the Holy Bible really is and that they can know God Almighty beyond all doubt and MUST know Him for their own good now and forever.

Knowing our Eternal Creator, enables you to be absolutely certain about the things that matter most. He defines Himself as Truth and because He and His Words are the reason for creation, He is the Definer of what is True about it. (not any opinions from fallible people, "scientific" or otherwise.) In other words, when you know God, when you know Jesus Christ personally, you can ask the ULTIMATE AUTHORITY in all the universe about anything! So, you can verify word by word the contents of the Holy Bible with Him and is why I say those contents are VERIFIABLY Divinely Inspired, because I have verified them with Him, at least sufficiently enough to testify that the

Words of God in the Holy Bible test and try all other spoken or written opinions from anyone (including me) past, present and future. GOD DOESN'T LIE! He alone understands all things; He alone knows the meanings and intentions of His Own Words in the Holy Bible, perfectly. (no one He created and made and is walking around in flesh and bone does, so more often than not, those disdaining Holy Writ, simply are failing to understand what is written therein correctly.)

     Since we know only God Almighty perfectly understands all things, including the contents of the Holy Bible, we all NEED to be learning from Him personally!

     I've encountered people calling Jesus Christ a false prophet, because they're misinterpreting His Prophecies, and likewise, I've experienced being misunderstood even by other Brothers and Sisters in Christ.

     For example, I can remember that part of my own calling and training by God was when He had taught me that dreams and visions have three sources: Firstly, God Himself, through His Holy Spirit of Truth and so those dreams and visions are absolutely true and stand upon His Words in the Holy Bible. Secondly, the lying devil, by his spirit of err. The deceptions from the devil might be obvious to someone else, but not so obvious to you; sometimes lies are very easy to discern, other times not so easy. The most devious deceptions are ones that include partial truth, just look at how the devil twisted the Words of God when he deceived Eve in the Holy Bible. Thirdly, our own imaginations. After He had taught me how to discern which is which, I then was given what seemed like years of them in order to see if I could apply correctly what our Lord had taught me.

As stated, some lies and deceptions are very easy to discern. If you have a dream or vision enticing you to any kind of evil, break any Divine Commandments, well then immediately you can dismiss it as from the devil, but again not all of his deceptions are so simple to recognize or everyone would already know the One True God, Jesus Christ.

If you can control the imagery in the dream or vision, that is definitely coming from your own imagination. Anything evil or deceptive, enticing you to do evil in any way is of the devil. And anything that is true, enticing you to love and serve God, is a revelation that is built upon the Foundation of TRUTH laid for us in the Holy Bible, is from God. Sometimes, you might not know if something lines up with the scriptures or not, or is a truthful revelation, because you don't know enough yet, those are the ones you have to pray to God to interpret for you or if He will interpret them for you. Like Daniel prayed for interpretation, we all are still learning from God.

Most dreams or visions that come from God have some kind of Biblical support, but not all, sometimes God is teaching you about your own personal calling, or details about this life that are not necessarily clearly foretold in the scriptures. So, you have to pray and ask God for confirmation about the more difficult ones.

I was sharing this part of my training with a Brother and Sister in Christ and gave an example about one dream I had that seemed very important and seemed as if it had come from our Eternal Creator (the Light EXPOSES the darkness) and so in this particular dream, I was shown the earth opening up and flames of fire and smoke belched out, with demons and devils flying up out of the abyss into this world, and I saw the devil, the antichrist, abaddon, apollyon, the destroyer rising up on a jagged, rocky, spire in the center of what seemed like hell itself opened up to let the foul and unclean spirits there loose into this world. I heard powerful words saying that the antichrist will stand in the midst of hell opened up in the land of jorghal. It sounded like jor-gall (I have difficulty even spelling out the phonetic pronunciation of the word, similar to Jordan, only Jor-ghal). As I was hearing the words, I saw a cover of

Time magazine with the date of July 1996 and I saw a picture of a wealthy man wearing a turban in the upper right corner with a long first name and the letter "Al" and an even longer last name. When I saw the name, I got the impression that was not how he is called in this life, but that his name in the dream meant something, just like his other names and titles in the scriptures. (abaddon, apollyon, satan, deceiver, destroyer, antichrist, evil one, devil, etc.) I had this dream long before islam began to invade the west in recent history or personally ever seeing or reading islamic names.

Now do you understand how easy it is to misinterpret dreams and visions? I thought that God was using a visual aide to tell me about when hellish things were going to begin in the Middle East and begin spreading from there into the world. I thought MAYBE there might be a real Time magazine edition, which I looked for during the Summer of 1996, but didn't have what I had seen in my dream previously on the cover. MOST ALL DREAMS OR VISIONS, not just in the Holy Bible, MEAN SOMETHING OTHER THAN THE IMAGES DESCRIBED! you have to READ THE DIVINE DEFINTIONS OF THOSE WORDS/IMAGES IN THE HOLY BIBLE TO UNDERSTAND THEM CORRECTLY! Likewise, in my own experience, seeing a Time Magazine Cover was only a way of showing me a date, and that the antichrist, is ever like those with delusions of grandeur in the past: wealthy, arrogant, wicked, selfish, greedy, full of vices, and although they may even look charismatic, they are dangerous, wicked and evil (those who demonstrate such vices, tend to be both deceptive and manipulative/controlling even murderous/genocidal) not actually that there would be such an edition in print. But even though I told my Brother and Sister in Christ, that I had prayed for confirmation and never gotten it, just sharing one of many dreams is enough to get people to imagine you're a false prophet or false teacher, when the truth is most people simply don't understand what they read or even what they're shown by God. Even Daniel is noted as needing to pray for understanding. Sometimes God answers quickly and other times the answer comes later. There are even sometimes when we have to rely only upon His Words. I have found He tests us all, and the prophets are tested and tried perhaps even more, because of their calling, their duties and responsibilities. Remember, that the devil tried to deceive even our Lord Jesus Christ, showing Him visions in Matthew Ch. 4. So yes, God teaches us by dreams and visions (Acts 2:17-18), but just because we have His Holy Spirit, doesn't mean that the devil doesn't try at times to deceive us, or that we ourselves cease to have our own imaginations. Becoming a Disciple of Christ is similar to how we learn and grow in Wisdom, Knowledge and Understanding not just according to our learning in this world but from the Holy Spirit of our Lord Jesus Christ. (Not just physical, earthly knowledge, but Spiritual.)

That particular dream while not 100 percent positive, I'm still convinced is true, but after even decades of prayer and research I also still don't understand it fully. NOTICE THAT I DID NOT SAY THIS DREAM WAS GIVEN ME BY GOD AS I HAVE NEVER RECEIVED CONFIRMATION OF THAT FACT. I looked for ancient maps to see if I could find any mention of Jorghal and to this date have never found it. It SEEMED to be in the region of ancient Edom, upper Saudi Arabia/Jordan and perhaps as far north as Syria, but not finding any ancient reference for any mention of any land or nation by that name has left me puzzled. But the reason I think of it as true is due to the events that have been unfolding on earth since the Summer of 1996; particularly with the resurgence of islamic aggression not just against Israel but into Europe and the USA, the rest of the world.

islam has always been an antichristian, demonic, devious, violent cult. Please read my book **_Save the World from islam._**

Muslims openly DENY their imaginary "allah" is the one true God every time they mention allah has no children and no partners. In addition, "allah" of the quran and islam, smacks of the same kind of sexual idolatry of ancient baalism, that God confronted so long ago. When muslims openly deny their god has no children and no partners, they are saying their god isn't the REAL GOD at all. THE REAL GOD made an entire world full of children who all belong to Him. Jesus Christ even says so in Mt 19:14. And when muslims say their god has no partners, NOT ONE MUSLIM SHOULD DO ANYTHING their imaginary allah commands or they are partnering with him by definition! When the god "allah" promised them with perpetual erections to molest virgins with that is definitely a revival of baalism. Their god is not the true god at all. Jesus Christ is the true God 1Jn 5:20, Acts 4:12. You'll need to read my book to see just how muslims universally twist the scripture and how to avoid anything islamic, it's a sure way to end up in hell fire.

My point is that just because we know God, doesn't mean we know everything instantly, there are some things He doesn't want mankind to know (like the day and hour of His Return Acts 1:7-11). But once you know God, Jesus Christ, personally, you know what is most important! And you have the ability to ask Him about anything. Sometimes He answers quickly; other times you might pray for months to years about something and seem to get no answer. When it seems as if God isn't answering us, I think are things like when our parents knew answers to our questions as young children, but refuse to tell us until they know we're older and ready for such knowledge. God has already taught me so much that I cannot convey everything I've learned in my brief incarnation, so now it's simply my duty to share what I believe is most important or that He tells me to make public.

IT IS MOST IMPORTANT FOR EVERYONE TO KNOW OUR LORD JESUS CHRIST, THE ONE TRUE GOD, PERSONALLY!!!!!!!!

His specific instruction, His Divine Commandment in that regard, is for EVERYONE to REPENT and Believe in Him and His Words in the Holy Bible. (Gospel is archaic for "God-speaks" some equate the meaning to Good News, but the Gospel of Jesus Christ even though summarized in 1Cor 15, is actually the Words of God, the contents of the Holy Bible.) When the scriptures talk of "no other Gospel" in Galatians, again, specifically nothing contrary to 1Cor 15 but generally nothing contrary to the entire contents of the Holy Bible. For example, the quran is a different gospel, one completely contrary to that of the Words of God in the Holy Bible. It specifically denies the Gospel of Jesus Christ - 1Cor 15 and much of the Divine Commandments in the Holy Bible, including the identity of the One True God, and puts an evil imposter, an imaginary wicked god in Place of our Lord Jesus Christ and as such, is false and should be rejected by everyone. The quran specifically CONTRADICTS the Commandments and Teachings of our LORD JESUS CHRIST! We demonstrate we have repented and are ready to listen to and obey God, our Lord and Savior, JESUS, the Christ, when we force our bodies to go and GET BAPTIZED IN HIS NAME! (Matthew 28:18-20; Mark 16:15-16 and Acts 2:38-39; 4:12) So if muslims really loved Jesus Christ, they would all be Christians.

WHEN WE OBEY HIM, THEN GOD KEEPS HIS PROMISE AND GIVES US HIS OWN HOLY SPIRIT OF TRUTH. (Acts 2:38-39; Luke 11:13) The Holy Spirit of our Lord Jesus Christ who is the Truth (John 14:6-9; 8:32-36) is who God is without His Visible Body, just like your spirit is who you are without yours. YES, WE ALL HAVE SPIRITS! LIFE IS MORE THAN PHYSICAL MATTER! How do we easily know that? BECAUSE PEOPLE DIE!

Some might be lost when I make that statement as to how that proves we have spirits, and life is more than just physical substance. THINK! the instant BEFORE DEATH that person has all the cells, all the organs, all the matter in their bodies that they have the instant AFTER DEATH; so obviously life is more than just our physical bodies.

In addition, studies of people who have died and been resuscitated, like myself, have given much evidence to the fact we have spirits, exactly as God tells us in the Holy Bible (Ecclesiastes 12:7 and James 2:26).

Some might STILL have difficulty understanding how life is more than our physical bodies by looking at death, so then look at birth! It isn't until the babe takes his or her first breath that we see the child is alive! (until then it has all the physical matter necessary for life but we're alive in our bodies from our first breath until our last breath; so, it's no wonder in the ancient Hebrew the word for breath and spirit is the same).

https://biblehub.com/hebrew/7307.htm - yes, there are other words for wind, breath and spirit but this is one of the most common and indicates that God Himself breathes life into our bodies, just like He Created and Made the first man in His Image, Adam:

7Then the LORD God formed man from the dust of the ground and breathed the breath of life into his nostrils, and the man became a living being. https://biblehub.com/genesis/2-7.htm

Until the moment the infant takes his or her first breath after delivery, everyone is concerned because the mother was doing the breathing for the child while he or she was still in the womb. So, from our first breath until our last God is showing us, we are more than just physical bodies, we have spirits, just as He tells us and just as so many have now testified in NDE/"Beyond and Back" studies.

In addition, God, Jesus Christ, refers to Himself as the Vine (Jn 15) and calls Eve the mother of all Living (Gen 3:20), just as genetics has confirmed that everyone living today all come from one mother in the past. Every person born is attached to their mother by the umbilical cord, so from Adam and Eve mankind is connected by that Living Vine who brought us all into existence - GOD, the God who declares Himself in His Creation and by His Words recorded in the Holy Bible.

Not one thing in all creation contradicts what God Almighty plainly tells us in the Holy Bible. All true knowledge, all actual science plainly confirms those contents. Any opinions from anyone, scientific or otherwise, contrary to what God tells us in the Holy Bible are simply wrong. (errs, lies and deceptions.) The Words of God in the Holy Bible have been right historically and scientifically throughout all the generations of mankind, even when scientists were wrong and that's still the case today (and forever). If ANYONE has an idea, a theory, a notion, an imagination contrary to what God tells us in the Holy Bible, they're mistaken, wrong, deceived and/or self-deluded.

I repeat, since God, Jesus Christ, is alive forever, He can answer your questions and you can personally verify with Him that the Words in the Holy Bible come from Him. When He gives you His Holy Spirit of Truth and speaks to you personally, then you will understand how He commanded the Prophets to speak and write His Words in the past. And why God tells us through them:

Eyewitnesses of His Majesty
...**20**Above all, you must understand that no prophecy of Scripture comes from one's own interpretation. **21**For no such prophecy was ever brought forth by the will of man, but men spoke from God as they were carried along by the Holy Spirit. https://biblehub.com/2_peter/1-21.htm

All Scripture is God-Breathed
...**15**From infancy you have known the Holy Scriptures, which are able to make you wise for salvation through faith in Christ Jesus. **16**All Scripture is God-breathed and is useful for instruction, for conviction, for correction, and for training in righteousness, **17**so that the man of God

may be complete, fully equipped for every good work....
https://biblehub.com/2_timothy/3-16.htm

And is why when God came in the flesh, He told us those scriptures are all about Him (because they come from Him):

John 5:39-40

39 You search the Scriptures because you think that in them you have eternal life; and it is they that bear witness about me, **40** yet you refuse to come to me that you may have life.

Jesus Opens the Scriptures
...**26**Was it not necessary for the Christ to suffer these things and then to enter His
glory?" **27**And beginning with Moses and all the Prophets, He explained to them what was
written in all the Scriptures about Himself. https://biblehub.com/luke/24-27.htm

Only God Almighty understands all His Words perfectly and so can fulfill them all:

The Fulfillment of the Law
16In the same way, let your light shine before men, that they may see your good deeds and glorify your Father in heaven. **17**<u>Do not think that I have come to abolish the Law or the Prophets. I have not come to abolish them, but to fulfill them.</u> **18**For I tell you truly, until heaven and earth pass away, not a single jot, not a stroke of a pen, will disappear from the Law until everything is accomplished…. https://biblehub.com/matthew/5-17.htm

And only God can keep His Words forever:

33 <u>Heaven and earth will pass away, but My words will never pass away.</u> https://biblehub.com/luke/21-33.htm

So, when the One True God said:

10<u>And the gospel must first be proclaimed to all the nations.</u> https://biblehub.com/mark/13-10.htm

And then the contents of the Holy Bible inspired the printing press with moveable type and so modern books came into existence. Afterward the Holy Bible has been translated into over 5000 languages worldwide and over five billion copies of the Holy Bible are in circulation today. The Holy Bible is the most studied and verified reference book in all the world by far. It is cited in more books and other forms of media than any other book in all the world; in my own research, I believe it's generated more books and citations than all other books on earth combined.

The Gospel of Jesus Christ is broadcast 24/7 in the most spoken languages on earth. It is even broadcast at wavelengths so that people at sea and even in submarines can receive the transmissions. God has moved on missionaries to search the globe to proclaim His Gospel and as such translators found a remote tribe that didn't even have a written language yet. One was created just for them to give them the Words of God Almighty in the Holy Bible.

So, when God told us His Words must be proclaimed to all nations and it has come to pass, people SHOULD be noticing how astonishing that is! Even where the Holy Bible is banned (some islamic nations are so evil they banned the Word of God) His Gospel is proclaimed. Enough to examine the rest of what Jesus Christ, the One True God, has been telling us for millenniums in the Holy Bible. And when one seriously examines the Words of God in the Holy Bible, what God tells us therein is truly amazing!

    The Holy Bible is VERIFIABLY Divinely Inspired because Jesus Christ ever lives to keep His Words and Promises to us and He ever lives to answer those who call upon Him. To be sure, God did not entertain the proud and arrogant when He walked in the flesh; Herod who demanded God perform some miracle for him, and nor does He respond to the proud and arrogant today. He does keep His Words and His Promises to us, provided we fulfill the conditions He has given us. We must seek Him, we must do so humbly and reverently, that in knowing Him, we will obey Him as the One True God that He is. Over 2000 years ago, God told us His Commandments and the Gospel of His Salvation would be proclaimed among all nations! And we are seeing it done today!

    I do not worship Jesus Christ, the One True God, because He is on any kind of an ego trip as some falsely accuse, I worship Him because frankly by knowing Him as He truly is, He is WORTHY! GOD! the ETERNAL CREATOR! the One who but speaks and Created the Heavens and earth! The TRUTH! The LIFE! EVERYTHING GOOD! LOVE, PEACE, JOY, ALL THE VIRTUES! No wonder those who know Him Praise Him forever! HE IS WORTHY!

God tells us no one has any excuse in the Holy Bible because He has plainly made Himself known:

God's Wrath against Sin
…**19**For what may be known about God is plain to them, because God has made it plain to them. **20**For since the creation of the world God's invisible qualities, His eternal power and divine nature, have been clearly seen, being understood from His workmanship, so that men are without excuse. **21**For although they knew God, they neither glorified Him as God nor gave thanks to Him, but they became futile in their thinking and darkened in their foolish hearts.… https://biblehub.com/romans/1-20.htm

So, anyone I encounter willfully ignoring God and His Words in the Holy Bible, I respond by ignoring them. (All such persons are dead to God, lost in their sins.)

…**22**For Moses said, 'The Lord your God will raise up for you a prophet like me from among your brothers. You must listen to Him in everything He tells you. **23** Everyone who does not listen to Him will be completely cut off from among his people.'
https://biblehub.com/acts/3-23.htm

Any and all persons REFUSING to listen to the Words of God in the Holy Bible are headed for His Wrath!

Deuteronomy 18:19
And I will hold accountable anyone who does not listen to My words that the prophet speaks in My name.
https://biblehub.com/acts/3-23.htm

...**35**The Father loves the Son and has placed all things in His
hands. **36**Whoever believes in the Son has eternal life. Whoever rejects the Son will not see life. Instead, the wrath of God remains on him." https://biblehub.com/john/3-36.htm

Matthew 25:46
And they will go away into eternal punishment, but the righteous into eternal life."

2 Thessalonians 1:8-9

[8] In flaming fire taking vengeance on them that know not God, and that obey not the gospel of our Lord Jesus Christ:

⁹ Who shall be punished with everlasting destruction from the presence of the Lord, and from the glory of his power;

NOTICE THAT THE WRATH OF GOD IS UPON THOSE WHO DO NOT KNOW HIM! DO YOU KNOW HIM? KNOW HIM!

Mourning Turned to Joy
...**33**"But this is the covenant I will make with the house of Israel after those days, declares the LORD. I will put My law in their minds and inscribe it on their hearts. And I will be their God, and they will be My people. **34**No longer will each man teach his neighbor or his brother, saying, 'Know the LORD,' because they will all know Me, from the least of them to the greatest, declares the LORD. For I will forgive their iniquities and will remember their sins no more."
https://biblehub.com/jeremiah/31-34.htm

Since none of us are guaranteed another day, I encourage everyone in the strongest terms that if you have not yet obeyed God's Commandment to Repent and Be Baptized in His Name, that you do so IMMEDIATELY! DON'T PUT IT OFF! THERE IS NOTHING MORE IMPORTANT THAN KNOWING OUR ETERNAL CREATOR, LORD AND SAVIOR, JESUS, THE CHRIST!

Heaven is real and so wonderful that words fail to describe how awesome God has made Creation for those who have the sense to love and obey Him, but also the lake of fire is very real and how awful to incur the Wrath of the Almighty! REPENT! GET BAPTIZED IN HIS NAME TODAY AND PRAY TO RECEIVE HIS HOLY SPIRIT! Keep seeking Jesus Christ, the One True God, until you know beyond all doubt that He has given you His Holy Spirit of Truth and you are learning from Him personally. Then study His Words in the Holy Bible and apply them to your existence now and forever.

Have the good sense to ask God not only to forgive you of all your sins and to save you, but to save and keep you and your loved ones forever. CALL ON OUR LORD JESUS CHRIST! Ask Him to make sure you go to Heaven and to never let you go to any of the places of the damned! Ask Him to fill you with His Holy Spirit and His Virtues; especially His Love to love Him with and to love all your Brothers and Sisters in Christ.

Remember none of us in the flesh have been perfected by Him yet, which is why He Commanded us to practice forgiving each other as often as necessary.

So again, the HOLY BIBLE is VERIFIABLY DIVINELY INSPIRED, JUST BY KNOWING JESUS CHRIST, THE ONE TRUE GOD! (it's one thing to hear about someone from others, it's another to meet them personally). So, when I say, "KNOW THE LORD!" I am saying you need to OBEY HIS INSTRUCTIONS, HIS COMMANDMENT TO REPENT AND BE BAPTIZED IN HIS NAME, SO THAT HE WILL GIVE YOU HIS OWN HOLY SPIRIT OF TRUTH AND REVEAL HIMSELF TO YOU! Mt 26:18-20, Acts2:38-39, Jn 14:20-26

Then you will understand that the Holy Bible is indeed verifiable with the Author. That Author gave us proof that the Holy Bible comes from Him; which brings me to the next chapter.

Chapter 3 The Holy Bible is Provably Divinely Inspired

Divine Prophecies that Accurately come to pass throughout history to this day are one of those most obvious proofs that the contents of the Holy Bible come to us from the One True God.

The Holy Bible is unlike any other book in all the world in that the Old Testament was written over centuries of ancient history and records our Eternal Creator, (English - JESUS, the Christ) communicating with Adam and Eve, the first man and woman and then chosen Prophets, Kings and Judges over the generations of mankind leading up to His Incarnation as the Messiah.

YES! JESUS CHRIST IS GOD/YHWH WHO WAS SPEAKING WITH US FROM THE BEGINNING!

24That is why I told you that you would die in your sins. For unless you believe that I am He, you will die in your sins." **25**"Who are You?" they asked. "Just what I have been telling you from the beginning," Jesus replied.... https://biblehub.com/john/8-25.htm

God, Jesus Christ, told the Prophets, when He would come in the flesh as the Messiah centuries before He did so. He even created and made the stars above to teach His Gospel Message, so that the wise could simply look up to the heavens above and learn from our Eternal Creator. So, He had the Prophets record His Law and Prophecies in the Old Testament and is why when He came in the flesh, He plainly stated that the Sacred Scriptures were all about Him, the One who has Eternal Life and the One everyone must come to in order to have that Life.

In other words, not just the Holy Bible but the stars above us testify that Jesus Christ is the One True God, our Eternal Creator.

Do you understand that the Old Testament was compiled centuries before the Advent of God Almighty in the flesh, walking upon this world He Created and Made?

https://biblearchaeology.org/research/new-testament-era/4022-a-brief-history-of-the-septuagint - the contents of the Old Testament, including the many prophecies that plainly tell us Jesus Christ is the One True God, were compiled centuries before God came in the flesh and showed and proved Himself to His Creation.

These many hundreds of prophecies that Jesus Christ fulfilled are proof beyond any reasonable doubt of His Divinity as the One True God who has been speaking with mankind from the moment He Created and Made Adam and Eve. The One True God plainly referred to the first man and first woman that He created and made in the Beginning, so the contents of Genesis and the Divine Creation of mankind are historic facts, not an allegory. (the Theory of Evolution is Wrong - God tells us WE ARE CREATED AND MADE IN HIS IMAGE, not some "evolved" monkey/ape or microbe!)

https://www.accordingtothescriptures.org/prophecy/353prophecies.html - anyone denying Jesus Christ is the One True God who came in the flesh is not comprehending that He told His Prophets what He would say and do centuries in advance as proof of His Identity.

THERE IS NO OTHER BOOK IN ALL THE WORLD LIKE THE HOLY BIBLE THAT RECORDS OUR ETERNAL CREATOR FACTUALLY SPEAKING WITH MANKIND THROUGHOUT HISTORY AND TELLING US THE TRUTH ABOUT CREATION BEFORE OUR VERY EYES! THERE IS NO OTHER BOOK IN ALL THE WORLD THAT HAS THESE DIVINE PROOFS OF AUTHORSHIP; TELLING US WHO GOD ALMIGHTY IS AND HOW TO KNOW HIM PERSONALLY BEYOND ALL DOUBT!

Though billions testify and billions of blogs/books/pamphlets have been written about Him, the Holy Bible is unique in that it records God, Jesus Christ, interacting with His Creation FROM THE BEGINNING and throughout all ancient history until He appeared in the flesh and said and did exactly what He foretold in the contents of the Old Testament.

If anyone tries to argue that anyone could fulfill their own prophecies about where and when they would be born, how they would die, along with the details of their entire life in the flesh BEFORE they were even born, ask them to PROVE IT! JESUS CHRIST IS GOD ALMIGHTY, no ifs, ands or buts.

https://www.icsv.at/one-chance-in-a-trillion-trillion-trillion-trillion-trillion-trillion-trillion-trillion-trillion-trillion-trillion-trillion-trillion - although this website is pointing out how ridiculous it is to deny Jesus Christ as the One True God, there is no random possibility whatsoever of anyone but God Almighty, the One True God, fulfilling all His Prophecies. NONE! So, when Jesus Christ says He is the fulfillment of the Law and Prophets, that is just another way of telling us HE IS GOD!

The Fulfillment of the Law

16In the same way, let your light shine before men, that they may see your good deeds and glorify your Father in heaven. **17**Do not think that I have come to abolish the Law or the Prophets. I have not come to abolish them, but to fulfill them. **18**For I tell you truly, until heaven and earth pass away, not a single jot, not a stroke of a pen, will disappear from the Law until everything is accomplished.... https://biblehub.com/matthew/5-17.htm

So yes, specific prophecies given us from God about Himself for centuries of ancient history and about the future of His Creation is indeed proof of the Divine Inspiration of the contents of the Holy Bible and when God appeared in the flesh and confirmed His Words as facts of history, then it's wrong to imagine that they aren't.

Matthew 19:4-6

[4] He replied, "Have you never read that He who created them from the beginning made them male and female, [5] and said, 'For this reason a man shall leave his father and mother and shall be joined inseparably to his wife, and the two shall become one flesh'? [6] So they are no longer two, but one flesh. Therefore, what God has joined together, let no one separate."

COMPREHEND THIS FACT! NO ONE ELSE IN ALL HISTORY BOTH STATED AND PROVED THEY ARE GOD ALMIGHTY LIKE JESUS CHRIST! Therefore, no one should be believing anyone over Him! Jesus Christ, the One True God, and His Words in the Holy Bible is the Divine Standard of Truth! no ifs, ands, or buts!

Eyewitnesses of His Majesty

...**18**And we ourselves heard this voice from heaven when we were with Him on the holy mountain. **19** We also have the word of the prophets as confirmed beyond doubt. And you will do well to pay attention to it, as to a lamp shining in a dark place, until the day dawns and the morning star rises in your hearts. **20**Above all, you must understand that no prophecy of Scripture comes from one's own interpretation. **21**For no such prophecy was ever brought forth by the will of man, but men spoke from God as they were carried along by the Holy Spirit....
https://biblehub.com/2_peter/1-19.htm

So yes! Divine Prophecies from God Almighty that have come to pass throughout history ARE PROOF HE IS GOD! If mankind could all on their own accurately foretell the future many hundreds of times over, then the whole world would be filled with books like the Holy Bible BUT THE HOLY BIBLE IS UNIQUELY PROVABLY AND VERIFIABLY DIVINELY INSPIRED! (There are no other books like the

Holy Bible, whose contents span millenniums of ancient history and have prophecies in them still coming to pass before our eyes even today, millenniums later.) Prophecies that foretold the advent of jets, smart missiles, nuclear weapons, specific wars, modern automobiles, tanks, and more thousands of years before such things ever came into existence. The prophecies were so ancient that those writing about such things, as God had commanded them, didn't even have specific words in their ancient language for what they were seeing and so had to describe what they were seeing as best they could in language now over 2500 years old!

https://www.youtube.com/watch?v=ICkKASOs2Wo - when I cite a person, it doesn't mean I agree with everything they teach; I am only citing that I agree that the prophets saw things like missiles, jets, tanks and future wars but didn't have specific words in their ancient languages for such things. Michael Rood has done some commendable research on the scriptures and as such deserves praise in that regard.

https://youtu.be/fyd3PDnYK2w?t=162 - I can remember reading:

4The chariots dash through the streets; they rush around the plazas, appearing like torches, darting about like lightning. https://biblehub.com/nahum/2-4.htm

and being reminded of:
https://www.youtube.com/watch?v=QNXtbsS633w

https://www.biblegateway.com/verse/en/Nahum%202%3A4 - no matter how the ancient text is rendered clearly it was prophetically speaking of modern automobiles (the ancient word chariot was what they had at the time since they didn't have a word like "cars" back then.)

    I am well aware of how others interpret such prophecies as being fulfilled long ago and have nothing to do with the present or our future, but I disagree. Time and again, God has shown me that what took place in the past was like a seed being planted for an even larger fulfillment in the future; hence the expression by some, "history repeats itself..." or "those who fail to learn from history are doomed to repeat it."

    The reason I associate such prophecies in the past with things in our present is due to the fact I have been shown things also from God and when He reveals things to me, it sometimes is just like a time-lapse of many events. Images that might refer to things in the near future or things that elapse over time. (Future history from the One who sees it all clearly and is why He tells us the End from the Beginning.) Just like the dream of Pharaoh that Joseph correctly interpreted by God's Grace, the dream itself was just brief images in one night that were about 14 years to come. And when you read the Divine Consequences that came upon ancient Egypt for oppressing the Israelites, and compare it to the Divine Consequences in Deuteronomy 28 and the Book of Revelation, along with the events surrounding the fall of Jericho, you can begin to see how that our Creator is warning the world by what He has done in the past and telling us that He will deal with all mankind in like manner. That in the end, the Oppressor will cease, and His People will Ascend Triumphantly!

…**9**Remember what happened long ago, for I am God, and there is no other; I am God, and there is none like Me. **10**I declare the end from the beginning, and ancient times from what is still to come. I say, 'My purpose will stand, and all My good pleasure I will accomplish.' **11**I summon a bird of prey from the east, a man for My purpose from a far-off land. Truly I have spoken, and truly I will bring it to pass. I have planned it, and I will surely do it.… https://biblehub.com/isaiah/46-10.htm

So, when I understood the ancient scriptures were clearly talking about things yet to come even centuries to millenniums later, I began to see more and more of those prophecies describing things that now presently exist.

Like the time I was telling a skeptic that the Holy Bible had prophecies in it that were clearly talking about things taking place right now and how he laughed and denied that statement. So, without knowing that God had ordained that conversation, I opened the Holy Bible and began reading out of Jeremiah at the exact moment news about the gulf war came on the television. (Again, I had no idea that the news was going to match what I was led by God to read to the skeptical man.)

https://biblehub.com/jeremiah/50-9.htm -
9For behold, I stir up and bring against Babylon an assembly of great nations from the land of the north. They will line up against her; from the north she will be captured. Their arrows will be like skilled warriors who do not return empty-handed.

The version of the Holy Bible I had been reading from at the time was closer to:

New Living Translation

For I am raising up an army of great nations from the north. They will join forces to attack Babylon, and she will be captured. The enemies' arrows will go straight to the mark; they will not miss!

And while I was reading the passage the news was talking about the coalition of nations that had come together because Iraq had come down to plunder Kuwait (which is the location of ancient Ur of the Chaldeans) and so the news showed a smart missile exactly hitting its target when I was reading the passage that said their arrows will hit their mark, they will not miss their target out of the Holy Bible.

https://biblehub.com/hebrew/chitztzav_2671.htm - notice the scriptures have passages like "he makes his arrows fiery shafts" (smart missiles that don't miss their targets) It's just when the scriptures were written that long ago, the prophets didn't have such words, so they used things like arrows to indicate they saw a weapon that flew through the air.

And then I went on to read:

30The warriors of Babylon have stopped fighting; they sit in their strongholds. Their strength is exhausted; they have become like women. Babylon's homes have been set ablaze, the bars of her gates are broken.
https://biblehub.com/jeremiah/51-30.htm

    And on the news, they were showing Iraqi soldiers laying down their weapons and surrendering amidst images of advancing tanks, buildings exploding and burning and Iraqi soldiers running away, hiding and retreating. Nothing really to be ashamed of, when they were fighting against superior air power and weapons, but nevertheless the news was corresponding to the scriptures as if on cue while the skeptic listened and watched. That particular guy didn't argue with me about prophecies in the Holy Bible pertaining to even recent history, the version of the Holy Bible I had at the time was perfectly matching the news before his own eyes.

    The scriptures use ancient words not only to describe future things like weapons and wars but also to describe locations, so knowing ancient maps helps to understand what nations the prophets are speaking of not just in history but today and into the future.

In addition, the scriptures talk about ancient empires, like Egyptian, Assyrian, Babylonian, Medo-Persian, Grecian, and Roman as heads belonging to "the beast" so the spirit of err has been uniting the ungodly against the Kingdom of God and His People down through history and is why whenever you read prophecies about "Pharaoh of Egypt" or "King of Babylon" or "spiritual Egypt" you need to understand that what was in specific localities in the past has expanded as we now have a global civilization and that such references are often prophetically talking about the devil within the antichrist and body of antichrists all over this world. That the real battle the Holy Bible is talking about is between those who know and love the One True God Jesus Christ and those who don't. Throughout history that has manifested as ungodly empires have persecuted and made war with Holy Bible believers. So, it is in the interest of those who know and love our Lord Jesus Christ and who honor and keep His Commandments in the Holy Bible to make sure their nation is full of like-minded people, or eventually conflict results, sometimes open persecution.

Everyone who knows the Lord, who knows our Eternal Creator, Lord and Savior, JESUS, the Christ, needs to do their best to tell everyone they can that they need to know Him also.

Heavenly Father, LORD JESUS, Glorify Your Name in and through all Your Children and all Creation; cause us all to bear much good fruit by Your Grace. Thank You, Lord Jesus; Amen.

Yes, I know we can be reasonably sure He went by Yeshua when He walked in the flesh, but God knows all languages and knows the details about all His Creation, past, present and future; so, He knew His Name would be translated, in the English, into JESUS the Christ from Yahoshuah/Yeshua Ha Mashiach.

The contents of the Holy Bible not only correspond to the most important facts of history; telling us the future accurately before it even happens, but to observable reality, even the stars above. This is another proof of Divine Inspiration in that the Divine Prophecies have been accurate about past, present and future history AND past, present and future REALITY. God Almighty declaring Himself to us not just with His Words, but with His Creation.

As long as you are referring to the One True God who declares Himself in the Holy Bible and in the Stars from Heaven Above, then He honors His Promise to give you His Holy Spirit when you Repent and are Baptized in His Name. (Matthew 28;18-20, Mark 16:15-16, Acts 2:38-39; 4:12) When God Almighty gives you His own Holy Spirit of Truth, you will know Him, He will be communicating with you, empowering you and teaching you personally. (John 14:20-26; 16:13)

So, you might be wondering how do the stars tell us about our Eternal Creator?

Some people who are desperately trying to deny the One True God, Jesus Christ, put out presentations like

Zeitgeist imagining they are casting doubt on the veracity of the Divinely Inspired Holy Bible, but instead they are pointing out that our Eternal Creator wrote His Gospel Message in the stars He Created and Made. His Divine Message was so clear that ancient civilizations all over the world understood it. While the presentation is incorrect in its assertions that anyone else but Jesus Christ is the fulfillment of that Divine Message given mankind, it suffices to let us all know that God speaks to us not just by His Holy Spirit, not just by those who know Him, the Prophets, but by His Creation, the stars from Heaven Above, giving us light even in the darkest night.

The ancients knew that mankind was Created and Made by our Eternal Creator and that He designed the stars not just for the telling of the times and seasons, but to give us His Light of Truth, even in this present darkness of still too much ignorance and wickedness on earth. This is why the word stars in the scriptures is not just referring to the burning lights we see each night as we look up, but to those who know the One True God, Jesus Christ, and are filled with His Light, His Truth. So, the ancients understood the Celestial and Terrestrial connection how that our spirits are presently residing in these earthly tabernacles. And so is how the wise men understood that the Messiah, God in the flesh, had arrived on earth by looking up and watching the stars above them.

The scriptures plainly record that an extremely bright star appeared when God came in the flesh and that there were also signs in the heavens and earth during His Crucifixion and death on the Cross. So, Creation testifies of our Creator and His Words in the Holy Bible have always corresponded with observable reality, because God and His Words are the reason Creation exists as it exists. The evil in this world is the result of not just our own evil thoughts, words, ways and deeds, but Divine Consequences have come upon us due to those wicked thoughts, words, ways and deeds. So, this present world is fallen and is a battleground between those who choose to love and obey our Eternal Creator, Lord and Savior, JESUS, the Christ and those who don't. God refers to those who love and obey Him as His Children, and He calls those who refuse to do so, and are deliberately evil and wicked, children of the devil. It is this ongoing conflict throughout history to this day and until our Lord returns in Glory that the Battle of Armageddon is really about.

Heavenly Father, LORD JESUS, make those of us who are trusting in You to Save, Keep and Bless us forever to be Faithful and True like Yourself. Thank you, My Lord; Amen.

Now when I reviewed some presentations about how the stars were named and proclaim the Divine

Message that's also recorded in the Holy Bible, I found discrepancies between various presenters on the subject, but I cite them regardless, because between them, they are getting closer to Divine Truth; perhaps it is the astronomical software they are using and perhaps they all just haven't collaborated with scholars of Biblical history enough to see precisely the reason why people haven't come to strong agreement yet on the precise timing that both the scriptures and the stars indicated regarding the Incarnation, Crucifixion, Resurrection and Ascension of the Messiah, Jesus Christ, God Almighty who came in the flesh.

https://www.youtube.com/watch?v=PHCftvj_Prw - Chuck Missler gives a presentation on the topic of how the constellations and stars were named specifically to tell us about God and His Divine Work of Salvation in coming in the flesh to suffer and die in behalf of mankind.

    When the scriptures tell us He condemned sin in the flesh, God proved to mankind His Commandments can be kept as a Man! (so none of us can falsely accuse Him of giving us impossible commandments to keep, since we all failed to do so) He wasn't just fulfilling His Law of Redemption and Prophecies of Salvation, He was proving by publicly dying and raising His own Body from the Grave, Transfiguring it and Ascending into Heaven in front of eyewitnesses that He is indeed the One True God, the One who has Eternal Life and is the Way to Heaven that He claimed to be.

By the way, the Shroud of Turin, according to the scientists is authentic, anyone claiming it was forged have at least 100 facts to overcome, including that it was made by a man who had been crucified exactly as the Holy Bible records Jesus was crucified, with fauna from the area of Jerusalem, and can tell how they forged it (who was actually crucified in the place of Jesus), since no one with modern technologies can do it.
https://youtu.be/LLnClp3OVmE?t=1884 and https://www.youtube.com/results?search_query=barrie+schwortz+shroud+of+turin+

https://www.khouse.org/search/content?keys=chuck%20missler%20signs%20in%20the%20heavens - you can search the website of the ministry of Chuck Missler for more of his perspective about how Creation and the Scriptures are connected: past, present and future. Again, when I cite someone, I am not saying I agree with all their personal beliefs and doctrines, I am only saying that I found at least some of what they teach commendable enough to reference them.

When I speak of discrepancies, examine these presentations and see if you can spot them:

https://bethlehemstar.com/ - I'm not saying anyone is deliberately misleading us, I'm suggesting that perhaps there's an error in the various astronomical software people are using. I haven't found anyone who has written about the correlation of an ancient ephemeris during the Advent of Jesus Christ in the flesh or about the reliability of such records. If modern software engineers are using reverse extrapolation to generate past movements of the stars in astronomical software, it would be interesting to see if their procedures concur with any ancient records in that regard. Since the "Bethlehem Star" is associated as a Sign in the Heavens that the Messiah is arriving, it seems prudent to correctly ascertain that Sign of the Messiah, since He told us it would precede His Return in Glory and Power with the Heavenly Host.

The Return of the Son of Man
...**29**Immediately after the tribulation of those days: 'The sun will be darkened, and the moon will not give its light; the stars will fall from the sky, and the powers of the heavens will be shaken.' **30** At that time the sign of the Son of Man will appear in heaven, and all the tribes of the earth will mourn. They will see the Son of Man coming on the clouds of

heaven, with power and great glory. **31**And He will send out His angels with a loud trumpet call, and they will gather His elect from the four winds, from one end of the heavens to the other....
https://biblehub.com/matthew/24-30.htm

https://www.youtube.com/watch?v=EUQEMqF5dL8 - there is no doubt the scriptures tell us the wise men followed the Sign of the Messiah, the "Star of Bethlehem" so it's reasonable to try and ascertain whether or not that Sign/Star is discernible through such research or to ponder if it was purely Supernatural. I personally think that the Sign of Messiah is indeed tied not just to one particular Star, but to the constellations that tell His Gospel Message which is why I am referencing both.

The Fourth Day
...**13**And there was evening, and there was morning—the third day. **14**And God said, "Let there be lights in the expanse of the sky to distinguish between the day and the night, and let them be signs to mark the seasons and days and years. **15**And let them serve as lights in the expanse of the sky to shine upon the earth." And it was so.... https://biblehub.com/genesis/1-14.htm

https://www.youtube.com/watch?v=JM1sY44_-74&list=PL6NNBo_y_fjOF3wwi-VsCOcCNUeFqFINs - then compare those who are using astronomical software to identify the precise timing of the historic events of the Messiah on earth with those who research the scriptures and believe they can date the events recorded to specific days in the past. There should be harmony and agreement within the Body of Christ, so it's wise to search these things out, until we all come to a proper understanding of them.

Nevertheless, our journey of incarnation is very brief so let everyone in Christ be fully persuaded of their calling and Divine Purpose and fulfill that to the Glory of God.

The point is HEAVEN testifies of JESUS CHRIST the Creator! Those who know Him testifies that Jesus Christ is the Creator. Acts 10:34-43, Acts 1:8, Acts 4:12 The Greatest Book in all the world, the Holy Bible, testifies that Jesus Christ is the Creator. YOU NEED TO KNOW HIM FOR YOUR OWN GOOD NOW AND FOREVER!

Supernatural Miracles that correspond to the God of the Holy Bible, Jesus Christ, are also proof of the Divine Inspiration of the Holy Bible, because the same God who declares Himself therein has been performing miracles throughout history to this very day.

Those who know our Eternal Creator, Lord and Savior, Jesus Christ, are all under a Divine Commandment and Duty to TESTIFY about Him to others. Mt 28:18-20, Rev 12:11 Whether that's by word of mouth as you walk through this world, writing a blog or book or posting a video or all the above, PLEASE CONTINUE TO PASS ON HIS COMMANDMENT TO EVERYONE THAT WE ALL MUST REPENT AND BE BAPTIZED IN HIS NAME AND PRAY TO RECEIVE HIS HOLY SPIRIT OF TRUTH UNTIL WE ALL KNOW GOD PERSONALLY!

I personally made t-shirts with letters you can iron on that says things like "Jesus Christ is Lord! DO YOU KNOW HIM?!", "Repent and Be Baptized in the Name of our Lord Jesus Christ, pray to receive His Holy Spirit!" and other important messages, so that every time I go out in public, I'm a witness to the Truth. Most of the time I go out into the world, I am pleased to report other brothers and sisters encourage me in that regard! I need all the encouragement I can get!

The War in Heaven

…**10**And I heard a loud voice in heaven saying: "Now have come the salvation and the power and the kingdom of our God, and the authority of His Christ. For the accuser of our brothers has been thrown down—he who accuses them day and night before our God. **11** They have conquered him by the blood of the Lamb and by the word of their testimony. And they did not love their lives so as to shy away from death. **12**Therefore rejoice, O heavens, and you who dwell in them! But woe to the earth and the sea; with great fury the devil has come down to you, knowing he has only a short time."… https://biblehub.com/revelation/12-11.htm

TESTIFY OF HOW OUR LORD JESUS CHRIST SAVED YOU! TELL OTHERS HOW HE HAS BLESSED YOU! DO YOUR BEST TO MAKE SURE EVERYONE KNOWS THAT THEY CAN AND NEED TO KNOW GOD ALMIGHTY PERSONALLY!

I've been Blessed to listen to testimonies from ex-prostitutes, ex-drug dealers, ex-assassins, ex-robbers, ex-murderers, ex-criminals on death row, but also from people who were raised in Christian homes who had never smoked, never drank any alcoholic beverage, never committed any crimes or done anything extremely sinful. I've listened to testimonies from people who survived wars, others who were suicidal, others who were homicidal, and still others who had never endured any such evil in this world at all. But every true Christian plainly states that our Lord Jesus Christ Saved them! (Acts 2:38-39; 4:12) He either turned their life around for the better when they were at their lowest or He was with them even from childhood and kept them from such suffering in this world. Either way, Christians Praise our Savior for Saving them personally!

I've listened to or read testimonies from mafia hit-men, cleaners and such, and from police officers and soldiers, people from all walks of life and from all the major worldviews. Religion can't save you, being irreligious can't save you; ONLY THE ONE TRUE GOD, JESUS CHRIST! Acts 4:11-13, Acts 10:34-43, 1Jn 5:20, Jn 8:32-36

Some people have been on television or written books how they were firm atheists but had a near death experience that changed their mind! Some say they went to hell and back! Out of all the "beyond and back" testimonies I've read or listened to online, the agreement that ex-atheists, ex-hindus, ex-buddhists, ex-muslims and even testimonies from people who thought of themselves as a Christian, but weren't; all have: is that their experience with nearly dying and being resuscitated caused them to realize that the Holy Bible is telling us all the Truth, JESUS CHRIST IS LORD! THE ONE TRUE GOD! HE IS THE ONLY ONE WHO CAN SAVE YOU AND YOUR LOVED ONES!

      Radically changed lives for the better, the SAVED, are definitely evidence of God, Jesus Christ, and the Divine Inspiration of the Holy Bible.   God Almighty and His Words are responsible for all the good in this world; throughout history, to this very day, and forever!

      Yes, there are people that use support groups in an attempt to try and overcome their own drug addictions or other self-destructive bad behavior, but it's when people who have tried everything else, finally humble themselves before God and ask Him to Save them that He changes us from the inside, our very desires until we love what's good and right and hate what's evil, so much so that our lives demonstrate Jesus Christ really came into our lives by His Holy Spirit, Saved and changed us by His Power for the better. People who don't believe in God should take some time listening to those who have died and been resuscitated talk about their experiences and also should listen to the many who testify of His Miracles and His

Salvation until they comprehend that most people who are denying God, simply have not learned enough about history and reality to understand that it makes them look ignorant, irrational, deceived and self-deluded to deny our Eternal Creator. In other words, all creation is evidence of His Existence and He has been talking with mankind and working Divine Miracles throughout all recorded history to this very day.

The Words of God Almighty have been given mankind in the contents of the Holy Bible and therein Jesus Christ, the One True God, tells us all plainly how to know Him; so, the Holy Bible is provably and verifiably Divinely Inspired. Those who have already done so are telling the rest of mankind that Greatest Truth and have been doing so ever since God came in the flesh, showed and proved Himself to us. If you don't know God personally yet, it's due to the fact you haven't obeyed His Instructions in that regard.

So, our Eternal Creator Created and Made the Heavens and the earth, all living things, including mankind and has been speaking with mankind since the Beginning. He chose certain people to give His Holy Spirit to in the ancient past and these are the men and women called Prophets and Prophetesses in the Holy Bible. They heard the Voice of God known in English as Jesus Christ, speaking to them and telling them what to say and write down. Those scrolls were compiled into the Septuagint at least two centuries prior to God coming in the flesh as the Messiah.

God came in the flesh and in front of eyewitnesses would speak and reality would change instantly. He healed entire crowds of all ailments, even people born blind, deaf and dumb. He raised the dead, turned water into wine, fed thousands just by speaking and blessing, stopped storms, walked on water and He even showed us that He Created Adam exactly as the scriptures tell us, when He took dirt from the ground; spit on it, turning it into mud, and rubbed in on the eyes of a man born blind. God gave the man new eyes that could see! Our Creator demonstrated He had power over all Creation, even walking on the water and according to at least one of those eyewitnesses actually did so many miracles just during His brief ministry that if they had all been written down not even the whole world could contain the books. Again, those who saw and heard Him first hand were so convinced that Jesus Christ is the One True God they accepted torturous demises rather than deny Him!

https://tile.loc.gov/storage-services/public/gdcmassbookdig/foxesbookofmart00fo/foxesbookofmart00fo.pdf

God has been healing people all over this world, there are numerous miracles mentioned even today with medical evidence, so if you need a miracle pray to Him.

https://youtu.be/rn73J9A0SnU - PhD Craig Keener traveled the world. There is no doubt that Jesus Christ has been doing miracles proving He is the One True God.

Some might say they prayed for a miracle perhaps their whole life and it never came. Only God knows why. Some of us He heals now and others of us He Promises to wipe away our tears and explain everything to us! He is our Healer! Sometimes it's just a matter of WHEN He will do so! I can say, that when I prayed on this issue God showed me several reasons, none of which were necessarily something we might think on. Some people built their ministries "on their disabilities" that made them to be inspirational to others! Somehow their disabilities inspired others to accept Christ for the fact He IS GOD, regardless of what He does for us! regardless if He heals us when we want!

Nevertheless, I am looking forward to that Day when He heals us all!

A New Heaven and a New Earth

…**3**And I heard a loud voice from the throne saying: "Behold, the dwelling place of God is with man, and He will dwell with them. They will be His people, and God Himself will be with them as their God. **4**' He will wipe away every tear from their eyes,' and there will be no more death or mourning or crying or pain, for the former things have passed away." **5**And the One seated on the throne said, "Behold, I make all things new." Then He said, "Write this down, for these words are faithful and true." **6**And He told me, "It is done! I am the Alpha and the Omega, the Beginning and the End. To the thirsty I will give freely from the spring of the water of life. **7**The one who overcomes will inherit all things, and I will be his God, and he will be My son. https://biblehub.com/revelation/21-4.htm

NO MORE DEATH! NO MORE CRYING OR PAIN! WE WILL INHERIT ALL THINGS! PRAISE HIS HOLY NAME! PRAISE YOU LORD JESUS! FOREVER!

So even in this life, it is as nothing compared to eternity! While I wish people wouldn't have martyred the saints throughout the ages, they knew GOD KEEPS HIS WORDS! It's just sad that people who hate, hate those who actually truly love them; telling them the truth that we all need God, to the point of killing them. The saints are praiseworthy in that they tell the Truth; despite knowing the risks. We are telling the whole world JESUS CHRIST IS LORD! ask Him to forgive you and come into your life by His Holy Spirit! Then tell everyone else how to know Him!

The Holy Bible is not just provably and verifiably Divinely Inspired, but is the most trustworthy reference book in all the world for accurate information about the things that matter most. It is written as historic non-fiction, the Gospels in the biographical, historic genre complete with genealogies of real people and real places. No other book in all the world has been as thoroughly scrutinized for centuries for its historicity and overall veracity like the Holy Bible. Anyone imagining it's a work of fiction or ancient mythology, frankly, needs to go back to grade school and demand a proper education; one in which the Holy Bible is the primary text book lifelong. Just the centuries of research of its contents have generated more commentaries, apologetics, scientific and historic literary works than any other book in all the world, by far. In my own research, the Holy Bible has generated more accurate knowledge, more books on science and all other subjects, than all the rest of the most popular books in all the world combined! Anyone disdaining its contents is making themselves look EXTREMELY foolish! (and, as stated, lacking a proper education completely.) Everything mankind has learned about reality and history only confirms the contents of the Holy Bible as absolutely true, the very Words of our Eternal Creator, telling us all about Himself and His Creation.

It is lies, mistaken imaginations, foolish notions, and all manner of deceptions that people mistake for knowledge, that contradicts the Truth, the Words of God, the Holy Bible; so, if you are one of those people who are disdaining the Holy Bible, you need to rethink what you think you know. Pay attention to what Creation Scientists are teaching about reality, why they say that knowledge, science, only confirms the Holy Bible. Stop listening to those who do not know God, who do not confirm His Words in the Holy Bible. Lies only turn you into a liar yourself and will result in your damnation. Rev 21:8 Whenever anyone places the opinions of fallible mortals above the Words of God Almighty in the Holy Bible is the moment they are committing idolatry and are being deceived. The Holy Bible has been right when opinions of scientists have been wrong throughout history and it's still so today. Correct information has only confirmed the contents of the Holy Bible as absolutely true. Any imaginations, even given in the name of science, that are contrary to the plain language of the Holy Bible are wrong; no ifs, ands or buts!

LET IT SINK IN! NO ONE IN ALL HISTORY BOTH CLAIMED TO BE AND PROVED THEY ARE GOD ALMIGHTY LIKE JESUS CHRIST! HE EVER LIVES TO ANSWER ANY AND ALL WITH ENOUGH SENSE TO SEEK TO KNOW HIM! With enough seriousness to actually Obey His Commandment to Repent of every wicked thought, word, way and deed and get baptized in His Name! PRAY TO RECEIVE HIS HOLY SPIRIT OF TRUTH UNTIL YOU KNOW GOD PERSONALLY THEREBY! Acts 2:38-39, Rom 8:9-15

And once you know Him and begin studying His Words in the Holy Bible most seriously, THEN you will wonder how you ever could have believed any of the nonsense wrongly being taught in the name of science currently. God, Jesus Christ, doesn't tell lies! He is Truth; so ALWAYS TRUST HIM AND HIS WORDS IN THE HOLY BIBLE ABOVE EVERYONE ELSE FOREVER!

Do you understand? God came in the flesh exactly as He told the Prophets He would and did exactly what He said He would do when He did. HE SPOKE AND STOPPED STORMS INSTANTLY showing He has Power over Creation to change it at His Will! So, when God spoke and reality instantly changed in front of crowds of people, that means He was letting us know that's exactly how He Created and Made the universe! HE SPEAKS! Just like the scriptures plainly state! "Let there be Light!" and LIGHT exists! (and all according to His Own Creative Divine Thought!) It's why the scriptures say "Created AND Made" over and over! Divine Thoughts Made Manifest, JUST BECAUSE JESUS CHRIST, THE ONE TRUE GOD, SAYS SO!

He tells us the evil in this world is due to the fact people are imagining (creating) and then acting (making) evil things and doing evil deeds. So, when people think good and right thoughts always and act on them, the world becomes more like Heaven, and when they think wickedly and act evilly, the world becomes more like hell, which is why the scriptures tell us of this battle between God and His Angels and the devil and his demons. Jesus Christ is the One who can set you free from the devil! (evil thoughts, vain imaginations, deceptions, delusions, wickedness) and once you are free from evil within your own person, then you will be able by His Grace and Power to tell others that they need to be free from the devil/evil also, so that the whole world becomes a better place! Holy Bible believers have founded and funded the largest number of humanitarian charities on earth! So clearly GOD IS GOOD! and His Commandments in the Holy Bible are Righteous and True Altogether!

He tells us His Two Greatest Commandments are to Love Him and Love each other and that all the rest of His Commandments are built on those Two! So, no one should find such honorable and righteous Divine Instructions objectionable in any way!

Recapping how Jesus Christ proved beyond reasonable doubt that He is the One True God:

No one in denial of our Eternal Creator has a rational explanation for the universe, reality before their own eyes. The One True God, Jesus Christ, is it!

https://www.facebook.com/photo/?fbid=6382847548460817&set=a.115635768515391 - the stories being told in the name of science today are laughable if it wasn't so sad people actually believe that nonsense. I'm not trying to insult anyone in saying this; remember, I was one of those children brainwashed in our public schools, taught this lying crap year after year, until I actually believed it myself! I'm only pointing out, and putting it down in laymen's terms to get you all to understand that it is actually lying garbage! To understand that no one should believe anyone denying our Eternal Creator and His Words, the Holy Bible!

God spoke with mankind from the moment He

Created Adam and Eve and told the Prophets to write down His Words in what have become the contents of the Holy Bible. The entire Old Testament was compiled in the Septuagint centuries before God came in the flesh, showed and proved Himself to mankind and told us all how to know Him personally beyond all doubt.

https://biblearchaeology.org/research/new-testament-era/4022-a-brief-history-of-the-septuagint - the many hundreds of prophecies from God telling mankind who He is, were fulfilled by Him when He came in the flesh as proof, He is the Eternal Creator who had been speaking with mankind from the Beginning. Jn 8:24-25

https://www.accordingtothescriptures.org/prophecy/353prophecies.html - God told His Prophets He would come in the flesh and did so precisely according to them, which is how the wise identified Him as God in the flesh even at His birth. (The prophecies and the stars He created and made announced His Incarnation in the flesh.)

When God walked among us in the flesh, He spoke and changed reality instantly, proving He is God. As His final proof before He returned to Heaven, He died publicly, then raised His Body from the Grave, transfigured it;

making it Immortal and Glorious and Ascended into Heaven in front of eyewitnesses. Those who saw and heard Him firsthand gave their lives telling everyone they had seen and heard the One True God and is how the contents of the New Testament came to be recorded.

https://tile.loc.gov/storage-services/public/gdcmassbookdig/foxesbookofmart00fo/foxesbookofmart00fo.pdf

So, the Holy Bible contains the most important information on earth and is why it's the most studied book in all the world by far.

24That is why I told you that you would die in your sins. For unless you believe that I am He, you will die in your sins." 25"Who are You?" they asked. "Just what I have been telling you from the beginning," Jesus replied....
https://biblehub.com/john/8-24.htm

Jesus Christ didn't just do miracles long ago; He has been doing them throughout history to this very day.

https://www.youtube.com/watch?v=rn73J9A0SnU - this

PhD scholar traveled the world documenting some of the most notable recent miracles, many of which came with not just testimonies, but medical records and other external methods of verification. Believe in God, and believe He is our Healer and Savior!

https://www.youtube.com/watch?v=X3wGdjYnWRI - miracles with medical records

https://sidroth.org - this guy regularly has people on his show that have experienced miracles.

Many of which are now called NDE (near death experiences) from people who have died all over the world and been resuscitated and come back telling us that they saw Jesus Christ, the One True God. (even die-hard former atheists)

https://www.youtube.com/results?search_query=atheist+dies+and+sees+Jesus+Christ - it's not just atheists that come back telling us the Holy Bible is telling us all the truth, but buddhists, hindus, and muslims as well. Even some monks in monasteries that had never even read a Holy Bible are online testifying that Jesus Christ is the One

True God.

I also died and found out the very hard way that our Eternal Creator most definitely exists. When I died as a young man, I was then believing in evolution and thought of myself as an agnostic. I simply didn't know whether or not there was an Eternal Creator, "God". I just hadn't learned enough by that age.

Anyway, when I died, I didn't go to hell, instead my spirit came out of my body and I went up and up past the galaxies to a place of complete void, absolutely nothing. (I later read in the Holy Bible that place is called "outer darkness".) Anyway, when I arrived there, God challenged me, "Alright wiseguy, if I don't exist, can YOU make the sun, moon and stars? can you make ANYTHING (by implication even an atom or quark) from this void of nothing? from nothing but your own spirit?"

God taught me in a nanosecond that He is very real, the universe doesn't exist without Him and also that I am not Him. (In other words, I knew that even if I tried for all eternity, I could not create anything of substance from nothing but my own spirit.) When God says He has All Power and Authority in Heaven and earth, that's the

Power He's talking about. We are not Him; none of us created the universe, He did.

And like I said, Jesus Christ proved beyond any reasonable doubt that He is the One True God, when He came in the flesh and healed crowds just by speaking from all ailments and birth defects, stopped storms, turned water into wine, raised the dead, and then after saying He is the One who has Eternal Life and the One everyone must come to in order to have that Life and that He is the Way to Heaven, PROVED it by publicly dying, raising His Body from the Grave, transfigured it, made it Immortal and Glorious and then Ascended into Heaven in front of eyewitnesses. Those who saw and heard Him were so convinced He is the One True God that they gave their lives to torturous demises rather than deny Him or one word of their testimonies which are now the contents of the New Testament.

https://tile.loc.gov/storage-services/public/gdcmassbookdig/foxesbookofmart00fo/foxesbookofmart00fo.pdf

So, the Holy Bible is the most studied and referenced book in all the world because it contains the most important information in all the world, how anyone can know God Almighty personally and begin learning from Him right here and now.

Not only has the Holy Bible been studied down to every letter it contains for millenniums for its historicity and veracity, but the most studied artifact on earth confirms the death and resurrection of Jesus Christ exactly as recorded in the Holy Bible.

https://youtu.be/LLnClp3OVmE?t=1884 - no, the Shroud of Turin isn't a forgery, no one even today with modern technology can recreate the scientific details discovered about the image on the burial cloth of Jesus Christ; so, it certainly isn't a medieval forgery like some falsely allege. THE IMAGE WAS IN FACT OF A MAN THAT WAS CRUCIFIED IN THE EXACT WAY JESUS CHRIST WAS CRUCIFIED, so anyone saying it was a forgery is claiming SOMEONE ELSE WAS CRUCIFIED IN THAT WAY... ridiculous!

https://www.youtube.com/watch?v=jvmxL4lCXpg - The Shroud has recorded history dating to the Burial and Resurrection of Jesus Christ, so any dating method that claims the Shroud came later in history is mistaken.

Again, God tells us all how to know Him personally in the Holy Bible. He commands everyone to Repent of every wicked thought, word, way and deed, including thinking we know better than Him, and to get Baptized in His Name. (Matt 28:18-20; Mark 16:15-16; Acts 2:38-39; 4:12)

So, the Holy Bible is provably and verifiably Divinely Inspired. Everyone needs to know God personally; not just their present quality of life, but their everlasting destiny depends on their relationship with Him.

There are other proofs of the Divine Inspiration of the Holy Bible.

Understand that there is no other book in all the world like the Holy Bible that was written from the most ancient history over centuries even millenniums telling us about how our very real Eternal Creator has been interacting with His Creation from the Beginning. Telling us absolute truth that He is the One who not only brought the heavens and earth into existence but that He created all living things on earth. He tells us He designed all living things with seed in themselves to bring forth like kinds of creatures unto themselves from generation to generation;

so, by Divine Design the notion of macro-evolution is impossible.

Read my book **The Theory of Evolution is Impossible.**

Whenever any opinion comes along from anyone, scientist or otherwise, that is contrary to the plain language of the Holy Bible, the well verified Words of God Almighty in the Holy Bible, that opinion is wrong! no ifs, ands or buts! If you want to know the most important truthful information in all the world, then STUDY THE WORDS OF GOD ALMIGHTY IN THE HOLY BIBLE AND ASK HIM TO GIVE YOU HIS UNDERSTANDING OF ALL THINGS!

When I say other Divine Proofs, I'm saying that the Holy Bible contains the VERIFIABLE Words of God Almighty, Jesus Christ, Himself: 1) ASK HIM! GOD WILL VERIFY HIS WORDS WITH YOU PERSONALLY! 2) GOD AND HIS WORDS HAVE BEEN RIGHT THROUGHOUT ALL GENERATIONS TO THIS DAY, even when so-called science has been wrong! NEVER BELIEVE ANYONE OVER GOD AND HIS WORDS IN THE HOLY BIBLE! NEVER! 3) While God was teaching us His Commandments giving us detailed accurate prophecies about the future (and no, no one contrived self-fulfilling prophecies when those prophecies were written thousands of years ago and have been coming to pass throughout history to this very day!) He included what some call "Divine Signatures" in the contents. 4) Divine Signatures are what serious scholars on the subject claim are irrefutable proofs of Divine Authorship of the contents of the Holy Bible.

      Some of these Divine Signatures are: 1) Bible Codes - encrypted Divine Messages indicating that the Words of God were dictated so precisely to the Prophets that even the letters therein and the order of the letters of every word have Divine Messages 2) Hidden mathematics like Pi and e, and "heptads" of scriptures found throughout the entire Holy Bible and in very specific locations (work of Mathematician Ivan Panin) Again, these were written in the scriptures long before they were discovered by mankind! The Holy Bible has been scientifically accurate in all respects long before science was able to verify it! SCIENCE IS STILL CATCHING UP WITH THE DIVINE KNOWLEDGE IN THE HOLY BIBLE; not the other way around like some wrongly imagine these days. 3) God, Jesus Christ, and His Words in The Holy Bible is the reason for the existence of modern books, the modern fields of science, and everything good in this world. So entire encyclopedic volumes exist describing how God and His Words relate not just to observable reality but virtually any and all fields of science and accurate knowledge on earth! If you are unaware of these facts, it's due to a lack of research on your part, not just regarding the most important things we can know about all history and present day, but about our future. Reading Isaac Newton's commentary on the Books of Daniel and Revelation had me rereading it over and over because his scholarship was so superior compared to the works of so many boastful persons of today. What I'm trying to say is that the Words of God in the Holy Bible pertain to all persons, all fields of study, everything in all creation, past, present and future and ALL that Divine Knowledge is clearly proof of its Divine Inspiration. (Mathematics, Numerology, Encryption, History, Medical Sciences, Biology, Genetics, Hematology, Proper Hygiene, Proper handling of the dead, it even has prophecies that sound like HAZMAT procedures for various types of warfare and diseases! Astronomy, Physics, Anthropology, Geology, Hydrology, etc. etc.) Get online and start reading the writings of the Biblical Monotheists Nobel Prize winning scientists! take a gander at the mass millions of Biblical Commentaries and Apologetics! No matter what your specialization is, GOD, JESUS CHRIST, KNOWS EVERYTHING! LEARN FROM HIM! Pray to receive His Holy Spirit of Truth and ask Him to teach you personally! (anyone disdaining the contents of the Holy Bible is lacking so much correct knowledge that they appear to have crammed their head only with inaccurate nonsense instead!) so YES, the Holy Bible is not just historic non-fiction, containing the most important facts of history, but is most definitely SCIENTIFICALLY ACCURATE! It has been FROM THE BEGINNING, throughout all recorded history, and will be FOREVER! Because, as redundantly stated, the Holy Bible contains the Words of our Eternal Creator, the One True God!

Fathers of the Sciences and Great Scientific Minds; In Their Own Words

Contrary to the opinion of far too many these days, science is in no opposition to God our Creator or the Divinely Inspired Biblical Account. In fact, science is the result of the inquisitive nature of mankind as he perceives all creation. The fathers of the many fields of science today mostly were just persons who sought to know what is Truth. You will find in their own words that they not only believed in the Biblical Account; but that they believe in the GOD, our Creator of the Biblical Account. As you read these quotes, understand their point and mine; and that is they sought to know more about our Creator by the study of His Creation; as should we all.

Sir Francis Bacon, known as the father of the scientific method, wrote: **"There are two books laid before us to study, to prevent our falling into error; first, the volume of Scriptures, which reveal the will of God, then the volume of the Creatures [Creation], which express His power."** - http://www.ucg.org/booklet/bible-true/one-worlds-most-popular-books/their-own-words-great-men-and-women-who-highly-resp/

http://www.brainpickings.org/index.php/2013/02/15/galileo-letter-to-duchess-of-tuscany/ - contrary to the title of this blog, **Galileo Galilei** was in no way opposing GOD and he said this plainly in his own words.

"I do not feel obliged to believe that the same God who has endowed us with senses, reason and intellect has intended us to forego their use and by some other means to give us knowledge which we can attain by them. He would not require us to deny sense and reason in physical matters which are set before our eyes and minds by direct experience or necessary demonstrations."

and

"People who are unable to understand perfectly both the Bible and the science far outnumber those who do understand them. The former, glancing superficially through the Bible, would arrogate to themselves the authority to decree upon every question of physics on the strength of some word which they have misunderstood, and which was employed by the sacred authors for some different purpose. And the smaller number of understanding men could not dam up the furious torrent of such people, who would gain the majority of followers simply because it is much more pleasant to gain a reputation for wisdom without effort or study than to consume oneself tirelessly in the most laborious disciplines."

and he goes on to state

"...nor is God any less excellently revealed in Nature's actions than in the sacred statements of the Bible."

he was even familiar with and understood the chief endeavor of the Holy Ghost (the Holy Spirit).

"Now if the Holy Spirit has purposely neglected to teach us propositions of this sort as irrelevant to the highest goal (that is, to our salvation), how can anyone affirm that it is obligatory to take sides on them, that one belief is required by faith, while the other side is erroneous?"

Being filled with the Holy Spirit myself; if present; I would have replied to him, that GOD our Creator has not *neglected* to teach us Truth in any way; but that we will be learning it from Him for all eternity. Our present limited understanding of what is Truth; is not to be laid in any way upon the Master of the Universe; as if our Creator has not made it plain before us; as we adventure in discovery of it;

by observing and meditating upon His Creation; including the diligent study of His Word given to us in the Holy Bible. Please do not sir, out of your own present ignorance, falsely accuse our Creator of some supposed negligence on His part; and I say the same to the many who are doing so today.

I will furthermore add, that if you THINK you have found something contrary to the Biblical Account in the study of Creation; then you should examine both what you THINK is contrary and your comprehension of what you read more thoroughly. Galileo did properly understand that most who argue from what is contained therein against fundamental, observable Truth; do so because they have incorrectly interpreted the meaning of what they read; even as he did in presupposing others before him had not observed such things as he had through his optics. (http://www.godempowersyou.com/documentation/HistoricalTestimonyandMinistry/MansChronologicalExistenceExplained.pdf) For contrary to what Galileo went on to state; (for which I would have rebuked him to his face sternly):

Galileo stated falsely; **"That the intention of the Holy Ghost is to teach us how one goes to heaven, not how heaven goes."**

Our Creator teaches us only Truth about **EVERYTHING!** As it is written:

"and the Comforter, the Holy Spirit, whom the Father will send in my name, he will teach you all things, and remind you of all things that I said to you." - http://biblehub.com/john/14-26.htm

"But whenever The Spirit of The Truth comes, he will lead you into the whole truth, for he will not speak of his own will, but he shall speak whatever he shall hear and he shall reveal the future to you." - http://biblehub.com/john/16-13.htm

Our Eternal Creator teaches us the Truth concerning everything! Lack of knowledge is apparent in us all because we are not our Perfect Eternal Creator; but it is most apparent in those who are choosing not to learn from Him directly (by the Presence of His Holy Spirit upon us http://www.biblegateway.com/passage/?search=Acts+2%3A38-39&version=KJV; diligent study of His Word http://biblehub.com/2_timothy/2-15.htm, the Holy Bible, and the confirming comparative, accurate observation of His Creation; the sciences http://biblehub.com/romans/12-2.htm)!

http://biblehub.com/1_john/2-27.htm and http://biblehub.com/hebrews/6-18.htm

It seems some people like to argue just for the sake of arguing. Heliocentric! Geocentric! Heliocentric! Geocentric! etc. but the Truth is that our entire solar system is in constant motion hurling through space like a complex bola. That BOTH the earth is revolving around the sun AND the sun around the earth; which is hurling around our galaxy; which is hurling through space itself in similar fashion. Our solar system is revolving around the Milky Way galaxy; the sun isn't motionless. Now these images are overstated, but you get the idea, the sun is in motion, the stars are in motion, the planets are in motion.

http://www.youtube.com/watch?v=RON9rWcALWc

The entire universe is like a massively complex bola of galaxies (more bolas) of solar systems (more bolas) of planetary systems (more bolas), etc.; that was sent spinning from the origin (the only stationary point in all time and space) and can be found at the intersection of time and space by reverse extrapolation of the expansion of the flung galaxies all flying outward from the origin. (http://www.youtube.com/watch?v=ri3R6vFVfEg and http://www.youtube.com/watch?v=u-xUAC9ya3o and http://www.facebook.com/photo.php?fbid=451991028213195&set=a.115635768515391.22520.100002069048072&type=3&theater) our Creator set the entire universe in motion and in a way that galaxies are revolving around the origin while revolving around each other as they expand outward in the void of space. In the galaxies, solar systems are doing the very same thing; including ours. These solar systems are in motion in such a way as while they are revolving around their respective galactic centers, they have smaller/larger solar systems all around them do the very same thing. The best analogy I could think of at present is the flung bola; while the sun is larger than the earth both are still in fact moving through space and revolving around each other as they do. God is stretching out the galaxies. From what I saw of how he could create a new heavens and earth; it was by centripetal force. The path through space is not such a smooth line as is often depicted in diagrams but has the same kind of wobbles to it that flung bolas do (to a greater or lesser extent). So actually the paths are not like the 3d models in grade school at all but more like bolas and if you were to follow the paths would look like spiral waves as these particles of dust and fire of various sizes expand explosively from the origin of the universe (the same way light is observed to travel - http://www.howstuffworks.com/light6.htm - because when we look into time and space (all that we perceive of visible creation) we are actually viewing those spiral waves of light trails; not the moving objects themselves). SOME visible elements are spinning in seeming opposite directions from the vast majority BECAUSE OF EXPLOSIONS AND COLLISIONS WITH OTHER SPINNING BITS OF MATTER in space that we call galaxies today. Likewise, SOME particles don't appear in the many clusters of galaxies because of EXPLOSIONS OF SUPERHEATED matter we call stars, novae, etc. SOME of those particulates then cool and even ice and we call those objects things like dark matter, planets, asteroids, comets, etc. BUT GENERALLY, in 360 degrees from the origin in great orbital (wobbling) planes around the origin galaxies are spinning and revolving at various velocities (DUE TO THE AMOUNT OF MATTER THAT BROKE OFF FROM THE ORIGIN WHEN THE UNIVERSE WAS ALL GATHERED TOGETHER IN ONE SUPER HEATED ENORMOUS MASS AND IF IN THE PROCESS IT BROKE AWAY SLOWLY (LOW VISCOSITY GALAXY) OR QUICKLY (HIGH VISCOSITY GALAXY) OR EVEN EXPLODED FROM THE ORIGIN. (At least if this universe was formed the way He showed me, He could create a new one.) To this day stars can and do explode (YES, BURNING LIQUIDS, GASES AND SOLIDS CAN DO THAT) and even galactic centers (JUST LARGER MASSES THAN THE STARS OF SOLAR SYSTEMS REVOLVING AROUND THEM) can do the same.

My point here is that most of us are like little children (even Galileo) that when we explore the universe in which we find ourselves and discover anything at all about it are likely to boast of it to others and in such a way as to become very defensive about our "new discovery" (http://biblehub.com/ecclesiastes/1-9.htm); so defensive we can fall into the same heresy we accuse others of practicing (that of ignorance; made worse by the mixture of arrogance in far too many). And in that boast make errors like thinking GOD doesn't mean what He states in His Word; when in fact it is appropriate that in some regards it talks of the heavens from a geocentric perspective; because that is where we live in flesh and blood and how we look out and perceive the celestial bodies. There is therefore no error in that perspective and no contradiction, scientifically speaking or in any other rational connotation, throughout the Holy Bible. If one takes a larger rock of more mass and ties it to a smaller and throws it in bola fashion both rocks still act upon one another to a greater and lesser extent; our solar system, while having more objects than just the two, operates in similar fashion; it is therefore neither heliocentric or geocentric, technically speaking. It only serves to discuss it as predominantly heliocentric; since that is the largest nearby mass affecting all the smaller rocks it acts upon; but never forget those smaller rocks we call planets are also acting upon it; together with nearby solar systems in our galaxy; along with all the other seen and unseen forces that exist by the Words and Power of our Creator http://biblehub.com/colossians/1-17.htm.

"As a man who has devoted his whole life to the most clear headed science, to the study of matter, I can tell you as a result of my research about atoms this much: There is no matter as such. All matter originates and exists only by virtue of a force which brings the particle of an atom to vibration and holds this most minute solar system of the atom together. We must assume behind this force the existence of a conscious and

**intelligent mind. This mind is the matrix of all matter." - -
Max Planck**
(founder of the quantum theory and one of the most important physicists of the twentieth century)

http://www.simpletoremember.com/articles/a/science-quotes/

The mass of our sun (and all stars) is burning off; if it loses its mass at a rate that it's gravitational force equals the centripetal force of those objects flying around it and whose velocities are slowing down, then harmony is maintained; but in the more likely event either velocities of planets change to upset that balance (most likely by collisions or near collisions) or the mass of the star(sun) explodes or burns off; the earth could find itself either flung off into space or pulled into the sun's burning flames. It is; after all, only a lake of fire.
http://biblehub.com/revelation/20-14.htm (I am NOT saying the sun is THE lake of fire); I am only saying it is A lake of fire (one of many billions of them) to make my point in how many people mock the Divinely Inspired Holy Scriptures while in the presence of such clear examples that such things as "lakes of fire" exist all around them; throughout the entire universe, and one very prominently viewed and experienced by all who dwell on earth day after day!

Albert Einstein

"In view of such harmony in the cosmos which I, with my limited human mind, am able to recognize, there are yet people who say there is no God. But what really makes me angry is that they quote me for the support of such views." -
http://www.einsteinandreligion.com/atheism.html

While what we may have of Einstein's quotes may not categorically place him easily in any labeled worldview; it is obvious He believed in a Creator; after giving thought to what he observed in creation. (and I hope for his sake he determined who that "Spirit" is; before he breathed his last)
http://www.clockbackward.com/2009/02/08/was-albert-einstein-religious/

"I want to know God's thoughts; the rest is just details." -
http://jick.net/~jess/p200/quotes.html

Too many today are treating science and scientists as if they are infallible and speak almost with reverence about science and scientists. Most doing so seem not to understand that scientists (and science thereby) are fallible; even Einstein:
http://www.facebook.com/notes/michael-swenson/emc2-is-rubbish/485479484864349 Too many championing science act as if they don't realize that even words and their definitions can change due to subjective opinions of people (including scientists) concerning them; let alone

"scientific laws" or "scientific theories" http://en.wikipedia.org/wiki/Superseded_scientific_theories And obviously, those revering fallible men (science and scientists) above the Divinely Inspired Record of God our Creator in the Holy Bible; don't realize that science and scientific discoveries are STILL trying to catch up with the knowledge in it! (knowledge that existed centuries or millenniums BEFORE scientists finally figure out the Truth of its contents): http://www.ucg.org/booklet/bible-true/bible-and-science/ It took the advent of supercomputers to find that there are prophetic encrypted messages within the Holy Bible placed there while it accurately recorded history and truth about creation simultaneously! https://www.google.com/search?q=the+bible+code+michael+drosnin&rlz=1C1GIGM_enUS535US535&oq=the+bible+code&aqs=chrome.2.69i57j0l5.8780j0j8&sourceid=chrome&espv=210&es_sm=93&ie=UTF-8 Very specific prophecies even with dates included in numerous instances!

    Back to my point, science and scientists who accurately study creation will only find it leads to the Creator; no matter what field of science one may specialize in. Science will only continually prove the validity of the contents of the Holy Bible as it is still acquiring the knowledge it contains so plainly in the Divinely Inspired words therein: http://www.facebook.com/notes/michael-swenson/prophecies-show-divine-inspiration-of-the-holy-bible/520171808061783   And all these fathers of the sciences understood that.

http://en.wikipedia.org/wiki/List_of_Christian_thinkers_in_science

Max Planck -

"Both religion and science need for their activities the belief in God, and moreover God stands for the former in the beginning, and for the latter at the end of the whole thinking. For the former, God represents the basis, for the latter – the crown of any reasoning concerning the world-view." -

http://withalliamgod.wordpress.com/2010/11/28/max-planck-on-god/

Carl Sagan

"Science is not only compatible with spirituality; it is a profound source of spirituality. When we recognize our place in an immensity of light-years and in the passage of ages, when we grasp the intricacy, beauty, and subtlety of life, then that soaring feeling, that sense of elation and humility combined, is surely spiritual...The notion that science and spirituality are somehow mutually exclusive does a disservice to both." -

http://www.youtube.com/watch?v=Ag6fH8cU-MU   As a

scientist you would think he could answer such simple questions he expressed in that video: http://www.facebook.com/notes/michael-swenson/acknowledging-the-eternal-creator-takes-no-faith-it-is-scientific-fact/491948024217495 and http://www.facebook.com/notes/michael-swenson/creation-v-evolution-please-use-your-intelligence-to-recognize-intelligence/566154943463469

Francis Collins

"Science is...a powerful way, indeed - to study the natural world. Science is not particularly effective...in making commentary about the supernatural world. Both worlds, for me, are quite real and quite important. They are investigated in different ways. They coexist. They illuminate each other."

--American physician-geneticist and director of the National Human Genome Research Institute

-

http://www.goodreads.com/author/quotes/20100.Francis_S_Collins

William H. Bragg

"From religion comes a man's purpose; from science, his power to achieve it. Sometimes people ask if religion and science are not opposed to one another. They are: in the sense that the thumb and fingers of my hands are opposed to one another. It is an opposition by means of which anything can be grasped."

--British physicist, chemist, and mathematician. Awarded Nobel Prize in 1915

- http://www.beliefnet.com/Faiths/Galleries/God-and-Science-What-Do-Scientists-Believe.aspx?p=9

And I agree that the way to grasp the Truth contained in writing within the Holy Bible comes from seeking answers from our Creator and by observing Creation in a rational manner; scientifically. Even our Creator told us that any claims that scientific findings were in anyway contradictory to His Divine Instructions for Life contained in the Holy Bible were false; as true science (factual observations of creation) will always confirm what our Creator has declared and made known to us. No one who long observes and meditates upon what he or she perceives can fail to see the Intelligence that made all things and holds all things together to this very moment. http://biblehub.com/1_timothy/6-20.htm

Fred Hoyle

"A junkyard contains all the bits and pieces of a Boeing 747, dismembered and in disarray. A whirlwind happens to blow through the yard. What is the chance that after its passage a fully assembled 747, ready to fly, will be found standing there? So small as to be negligible, even if a tornado were to blow through enough junkyards to fill the whole Universe."

"Life cannot have had a random beginning ... The trouble is that there are about 2000 enzymes, and the chance of obtaining them all in a random trial is only one part in 10^40,000, an outrageously small probability that could not be faced even if the whole universe consisted of organic soup."

"The notion that not only the biopolymer but the operating program of a living cell could be arrived at by chance in a primordial organic soup here on the Earth is evidently nonsense of a high order."

"Once we see, however, that the probability of life originating at random is so utterly miniscule as to make it absurd, it becomes sensible to think that the favorable properties of physics on which life depends are in every respect deliberate ... . It is therefore almost inevitable that our own measure of intelligence must reflect ... higher intelligences ... even to the limit of God ... such a theory is so obvious that one wonders why it is not widely accepted as being self-evident. The reasons are psychological rather than scientific."

B. Prokop said...

Add Fred Hoyle. British cosmologist; came up with the term "The Big Bang".

Fierce and vocal atheist for decades. Embraced theism late in life, after being convinced that Intelligent Design was the only rational belief.

(Also a great writer. Might I recommend "The Black Cloud".) -
http://dangerousidea.blogspot.com/2011/03/list-of-former-atheists.html
--English mathematician and astronomer.

-
http://www.goodreads.com/author/quotes/199992.Fred_Hoyle

      I'm former atheist/agnostic (the brainwashing in our American public schools is that effective; so effective I forgot about early childhood recurring nightly dreams from our Creator for many years).

Johannes Kepler

1571-1630 German Astronomer

(planetary orbits, optics, mathematical language of science)
The 3 laws of planetary motion. Advanced Copernicus' heliocentric theory.

"Since we astronomers are priests of the highest God in regard to the book of nature, it befits us to be thoughtful, not of the glory of our minds, but rather, above all else, of the glory of God."

"...the harmony in the universe is "a sacred sermon, a veritable hymn to God the Creator".... "Oh God, I am thinking thy thoughts after Thee" Johannes Kepler

"I believe only and alone in the service of Jesus Christ. In him is all refuge and solace."

http://www.valleypresbyterian.org/curriculum/science/quotes.htm

Isaac Newton

English mathematician & physicist, one of the greatest scientists of all time.
Laws of gravitation and motion, developed calculus. Major contributions to optics, physics, math and astronomy.

"He who thinks half-heartedly will not believe in God; but he who really thinks has to believe in God."

The solar system itself could not have been produced by blind chance or fortuitous causes but only by a cause "very well skilled in mechanics and geometry."

"There are more sure marks of authenticity in the Bible than in any profane history."

"No sciences are better attested to than the science of the Bible." "This most beautiful system of the sun, planets, and comets, could only proceed from the counsel and dominion of an intelligent and powerful Being.... This Being governs all things, not as the soul of the world, but as Lord over all; and on account of his dominion he is wont to be called Lord God." Isaac Newton; Principles.

"It must be expressed in the very form of sound words in which it was delivered by the apostles. For men are apt to run into partings about deductions. All the old heresies lie in deductions. The true faith was in the Biblical texts."

http://www.valleypresbyterian.org/curriculum/science/quotes.htm

"This most beautiful system of the sun, planets and comets, could only proceed from the counsel and dominion of an intelligent and powerful Being."

http://www.simpletoremember.com/articles/a/science-quotes/

James Clerk Maxwell

Scottish Physicist

discovered the relationships between electricity, magnetism and light and introduced the concept of field of EM force, devout Christian

"Happy is the man who can recognize in the work of today a connected portion of the work of life, and an embodiment of the work of Eternity."

"Think what God has determined to do to all those who submit themselves to his righteousness and are willing to receive his gift [of eternal life in Jesus Christ]. They are to be conformed to the image of his Son and when that is fulfilled and God sees they are conformed to the image of Christ, there can be no more condemnation."

"I think that men of science as well as other men need to learn from Christ, and I think that Christians whose minds are scientific are bound to study science that this view of the glory of God may be as extensive as their being is capable of."

"The more we enter into Christ's work He will have more room to work His work in us. For He always desires us to be one with us. Our worship is social, and

Christ will be where two or three are gathered together in His name."

http://www.adherents.com/people/pm/James_Clerk_Maxwell.html

http://www.valleypresbyterian.org/curriculum/science/quotes.htm

Michael Faraday

Discovered benzene and electromagnetic radiation, invented the generator and was the main architect of classical field
theory. One of the prominent experimental scientists of all time.

"Speculations, man, I have none. I have certainties. I thank God that I don't rest my dying head upon speculations for "I know whom I have believed and am persuaded that he is able to keep that which I've committed unto him against that day."

http://www.valleypresbyterian.org/curriculum/science/quotes.htm

http://www.icr.org/article/3958/

http://www.answersingenesis.org/articles/cm/v12/n4/faraday

Robert Boyle

Developed the idea of atoms. Boyle's law.

Wrote: *The Wisdom of God Manifested in the Works of Creation*. Governor of the Corporation for the Spread of the Gospel of Jesus Christ in New England.

"From a knowledge of God's work we shall know Him."

http://www.goodreads.com/quotes/144147-from-a-knowledge-of-god-s-work-we-shall-know-him

Arthur Compton

Nobel Prize-winning physicist for his discovery and explanation of the change in the wavelength of X rays when they collide with electrons. Compton effect confirmed the dual nature of electromagnetic radiation as both a wave and a particle.

"From earliest childhood I have learned to see in Jesus the supreme example of one who loves his neighbors and expresses that love in actions that count, who knows that people can find their souls by losing themselves in something of great value, who will die rather than deny the truth in favor of the popular view held by his most respected contemporaries. That Jesus lives so vitally in men today makes me hope that by following in his footsteps in my small way I also may live forever."

"For myself, faith begins with the realization that a supreme intelligence brought the universe into being and created man. It is not difficult for me to have this faith, for it is incontrovertible that where there is a plan there is intelligence. An orderly, unfolding universe testifies to the truth of the most majestic statement ever uttered: 'In the beginning God ... .'"

"In their essence there can be no conflict between science and religion. Science is a reliable method of finding truth. Religion is the search for a satisfying basis for life."

"What nobler ambition can one have than to cooperate with his Maker in bringing about a better world in which we can live? Science has created a world in which Christianity is a necessity."

"I believe that its insistence on the inherent value of individual men and women Christianity has the key to survival and the good life in the modern world."

http://www.doesgodexist.org/JulAug08/Nobel-Compton.html

J.J. Thompson

Discovered the electron

"In the distance tower still higher [scientific] peaks which will yield to those who ascend them still wider prospects and deepen the feeling whose truth is emphasized by every advance in science, that great are the works of the Lord." (Statement in *Nature*)

http://www.valleypresbyterian.org/curriculum/science/quotes.htm

Charles Coulson

Architect of molecular orbital theory.

"There were some ten of us and together we sought for God and together we found Him. I learned for the first time in my life that God was my friend. God became real to me, utterly real. I knew Him and could talk with Him as I never imagined it before and these prayers were the most glorious moment of the day. Life had a purpose and that purpose coloured everything."

http://www.valleypresbyterian.org/curriculum/science/quotes.htm

Robert Griffith, a member of our U.S. Academy of Sciences, Otto Stern professor of physics at Carnegie Mellon University received one of the most coveted awards of the American Physical Society in 1984 on his work in physical mechanics and thermodynamics. Physics Today said he is an evangelical Christian who is an amateur theologian and who helps teach a course on Christianity and science.

He recently said:

"If we need an atheist for a debate, I'd go to the philosophy department—the physics department isn't much use."

At Berkeley University, among 55 chemistry professors, we only had one who was willing to openly identify himself as an atheist, my good friend Bob, with whom I still have many discussions about spiritual things.

http://bib.irr.org/scientists-and-their-gods

Charles H. Townes

Nobel Prize winner. Inventor of the maser and laser. First to observe an interstellar molecule

"You may well ask, "Where does God come into this," to me, that's almost a pointless question. If you believe in God at all, there is no particular "where"—He is always there, everywhere….To me, God is personal yet omnipresent. A great source of strength, He has made an enormous difference to me." From *Making Waves*.

http://www.valleypresbyterian.org/curriculum/science/quotes.htm

"For successful science of the type we know, we must have faith that the universe is governed by reliable laws and, further, that these laws can be discovered by human inquiry. The logic of human inquiry is trustworthy only if nature is itself logical…. This is the faith of reason"

http:/benevolentbaptist.wordpress.com/2013/02/02/faith-within-reason-charles-h-townes-on-faith-in-scientific-thought/

Allan Sandage

One of the world's greatest observational cosmologists. Estimated the age of the universe.

"The world is too complicated in all its parts and interconnections to be due to chance…I am convinced that the existence of life with all its order and each of its organisms is simply too well put together."

http://www.valleypresbyterian.org/curriculum/science/quotes.htm

"I find it quite improbable that such order came out of chaos. There has to be some organizing principle. God to me is a mystery but is the explanation for the miracle of existence, why there is something instead of nothing."

- Alan Sandage (winner of the Crawford prize in astronomy) Willford, J.N. March 12, 1991. Sizing up the Cosmos: An Astronomers Quest. New York Times, p. B9.

http://www.simpletoremember.com/articles/a/science-quotes/

Ilya Prigogine (Chemist-Physicist)
Recipient of two Nobel Prizes in chemistry

"The statistical probability that organic structures and the most precisely harmonized reactions that typify living organisms would be generated by accident, is zero."

I. Prigogine, N. Gregair, A. Babbyabtz, Physics Today 25, pp. 23-28

http://www.simpletoremember.com/articles/a/science-quotes/

Christian de Duve

"*A Guided Tour of the Living Cell*" (Nobel laureate and organic chemist)

"If you equate the probability of the birth of a bacteria cell to chance assembly of its atoms, eternity will not suffice to produce one... Faced with the enormous sum of lucky draws behind the success of the evolutionary game, one may legitimately wonder to what extent this success is actually written into the fabric of the universe."

http://www.simpletoremember.com/articles/a/science-quotes/

"[Probably the leading paleontologist alive today, Simon Conway Morris, the scientist who discovered the significance of the Cambrian explosion of animal life, writes in his seminal book, Life's Solutions, that he is "convinced" that nature's success in the lottery of life has "metaphysical implications."]"

http://www.simpletoremember.com/articles/a/science-quotes/

Dr. Michael Denton (Australian microbiologist)

"...The capacity of DNA to store information vastly exceeds that of any other known system: it is so efficient that all the information needed to specify an organism as complex as man weighs less than a few thousand millionths of a gram. The information necessary to specify the design of all the species of organisms which have ever existed on the planet...could be held in a teaspoon and there would still be room left for all the information in every book ever written..."

http://www.simpletoremember.com/articles/a/science-quotes/

John O'Keefe (astronomer at NASA)

"We are, by astronomical standards, a pampered, cosseted, cherished group of creatures.. .. If the Universe had not been made with the most exacting precision we could never have come into existence. It is my view that these circumstances indicate the universe was created for man to live in."

- Heeren, F. 1995. Show Me God. Wheeling, IL, Searchlight Publications, p. 200

http://www.simpletoremember.com/articles/a/science-quotes/

Anthony Flew

Professor of Philosophy, former atheist, author, and debater

"It is, for example, impossible for evolution to account for the fact that one single cell can carry more data than all the volumes of the Encyclopedia Britannica put together."

"It now seems to me that the findings of more than fifty years of DNA research have provided materials for a new and enormously powerful argument to design."

http://www.simpletoremember.com/articles/a/science-quotes/

George Greenstein

"As we survey all the evidence, the thought insistently arises that some supernatural agency—or, rather, Agency—must be involved. Is it possible that suddenly, without intending to, we have stumbled upon scientific proof of the existence of a Supreme Being? Was it God who stepped in and so providentially crafted the cosmos for our benefit?"

(American astronomer) *Greenstein, George. The Symbiotic, Universe: Life and Mind in the Cosmos. (New York: William Morrow, (1988), pp.* 26-27

http://www.simpletoremember.com/articles/a/science-quotes/

Frank Tipler

"When I began my career as a cosmologist some twenty years ago, I was a convinced atheist. I never in my wildest dreams imagined that one day I would be writing a book purporting to show that the central claims of Judeo-Christian theology are in fact true, that these claims are straightforward deductions of the laws of physics as we now understand them. I have been forced into these conclusions by the inexorable logic of my own special branch of physics."

(Professor of Mathematical Physics) Tipler, F.J. 1994. The Physics Of Immortality. New York, Doubleday, Preface.

http://www.simpletoremember.com/articles/a/science-quotes/

William Phillips

Nobel prize for the development of methods to cool and trap atoms with laser light.

"God has given us an incredibly fascinating world to live in and explore."

Arthur Schawlow

Nobel Prize winner in Physics. Development of the laser and laser spectroscopy

"We are fortunate to have the Bible, and especially the New Testament, which tells so much about God in widely accessible, human terms."

Alexander Polyakov

Russian Physicist

"We know that nature is described by the best of all possible mathematics because God created it." The famous Russian physicist, Alexander Polyakov Fortune magazine (October, 1986),

Sir William Herschel

"All human discoveries seem to be made only for the purpose of confirming more and more the Truths contained in the Sacred Scriptures."

Sir William Herschel (1738-1822), English astronomer, he made numerous discoveries about the laws of the heavens.

C.F.Gauss

One of the greatest mathematicians of all time. Contributed significantly to pure mathematic and made practical applications of importance for 20th-century astronomy, geodesy, and electromagnetism.

"There are problems to whose solution I would attach an infinitely greater importance than to those of mathematics, for example touching ethics, or our relation to God, or concerning our destiny and our future; but their solution lies wholly beyond us and completely outside the province of science."

John Wheeler

Princeton University astronomer

"Slight variations in physical laws such as gravity or electromagnetism would make life impossible . . . the necessity to produce life lies at the center of the universe's whole machinery and design," stated John Wheeler, Princeton University professor of physics *(Reader's Digest, Sept., 1986).*

http://www.valleypresbyterian.org/curriculum/science/quotes.htm

Lord Kelvin

1824-1907 (William Thomson) British physicist; helped lay the foundations of thermodynamics.

First and second laws of thermodynamics. Absolute temp scale. Trans-Atlantic cable.

"I believe that the more thoroughly science is studied, the further does it take us from anything comparable to atheism."

Do not be afraid to be free thinkers. If you think strongly enough, you will be forced by science to the belief in God.

http://www.valleypresbyterian.org/curriculum/science/quotes.htm and http://www.valleypresbyterian.org/curriculum/science/science.htm

Blaise Pascal, *Pensées*

"There is a God shaped vacuum in the heart of every man which cannot be filled by any created thing, but only by God, the Creator, made known through Jesus."

-

http://www.goodreads.com/author/quotes/10994.Blaise_Pascal

About 80% of the listed 100 most influential persons in history acknowledge the Creator as the God of the Holy

Bible; most of the other 20% in this list were influential but in a detrimental way toward humanity and creation. http://www.adherents.com/adh_influ.html

It is evident that the greatest minds and most powerful persons in the history of the world have been deeply religious; purpose driven people. (even atheism is religious in nature in that they choose to believe in a concept that they can in no way prove and choose to believe in it; **even though science and rational thought proves their faith in the absence of an Intelligent, Eternal Creator is false -** But my point in this brief note on these scientific greats is that even the fields of science we have today would not even exist apart from those who wanted to know more about our Creator by the careful and meticulous observation of creation! That many today who so revere science and wrongly think it as adversarial to Truth and our Creator; don't even realize the science they believe in CAME FROM THE KNOWLEDGE of persons who KNEW AND OPENLY ACKNOWLEDGED OUR CREATOR! That SCIENCE itself COMES FROM OUR CREATOR; as well as the great minds who have recognized that fact in all of history.

The many fields of science ultimately owe their origins and continued existence to our Eternal, Intelligent Creator and to persons who; even though persecuted in varying degrees and some even murdered in the cause; still chose to Glorify GOD our Creator by the use of reason, rational thought, and meticulous observation of creation with lifelong meditation on the same! All who would be wise and knowledgeable do the same.

http://coldcasechristianity.com/2013/the-rich-historic-roll-call-of-great-christian-thinkers-and-scientists/

    This list is by no means exhaustive and is only the tip of the iceberg of all those who deserve to be recognized for their great achievements. If you are a scientist and by studying creation have discovered our Creator, I encourage you to write, publish, speak out about it; and try and monitor textbooks for our now faulty public indoctrination system; because we can save lives and souls from great suffering, great anguish; if we will only teach the children (and everyone) the Truth!

    People worldwide need to comprehend that the Holy Bible not only contains the most thoroughly researched and well verified history on earth, but Divine Knowledge even about the future! It has been studied for centuries, even millenniums down to every letter it contains! (so, when you find people today snickering and comparing the revered Words of God with a comic book, it frankly makes them look like an irreverent, sacrilegious, blasphemous fool! someone lacking so much knowledge, they need to go back to grade school and demand a proper education!) I encounter people that try to compare the Holy Bible to known fiction like Harry Potter, or other religious texts on earth and when they do so, they instantly are telling me they haven't read anything they're even talking about! or if they have, they lack so much proper reading comprehension, it's a wonder they've learned anything at all! If you have ever disdained the contents of the Holy Bible, you need to Repent immediately, humble yourself before the Living God and apologize to Him and for not esteeming His Words, His Holy Blood shed for you and the lives of all the saints that laid them down to give you His Words, the Holy Bible, throughout history.

https://www.ccel.org/ccel/v/vanbraght/mirror/cache/mirror.pdf - there has been a very real and very great Battle on earth between those who know and love the Living God and those wicked beings who refuse to live righteously as He Commands. Not just God Almighty, but the saints throughout history have been giving their lives to try and reach you all with the Truth. When God judges all souls, no one will have any excuse! So don't choose to be a willfully ignorant, self-destructive, deceived and self-deluded, unrepentant, wicked fool! SHOW SOME PROPER REVERENCE AND RESPECT FOR GOD, JESUS CHRIST, HIS

WORDS IN THE HOLY BIBLE, AND THE GREATEST SOULS WHO HAVE EVER WALKED ON EARTH!

OBEY HIS COMMANDMENT TO REPENT AND BE BAPTIZED IN HIS NAME, THE NAME OF OUR LORD JESUS CHRIST, AND PRAY TO RECEIVE HIS HOLY SPIRIT OF TRUTH! DO IT TODAY! DON'T PUT IT OFF! He warns us that anyone who procrastinates or hardens themselves against obeying Him, is in danger of falling under strong delusion that leads to the flames of damnation! SO, OBEY GOD AND BE QUICK ABOUT IT!

I repeat, the Holy Bible was not written like any other book in all the world! The Old Testament was written over centuries, even millenniums of ancient history! Passed on meticulously from generation to generation by scribes that were specially trained to handle the Words of God! Finally, the ancient scrolls were compiled into the Septuagint a few centuries before Jesus Christ, the One True God, came in the flesh, fulfilling His Words in that regard, that He had told the Prophets and had been recorded in those contents of the Tanakh/Miqra (Torah, Nevi'im and Ketuvim) - Old Testament.

https://www.accordingtothescriptures.org/prophecy/353prophecies.html - not only did Jesus Christ plainly state He is God fulfilling His Words, His Law and Prophecies but He PROVED it by doing Divine Miracles publicly; speaking and changing reality instantly just by doing so!

John 5:39-40

³⁹ You search the Scriptures because you think that in them you have eternal life; and it is they that bear witness about me, ⁴⁰ yet you refuse to come to me that you may have life.

The Fulfillment of the Law
16In the same way, let your light shine before men, that they may see your good deeds and glorify your Father in heaven. **17**Do not think that I have come to abolish the Law or the Prophets. I have not come to abolish them, but to fulfill them. **18**For I tell you truly, until heaven and earth pass away, not a single jot, not a stroke of a pen, will disappear from the Law until everything is accomplished.... https://biblehub.com/matthew/5-17.htm

The Hatred of the World
...**23**Whoever hates Me hates My Father as well. **24**If I had not done among them the works that no one else did, they would not be guilty of sin; but now they have seen and hated both Me and My Father. **25**But this is to

fulfill what is written in their Law: 'They hated Me without reason.'... https://biblehub.com/john/15-24.htm

Understand that Divine Creative Miracles like the Works of Jesus Christ are PROOF He is the ONE TRUE GOD! HE HAS BEEN DOING MIRACLES THROUGHOUT ALL HISTORY TO THIS VERY DAY!

https://www.youtube.com/watch?v=rn73J9A0SnU - Craig Keener PhD scholar has written a large volume documenting modern miracles by Jesus Christ, the One True God. Modern miracles often come with not just eyewitness testimonies but external evidence such as modern medical records.

https://www.youtube.com/watch?v=X3wGdjYnWRI

DON'T IGNORE BIBLICAL CONTENT! MEDITATE ON HIS WORDS!

Some wrongly imagine that the antichrist/devil can do such miracles. NO! the devil does not do the Divine Miracles of GOD! The wonders of the antichrist, the devil, are his evil deceptions! How he has been able to keep so many deceived despite the Words of God given us all in the Holy Bible, despite the Miracles of God, Jesus Christ, and despite all the efforts of the billions of us who know and love Him! The wonders of the devil are his evil deceptions like evolution, atheism, islam, buddhism, hinduism and anything keeping you from knowing the ONE TRUE GOD, JESUS CHRIST, personally!

The Abomination of Desolation
...**23**At that time, if anyone says to you, 'Look, here is the Christ!' or 'There He is!' do not believe it. **24**For false Christs and false prophets will appear and perform great signs and wonders that would deceive even the elect, if that were possible. **25**See, I have told you in advance.... https://biblehub.com/matthew/24-24.htm

The Man of Lawlessness
...**8**And then the lawless one will be revealed, whom the Lord Jesus will slay with the breath of His mouth and annihilate by the majesty of His arrival. **9** The coming of the lawless one will be accompanied by the working of Satan, with every kind of power, sign, and FALSE wonder, **10**and with every wicked deception directed against those who are perishing, because they refused the love of the truth that

would have saved them....
https://biblehub.com/2_thessalonians/2-9.htm

So, the devil and his false prophets and teachers use deceptions (anything he can to get you to fail to obey God, to fail to call upon Jesus Christ to Save you and your loved ones - SO IF YOU HAVE NEVER DONE THAT DO IT NOW WITH ALL SERIOUSNESS!)

Like how muslims are always dismissing the Words of God in the Holy Bible and wrongly claiming the lies in their quran are correct. They do that even though not one muslim, sees, hears or knows God! With exception to the ones that Jesus Christ is calling to Himself in dreams and visions. (obviously muslims are deceived) you can tell they are deceived the moment they tell you about their imaginary god, allah, the god that has no children and no partners, and gives them hundreds of clearly evil instructions in their qurans:

https://www.youtube.com/watch?v=htshvld51UE - Ann made me so joyful inside to see SOMEONE who is still thinking clearly and acting so righteously! islam and the quran has deceived and enslaved over a billion people today; leading them all into the flames of damnation! she is doing what should be done with all qurans!

https://www.thereligionofpeace.com/pages/quran/index.aspx - if the quran was ONLY evil lies, then everyone would recognize them, but the devil TWISTS the Words of God in the Holy Bible (includes just enough truth, to deceive people away from the Truth with his many inserted lies and clearly evil instructions).

It's not that wicked people are incapable of doing anything good or right, it's just that IF they do, they are doing it only with intent to deceive, like those criminal organizations that use fronts as a cover for their illegal activities or politicians who use polls and speech writers to tell the public what they imagine the public wants to hear, all while serving their own selfish interests behind the scenes.

So muslims throughout history infiltrate nations with intent of conquering them, but they wait for opportune moments to do so, which is why I encourage the world to recognize islam is a dangerous criminal organization bent on global conquest and ban it globally.

After the crusaders bravely gave their lives to keep Christian nations free from such demonic oppression, it looks like treason today to have muslims in our nations and mosques being built therein.

http://www.blastthetrumpet.org/PublicLetters/AAAUpdatedPublicAlertsMattersofLifeandDeath/Updates053016/Americans%20and%20Citizens%20of%20the%20World%20FREEDOM%20and%20LIFE%20Comes%20from%20GOD.pdf

For more details read my book **Save the World from islam.**

      Far too many people these days try to redefine terms, definitions of words such as "evidence" just to go around absurdly, falsely claiming there's no evidence of God or of the historicity of the Holy Bible. These people are making themselves all look extremely foolish, willfully ignorant, deceived and self-deluded. I'm not saying that people denying God Almighty, Jesus Christ, our Eternal Creator, Lord and Savior, are spiritually and mentally challenged or stupid, I'm saying they're giving the appearance of being such to everyone who knows better. They're letting the devil far too easily lead them into the flames of damnation with any of his many lies. Jesus Christ is the Truth everyone must know, in order to be set free and remain free from all the lies of the devil; lies that lead to suffering, death and destruction.

Evidence is evidence by definition; it's not up for revision based on yours or anyone else's vain imaginations. An apple is an apple whether it's presented by an infant or an elder, or by an imbecile or a genius.

https://www.facebook.com/photo/?fbid=977229375689355&set=a.115635768515391 - the evidence of God is so overwhelming that those denying Him, look as if they're lacking knowledge to such a degree that they need to go back to grade school and demand a proper education or that they have filled their heads with so much lying garbage, they've left no room for truth.

The contents of the Holy Bible have undergone more scientific scrutiny than any other recorded facts of history for veracity. Your lack of knowledge in that regard doesn't entitle you to claim those contents are merely stories or myths. Miracles have also been documented with medical records to verify them as authentic, your incredulity of the facts and evidence, does not entitle you or anyone to dismiss them.

https://www.facebook.com/photo/?fbid=969688109776815&set=a.115635768515391 - just two eyewitnesses are sufficient to send people to prison, but an entire world full of them isn't enough to convince the unreasonable skeptic of Jesus Christ, our Eternal Creator, Lord and Savior.

All verified facts (true science/accurate knowledge) support Biblical veracity (creation).

https://www.facebook.com/photo.php?fbid=4890242114388042&set=pb.100002069048072.-2207520000&type=3
and
https://www.facebook.com/photo.php?fbid=6382847548460817&set=pb.100002069048072.-2207520000&type=3

There are scientific and mathematic formulas for everything observed in the universe, proving Intelligent Design. Virtually everything manmade takes massive amounts of engineering, time, energy and resources (watch "How Its Made"); so, our universe complete with laws and formulas is obviously Engineered by our Eternal Creator.

https://www.youtube.com/watch?v=4wMhXxZ1zNM - it astonishes me that someone could believe we exist in a programmed simulation and yet still deny the

Programmer.

The Supremacy of Christ
…16For in Him all things were created, things in heaven and on earth, visible and invisible, whether thrones or dominions or rulers or authorities. All things were created through Him and for Him. 17 He is before all things, and in Him all things hold together.
https://biblehub.com/colossians/1-17.htm

"All matter originates and exists only by virtue of a force which brings the particle of an atom to vibration and holds this most minute solar system of the atom together. We must assume behind this force the existence of a conscious and intelligent mind. This mind is the matrix of all matter."
― Max Planck -
https://www.goodreads.com/quotes/1328821-all-matter-originates-and-exists-only-by-virtue-of-a

I met someone online recently that was complaining about how Galileo was investigated by the Catholic Church for his observations of our solar system and planets. He was blaming God and the Holy Bible for the actions that people take down here.

I told Him that some scriptures are written from a geocentric perspective because God placed man on the earth; not the sun. Whereas other scriptures speak to us from His Perspective as God, Pervading and Transcending His Creation, existing within and also apart from space and time, this fallen temporal creation subjected by Him to decay and death. Rom 8:20-28 He didn't understand my point and so asked if I was saying the Holy Bible is wrong?

I probably should have given him the old adage, "In the Holy Bible, God is telling mankind how to go to Heaven; not how the heavens go." But the reason I don't like to use that adage, is that then people somehow think less of the scriptures regardless and then also wrongly imagine that God doesn't teach us ALL TRUTH about His Creation; even if we can't find that information in writing in the Holy Bible, we find it in Him (Jn 14:26, Col 2:3). So, I repeated that in some locations of the scriptures God describes the heavens and the earth as separate in aspects from the heavens and tells us about the heavens from the perspective of being on earth because that is where He placed us and that is how mankind observes the heavens. So, theories about our solar system have nothing whatsoever to do with the fact we observe the apparent motions of the sun, moon and stars FROM earth and use them exactly as the scriptures plainly state:

The Fourth Day

...**13**And there was evening, and there was morning—the third day. **14**And God said, "Let there be lights in the expanse of the sky to distinguish between the day and the night, and let them be signs to mark the seasons and days and years. **15**And let them serve as lights in the expanse of the sky to shine upon the earth." And it was so.... https://biblehub.com/genesis/1-14.htm

     In other words, God is telling us the plain truth in the Holy Bible, and if you're filling your head with information of any kind that is detracting you away from His Words of plain truth, then that's just another tool of the devil, leading you astray into virtually meaningless, insignificant matters and into deceptive imaginations and delusions. Like wrongly imagining that the Holy Bible isn't telling us the Truth just because you THINK it should mention something that it doesn't, or that you haven't read yet in its contents. Another reason I don't like that old adage is due to the fact that the Holy Bible is given us from God Himself and so has Divine Perspective throughout, and in that manner, He tells us He is concerned about our spirits, because our earthly bodies and this entire fallen creation is passing away, but our spirits still exist long after the death of our physical bodies. Jesus Christ, God, plainly states His Words are Spirit and Life, Truth, they are meant to be SPIRITUALLY understood

(God defines His Own Terms in the contents of the Holy Bible). 1Cor 2:14, Rom 8:5-10, Jn 6:63 So, when you read a dream, vision or revelation in the scriptures, you should get a concordance and look up the Divine Definitions given us by God Himself in the contents of the Holy Bible of every word therein, to properly interpret and understand what He is actually teaching or showing us thereby.

      Understand that the Words of God in the Holy Bible are given us to lead everyone to a personal relationship with our Eternal Creator, Lord and Savior, the One True God, (in English, known as) our Lord Jesus Christ. Everything God tells us in the Holy Bible is factually true. Anything He doesn't mention in writing in the Holy Bible, He, Himself, still teaches all Truth (not vain imaginations from anyone else!)

...**2**that they may be encouraged in heart, knit together in love, and filled with the full riches of complete understanding, so that they may know the mystery of God, namely Christ, **3**in whom are hidden all the treasures of wisdom and knowledge. **4I say this so that no one will deceive you by smooth rhetoric....**
https://biblehub.com/colossians/2-3.htm

In other words, only by receiving His Holy Spirit of Truth and learning from God Almighty personally can anyone keep from being deceived by the devil, by other people, or their own vain imaginations. <u>**Jesus Christ, the One True God, is the Truth that sets and keeps us free from any and all lies and deceptions! Jn 8:32-36.**</u> So, there is no opposition of science, accurate knowledge, to the contents of the Holy Bible! Any opinions from anyone past, present or future that is in direct conflict with the Words of God in the Holy Bible ARE WRONG! They are NOT GOD! They did not walk on water, heal the sick raise the dead, publicly die and raise their own body from the grave, transfigure it and make it Immortal and Glorious and then Ascend into Heaven in front of eyewitnesses! JESUS CHRIST DID! Don't trust ANYONE past, present or future over Him and His Words in the Holy Bible! NEVER! (So, that's why I really don't like that adage about what God teaches us or doesn't teach us in the Holy Bible, when in fact He teaches us all things, TRUTH.) His Knowledge is infinite, the whole world could not contain the books if God had given us everything He knows in writing, we will be learning from Him forever. The Holy Bible is the literary FOUNDATION OF TRUTH given us by God, Jesus Christ, by which all other opinions spoken or written are tested and tried by! Jn 12:48-50; 17:17, Lk 21:33 **I repeat! God and His Words Reign Supreme in all creation, any opinions from anyone else contrary to Him and His Words given us in the Holy Bible are wrong.**

So, God designed His Creation to TEACH MANKIND THE MOST IMPORTANT TRUTHS, to focus on our character and conduct, to focus on the Virtues, to focus on SPIRITUAL things, because this present physical reality is decaying and passing away! **(this incarnation is very brief on purpose, it's full of trials, toils and troubles, so get right with God today)! OBEY HIS COMMANDMENT TO REPENT AND BE BAPTIZED IN HIS NAME AND PRAY TO RECEIVE HIS HOLY SPIRIT OF TRUTH, THEN STUDY HIS WORDS IN THE HOLY BIBLE AND ASK HIM TO GIVE YOU HIS UNDERSTANDING OF ALL THINGS!** Apply His Commandments to your existence, ask Him to transform and perfect you, to fill you with His Love to Love Him and His Sons and Daughters with and to cause you to be quick to obey His Righteous Commandments now and forever! EVERYTHING GOD ASKS OF US IS INTENDED FOR OUR OWN GOOD AND THE GOOD OF ALL HIS CREATION! Since this earthly incarnation is so brief and since fallen creation is decaying and passing away, we shouldn't be dwelling on our physical solar system, motions thereof, so much as learning from God WHY He designed the Sun, moon and stars the way that He did, and what He is teaching us AS VIEWED FROM EARTH!

I summarize:

http://biblehub.com/jeremiah/9-24.htm - 23Thus says the LORD, "Let not a wise man boast of his wisdom, and let not the mighty man boast of his might, let not a rich man boast of his riches; 24but let him who boasts boast of this, that he understands and knows Me, that I am the LORD who exercises lovingkindness, justice and righteousness on earth; for I delight in these things," declares the LORD.

THERE IS NO DOUBT WHATSOEVER THAT YAHOSHUAH (English - JESUS the CHRIST) BOTH DECLARED AND PROVED HE IS THE ONE TRUE GOD!!!!!!!! http://www.icr.org/article/i-ams-christ/ and http://www.letusreason.org/trin16.htm and http://biblehub.com/1_john/5-20.htm that HE ALONE is the WAY to ETERNAL LIFE!!!!!!!! https://www.facebook.com/notes/michael-swenson/christ-crucified/735365403209088 and https://www.facebook.com/notes/michael-swenson/holy-bible-versus-the-quran/719366671475628 and https://www.facebook.com/notes/michael-swenson/evidence-of-god-our-creator/568134419932188 (if STILL unavailable - http://www.blastthetrumpet.org/PublicLetters/AAAUpdatedPublicAlertsMattersofLifeandDeath/MoreUpdates031315/Evidence%20of%20GOD%20our%20Creator.pdf)

http://vimeo.com/17960119

http://www.biblehub.com/aramaic-plain-english/john/8.htm

https://www.youtube.com/watch?v=uGu-QmfNNSQ

https://www.facebook.com/photo.php?fbid=1595242210744694&set=gm.482201258613094&type=1&theater

"What about baptism what name to be used Jesus' name or Father, Son and Holy Spirit?" - anonymous

YAHOSHUAH said He came in His Father's Name, Yahovah! https://youtu.be/EUQEMqF5dL8?t=770 Yaho - I AM - shuah SALVATION so the Name of the Father, Son and Holy Spirit IS YAHOSHUAH (that is Yah - I AM - shuah - Salvation (and Breath of Life) when the root is further researched. So, Baptism is performed in the Name of the Father, the Son and the Holy Spirit; when it is done in the Name of YAHOSHUAH Ha Mashiach (which transliterates by root word research to "I AM SALVATION, the ONE and ONLY Messiah")

YAHOSHUAH has been translated into many names depending on the language but I prefer to stick with YAHOSHUAH (English, Jesus the Christ). Some prefer the shortened version Yeshua like how many shorten our own names from Joshua to just Josh or Michael to just Mike or Jonathan to just Jon etc. but Yahoshuah is Yahovah (YHWH) who came in the flesh.

the SIGN
(http://biblehub.com/isaiah/7-14.htm - The Sign of Immanuel
...13Then he said, "Listen now, O house of David! Is it too slight a thing for you to try the patience of men, that you will try the patience of my God as well? 14"Therefore the Lord Himself will give you a sign: Behold, a virgin will be with child and bear a son, and she will call His name Immanuel. Some CLAIM it should read "young woman" instead of virgin. (WHY would GOD say the SIGN from HIM would merely be a "young woman", young women are all over the planet giving birth, that would be no SIGN at all! rather more like an act of frustration in search of the Messiah among billions of young women! RIDICULOUS! - GOD tells us the STARS are the signs!) That is how the wise seers KNEW the Messiah had been born!

GOD Incarnating was TIMED BY HIM; according to and coinciding with the SIGNS He made for mankind: (http://biblehub.com/genesis/1-14.htm - The Fourth Day: Sun, Moon, Stars

14Then God said, "Let there be lights in the expanse of the heavens to separate the day from the night, and let them be for signs and for seasons and for days and years; 15and let them be for lights in the expanse of the heavens to give light on the earth"; and it was so....)

Such that when YAHOSHUAH Incarnated (Immanuel - The Birth of Jesus)

...22Now all this took place to fulfill what was spoken by the Lord through the prophet: 23"BEHOLD, THE VIRGIN SHALL BE WITH CHILD AND SHALL BEAR A SON, AND THEY SHALL CALL HIS NAME IMMANUEL," which translated means, "GOD WITH US." http://biblehub.com/matthew/1-23.htm)

People all over the world would KNOW this is GOD in the flesh! https://www.youtube.com/watch?v=ff-Gp194XUU and https://www.youtube.com/watch?v=BJ6szvfApNM and https://www.youtube.com/watch?v=CtJ8Jjma5cM

GOD not only tells His Story in the Holy Bible and throughout history but in His Creation, day unto day, night unto night, DIVINE KNOWLEDGE is given to us all.

https://www.youtube.com/watch?v=kxgMR6cB1js

No one but GOD ALMIGHTY could predict His entire Incarnation in detail. (http://www.accordingtothescriptures.org/prophecy/353prophecies.html and https://www.facebook.com/notes/michael-swenson/prophecies-show-divine-inspiration-of-the-holy-bible/520171808061783) And have the STARS TELL the Gospel, AND not just tell the Gospel but coincide DIRECTLY with the Divine Incarnation, Crucifixion and Resurrection. (https://www.youtube.com/watch?v=ff-Gp194XUU and https://www.youtube.com/watch?v=BJ6szvfApNM and https://www.youtube.com/watch?v=CtJ8Jjma5cM) Watch those three presentations and stop saying you have never seen evidence of the Divine or Supernatural. Supernatural events are documented by the millions! https://www.youtube.com/watch?v=LYBnJF2P_WQ There are other views about the Star over Bethlehem (https://answersingenesis.org/christmas/an-evaluation-of-the-star-of-bethlehem-dvd/) I just want people to comprehend that God Created the Stars and the Stars tell His Gospel Message and have been doing so throughout history. https://www.youtube.com/watch?v=PHCftvj_Prw

Why not become a personal eyewitness of the Messiah today, call on YAHOSHUAH and ask Him if He is the ONE TRUE MESSIAH to forgive you your sins and unbelief and to please reveal Himself to you, so that you can KNOW Him! Then you will join the billions of us worldwide who already do!
http://biblehub.com/jeremiah/31-34.htm

Some try to dismiss the obvious: NO ONE ELSE IN ALL HISTORY DID THE MIRACLES OF INSTANTLY TRANSFORMING OBSERVABLE REALITY AT HIS WORD, LIKE JESUS CHRIST DID; PROVING HE IS THE ETERNAL CREATOR WHO HAS POWER OVER ALL HIS CREATION!

The Way, the Truth, and the Life
6 Jesus answered, "I am the way and the truth and the life. No one comes to the Father except through me. 7 If you really know me, you will know[a] my Father as well. From now on, you do know him and have seen him."8 Philip said, "Lord, show us the Father and that will be enough for us."9 Jesus answered: "Don't you know me, Philip, even after I have been among you such a long time? Anyone who has seen me has seen the Father. How can you say, 'Show us the Father'? 10Do you not believe that I am in the Father and the Father is in Me? The words I say to you, I do not speak on My own. Instead, it is the Father dwelling

in Me, performing His works. 11Believe Me that I am in the Father and the Father is in Me—or at least believe on account of the works themselves.... https://biblehub.com/john/14-10.htm

24If I had not done among them the works that no one else did, they would not be guilty of sin; but now they have seen and hated both Me and My Father. https://biblehub.com/john/15-24.htm

      Those STILL in denial of the Divinity of YAHOSHUAH are dismissing REALITY! (they are choosing to live in their delusions; regardless of history and observable creation) some WRONGLY say if Jesus, a human, could become GOD, why not me? so I reply to them (although it will be a miracle if any such mad fools come to their senses; so, I write more hoping no one else chooses to be so delusional) human did not BECOME God! GOD chose to Incarnate TO DECLARE HIMSELF PLAINLY to us all! https://www.facebook.com/notes/michael-swenson/god-part-1/719346771477618 the day you HEAL every disease, malady, sickness known to man (LIKE YAHOSHUAH - http://biblehub.com/matthew/4-23.htm), the day you stop storms (LIKE YAHOSHUAH http://biblehub.com/matthew/8-27.htm), the day you raise the dead (LIKE

YAHOSHUAH http://biblehub.com/john/11-43.htm and http://biblehub.com/john/11-25.htm), the day you speak only TRUTH, words of GOD (LIKE YAHOSHUAH - http://biblehub.com/john/12-49.htm and https://www.youtube.com/watch?v=eqnNuQ6S5OA), the day you create substance and transform substance (LIKE YAHOSHUAH - https://www.biblegateway.com/passage/?search=John+2:1-11 and https://www.biblegateway.com/passage/?search=Matthew14:13-21), the day you lay down your own life and raise it up again (LIKE YAHOSHUAH http://biblehub.com/john/10-18.htm and https://www.youtube.com/watch?v=ay_Db4RwZ_M and https://www.facebook.com/notes/michael-swenson/god-part-2/830858016993159) is the day your presently mad claim to being a god or goddess or any other fantasy, myth, delusion you might claim, might be considered. THE moment ANYONE can show THEY or some other FULFILLS ALL THE MESSIANIC PROPHECIES SINCE THE BEGINNING, LIKE YAHOSHUAH, https://www.accordingtothescriptures.org/prophecy/353prophecies.html, is the day even I, who have seen the Risen LORD of Creation face to face, will humor their rantings and ravings; otherwise, RIGHT NOW IT JUST MAKES all such persons LOOK AS IF THEY ARE DETERMINED TO PRESENT THEMSELVES AS EXTREMELY IGNORANT AND HELL BENT ON BEING HELL BOUND!!!!!!!!

https://www.youtube.com/watch?v=vQ8TEGMj-jc

In the contents of the Holy Bible, Jesus Christ, the One True God, plainly tells us all how to know Him personally beyond all doubt; so, no one has any excuse.

https://www.facebook.com/photo.php?fbid=6609426679136235&set=pb.100002069048072.-2207520000&type=3

Do you understand? The Sun, Moon and Stars are to teach us about GOD! not for people to get lost in their wild imaginations about how they move or came to be. It's why the most ancient writings and civilizations focused on the stars, because GOD TEACHES US THROUGH OBSERVING THEM FROM RIGHT HERE ON EARTH! The names of the constellations and stars all tell us His Gospel Message (if you skipped over them watch the citations just mentioned above), they corresponded precisely to the Incarnation of our Eternal Creator in this world He Created and Made! So the ancients knew we come from God, from Heaven Above, and when we die we return to Him and is why they named some stars after some people and referred to some people/stars as gods and goddesses because we are made in the Image of God who is the Light of lights, the Sun of suns, the Star of stars, the God of gods, the Man of men, the Spirit of spirits, Father of fathers, Son of sons, Angel of angels, etc. etc. IN ALL THINGS HE IS SUPREME!

Colossians 1:15-19

The Supremacy of the Son of God

[15] The Son is the image of the invisible God, the firstborn over all creation. [16] For in him all things were created: things in heaven and on earth, visible and invisible, whether thrones or powers or rulers or authorities; all things have been created through him and for him. [17] He is before all things, and in him all things hold together. [18] And he is the head of the body, the church; he is the beginning and the firstborn from among the dead, so that in everything he might have the supremacy. [19] For God was pleased to have all his fullness dwell in him,

   EVERYTHING GOD DESCRIBES HIMSELF AS IN THE SCRIPTURES, WE ALL ARE TO A LESSER EXTENT BECAUSE HE CREATED AND MADE US IN HIS IMAGE! Gen 1:27 which means Creation is an expression of our Eternal Creator and He intends it to be Perfect and Glorious, the presence of evil is due to our own evil imaginations, words and deeds. So, this present creation is fallen (decaying and dying, passing away) and only those who choose to Love and Be Perfected will remain with our Eternal Creator in Paradise, Creation Perfected. All who refuse to repent of their wicked thoughts, words, ways and deeds will be cast into the lake of fire. YES! God has EVERY RIGHT to determine who will and who will not spend eternity with Him! You don't surround yourself with people who hate you, so don't be a hypocrite about God! LOVE HIM AND LOVE EACH OTHER is what He commands, if you want to be around in a good way forever!

When I encounter anyone online or off, hating on the One who Created and Made them and gives them every breath they take, I think to myself what an incredibly ungrateful, demonic fool, I'm surprised God doesn't cause such wicked souls to burst into flames and turn into piles of ash just to warn the rest of mankind not to become so self-destructively evil and foolish. So, I tell everyone: Heaven is most definitely very real, I have been blessed with visits there and so I know from personal experience that when God tells us in the Holy Bible that words fail to describe how wonderful it is, He is telling us the Truth! NO ONE SHOULD MISS OUT ON HEAVEN! and likewise, I tell everyone: the lake of fire is very real, God showed me part of the Final Judgment and people were wailing before Him when they saw the smoke and felt the heat of the flames coming up from the pit of damnation in which agonizing screams of the damned could be heard. **DON'T BE AN UNREPENTANT, WICKED FOOL! REPENT! AND ASK GOD TO PERFECT YOU ACCORDING TO HIS WILL AND WORDS, BY HIS GRACE AND POWER! GET BAPTIZED IN HIS NAME**

AND PRAY TO RECEIVE HIS HOLY SPIRIT OF TRUTH! DON'T PUT IT OFF! <u>This life is very short but your decision to love and obey God Almighty, Jesus Christ, or not, has everlasting ramifications of the most serious kind.</u>

Filling your head full of fallible notions, virtually meaningless knowledge, while ignoring what's most important is why God says:

Romans 1:22-32

King James Version

[22] Professing themselves to be wise, they became fools,

[23] And changed the glory of the uncorruptible God into an image made like to corruptible man, and to birds, and fourfooted beasts, and creeping things.

[24] Wherefore God also gave them up to uncleanness through the lusts of their own hearts, to dishonour their own bodies between themselves:

[25] Who changed the truth of God into a lie, and worshipped and served the creature more than the Creator, who is blessed for ever. Amen.

[26] For this cause God gave them up unto vile affections: for even their women did change the natural use into that which is against nature:

27 And likewise also the men, leaving the natural use of the woman, burned in their lust one toward another; men with men working that which is unseemly, and receiving in themselves that recompence of their error which was meet.

28 And even as they did not like to retain God in their knowledge, God gave them over to a reprobate mind, to do those things which are not convenient;

29 Being filled with all unrighteousness, fornication, wickedness, covetousness, maliciousness; full of envy, murder, debate, deceit, malignity; whisperers,

30 Backbiters, haters of God, despiteful, proud, boasters, inventors of evil things, disobedient to parents,

31 Without understanding, covenant breakers, without natural affection, implacable, unmerciful:

32 Who knowing the judgment of God, that they which commit such things are worthy of death, not only do the same, but have pleasure in them that do them.

and also, plainly states:

God's Wrath against Sin
...**19**For what may be known about God is plain to them, because God has made it plain to them. **20**For since the

creation of the world God's invisible qualities, His eternal power and divine nature, have been clearly seen, being understood from His workmanship, so that men are without excuse. **21**For although they knew God, they neither glorified Him as God nor gave thanks to Him, but they became futile in their thinking and darkened in their foolish hearts.... https://biblehub.com/romans/1-20.htm

Far too many today are acting like God didn't show Himself to mankind and prove He is God beyond all reasonable doubt! These incredibly ignorant or deliberately evil fools are actually likening the well verified history of the Holy Bible to a comic book, calling it all myths and legends. THE PROBLEM IS SO PERVASIVE I BLAME OUR PUBLIC SCHOOLS FOR SUCH WIDESPREAD IDIOCY! PUT THE HOLY BIBLE BACK IN OUR SCHOOLS AS THE PRIMARY TEXT BOOK OF TRUTHFUL INFORMATION THAT IT IS! THE MOST IMPORTANT INFORMATION WE ALL NEED TO KNOW! DO IT NOW BEFORE WE HAVE AN ENTIRE WORLD OF PEOPLE ACTING LIKE SELF-DESTRUCTIVE, WICKED FOOLS THAT WILL DOOM THEMSELVES TO SUFFERING, DEATH AND DESTRUCTION!

EVERYONE NEEDS TO COMPREHEND THAT GOD, JESUS CHRIST, TOLD US ALL HOW TO KNOW HIM PERSONALLY AND LEARN FROM HIM PERSONALLY

BEYOND ALL DOUBT! THAT'S WHY HE STATES THAT NO ONE HAS ANY EXCUSE! AND THAT IF YOU DON'T BELIEVE HIM, YOU WILL DIE IN YOUR SINS! (ending up in the lake of fire, instead of Heaven). Jn 3:15-36; 2 Th 1:8-9; Rev 21:8, Jn 8:24-25

EVERYONE MUST! I REPEAT MUST! OBEY HIM FOR YOUR OWN GOOD! Repent and Be Baptized in His Name as He Commands us all! Mark 16:15-16, Matthew 28:18-20, Acts 2:38-39; 4:12 And pray to receive His Holy Spirit of Truth whereby you will KNOW HIM! Luke 11:13, John 14:20-26 and John 16:13 He will teach you personally, just like He taught the Prophets recorded in the Holy Bible! THE GOSPEL OF JESUS CHRIST IS GOOD NEWS FOR MANKIND ABOUT GOD RESTORING US BACK TO FELLOWSHIP WITH HIM, EVEN THOUGH WE WERE ALL LOST IN OUR SINS, DEAD TO HIM! Eph 2:1-10 Don't pass up KNOWING GOD! No matter what your specialization is, GOD KNOWS MORE (much more)! He is the ONLY ONE who can perfect you!

8But now, O LORD, You are our Father; we are the clay, and You are the potter; we are all the work of Your hand. https://biblehub.com/isaiah/64-8.htm

No other book in all the world told us what reality would be like millenniums in advance. There are televised programs that take modern headlines daily from around the world and show you where God told us this is what would happen in the Holy Bible like *Prophecy in the News* and *Jack Van Impe Presents*. Follow the Instructions of God on how to know Him personally beyond all doubt.

https://www.accordingtothescriptures.org/prophecy/353prophecies.html - these hundreds of prophecies God fulfilled when He came in the flesh are proof of the Divine Inspiration of the contents of the Holy Bible (God told us precisely where He would be born and when before He did so, He told us precisely how He would suffer and die before He did so, He not only did Miracles no one else in the entire history of the world has done as proof He is God (any miracles the Prophets, Apostles and Disciples do, they do because GOD JESUS CHRIST is living inside of them and they do those miracles IN HIS NAME! - Book of Acts throughout), but the hundreds of prophecies He fulfilled JUST DURING HIS BRIEF INCARNATION make the identity of the One True God a mathematic certainty.)

https://www.icsv.at/one-chance-in-a-trillion-trillion-trillion-trillion-trillion-trillion-trillion-trillion-trillion-trillion-trillion-trillion-trillion

Yes, the entire Old Testament, Divine Law and Prophecies, was compiled centuries before God came in the flesh and fulfilled hundreds of them (He is still fulfilling others He gave us throughout history.)
https://biblearchaeology.org/research/new-testament-era/4022-a-brief-history-of-the-septuagint

One of the more detailed and obvious prophecies God fulfilled in the sight of the entire world was the reformation of the nation of Israel in its ancient location.

https://www.google.com/search?client=opera&q=Israel+reformed+to+the+day+prophesied&sourceid=opera&ie=UTF-8&oe=UTF-8#ip=1 - Grant Jeffrey wrote a book called "Armageddon, Appointment with Destiny" in which he showed the prophecies of how the Israelites would be scattered among the nations (known as the Diaspora) and then regathered in the reformed nation of Israel. He shows the prophecies that they would be punished for a specific amount of time and then shows the dates of the destruction of Jerusalem and the nation of ancient Israel and the date of its reformation. (not many people have made these calculations) and argues to the day. I read the history, the prophecies and followed those calculations and it appears the nation of Israel was reformed to the day

God told us MILLENNIUMS ago! TO THE DAY! https://www.amazon.com/Armageddon-Appointment-Grant-R-Jeffrey/dp/0921714408 Michael Rood is another one who argues that God fulfills His Prophecies precisely - https://www.youtube.com/watch?v=JM1sY44_-74&list=PL6NNBo_y_fjOF3wwi-VsCOcCNUeFqFINs

No other book in all the world told us what reality would be like millenniums in advance. When I tell someone that there are televised programs that take modern headlines daily from around the world and shows you where God told us this is what would happen in the Holy Bible, and they don't even bother to take the time to consider the possibility and actually watch them, they are demonstrating willful ignorance with regards to their own soul. People demonstrating that they don't care about their own soul enough to watch and learn, are demonstrating not just a lack of knowledge, but are willfully ignoring God and his words because they don't want to repent. Anyone demonstrating they are hardening themselves to the Truth that much means you should spend time elsewhere because those people are making themselves unteachable by hardening themselves against the Truth/God. They are damning their own souls.

http://www.blastthetrumpet.org/PublicLetters/AAAUpdatedPublicAlertsMattersofLifeandDeath/Prophecies%20Sho w%20Divine%20Inspiration%20of%20the%20Holy%20Bibl2.pdf

I could be writing the rest of my life and still not cover all the proofs of Divine Inspiration given us by God in His Words in the Holy Bible, but it is safe to say that people who doubt His Prophecies are in fact proof of Divine Inspiration of the Holy Bible are leaving reasonable thought far behind them and embracing the absurd. https://biblehub.com/kjv/2_peter/1-19.htm There is simply no other book in all the world that rises to the Divine Authority, the plain truthful merit of the Holy Bible, it towers in trustworthiness about the most important knowledge on earth over all other books in the world, BY FAR! (The world is filled with millions of apologetics that cover the Divine Inspiration of the Holy Bible, that sadly far too many fail to even glance at during their entire life.)

https://www.google.com/search?client=opera&q=evidential+apologetics&sourceid=opera&ie=UTF-8&oe=UTF-8 and https://www.google.com/search?client=opera&q=classical+apologetics&sourceid=opera&ie=UTF-8&oe=UTF-8

https://www.facebook.com/photo.php?fbid=4890242114388042&set=pb.100002069048072.-2207520000&type=3 - The Holy Bible comes from God who doesn't lie. Don't trust the spoken or written opinions from anyone over our Lord Jesus Christ, the One True God!

A skeptic ripped one prophecy out of context from the hundreds listed that Jesus Christ fulfilled just during His Incarnation as the Messiah. People seem not to comprehend that God came in the flesh as a Man, declared and proved Himself to us, so that no one has any excuse.

So, the prophecy he ripped out of context was the prophecy about the enmity between the seed of the woman and that of the devil. Whenever someone rips any scripture out of the context of the entire Holy Bible, don't just put it back into context in that particular passage, but put it back into the entire Holy Bible!

It's clear enough when you don't ignore the rest of the scriptures.

16 The promises were spoken to Abraham and to his seed. The Scripture does not say, "and to seeds," meaning many, but "and to your seed," meaning One, who is Christ. https://biblehub.com/galatians/3-16.htm

https://www.biblegateway.com/verse/en/Revelation%2022%3A16 - the reason why the prophecies in the Holy Bible pertain to Jesus Christ, is due to the fact He gave those prophecies as the One True God that He is and is the reason only He fulfills them.

John 5:39-40

39 You search the Scriptures because you think that in them you have eternal life; and it is they that bear witness about me, 40 yet you refuse to come to me that you may have life.

Matthew 5:17-18

Christ Came to Fulfill the Law

17 "Do not think that I have come to abolish the Law or the Prophets; I have not come to abolish them but to fulfill them. 18 For truly, I say to you, until heaven and earth pass away, not an iota, not a dot, will pass from the Law until all is accomplished.

Jesus Opens the Scriptures

…26Was it not necessary for the Christ to suffer these things and then to enter His glory?" 27And beginning with Moses and all the Prophets, He explained to them what was written in all the Scriptures about Himself. https://biblehub.com/luke/24-27.htm

Taking one phrase or verse out of the Holy Bible is worse than the five blind man approach to the elephant. God, Jesus Christ, is telling us all about Himself and how to know Him personally from Genesis to Revelation. It is a must to read ALL of the Holy Bible IN CONTEXT in order to understand Him and His Words given us.

So, skepticism might seem rational to someone ignoring the content, the rest of the entire Holy Bible, but when put in context becomes nothing but a display of willful ignorance, deception and self-delusion. God came in the flesh, fulfilled prophecies He gave to mankind over millenniums of ancient history, even the stars He Created and Made identified Him (why the wise men came and worshiped Him as a babe). He spoke and instantly changed reality in front of crowds of eyewitnesses. Jesus Christ is God. Anyone denying Him has no excuse whatsoever. Anyone disobeying Him is a fool on their way to the flames of damnation.

Common Questions

Unbelievers often ask, "If Jesus Christ is God, who was taking care of the universe when He died on the cross?" and also, "Why should we trust in God, when He didn't save His Son?"

God does not define death the way some imagine it to be defined. In other words, nowhere in the Holy Bible does God tell us the death of our bodies mean we cease to exist. Instead, He tells us our spirits separate from our bodies that return to the dust at that point.

26 As the body without the spirit is dead, so faith without deeds is dead. https://biblehub.com/james/2-26.htm

Remember Your Creator
…6Remember Him before the silver cord is snapped and the golden bowl is crushed, before the pitcher is shattered at the spring and the wheel is broken at the well, 7before the dust returns to the ground from which it came and the spirit returns to God who gave it.
https://biblehub.com/ecclesiastes/12-7.htm

So, the death of Jesus Christ on the cross, does not mean Jesus Christ, God, ever ceased to exist.

As to your next point, it never was the intention of God to be saved from Crucifixion -

Jesus the Good Shepherd
…17The reason the Father loves Me is that I lay down My life in order to take it up again. 18No one takes it from Me, but I lay it down of My own accord. I have authority to lay it down and authority to take it up again. This charge I have received from My Father."
https://biblehub.com/john/10-18.htm

Matthew 26:53
Are you not aware that I can call on My Father, and He will at once put at My disposal more than twelve legions of angels?

John 2:19
Jesus answered, "Destroy this temple, and in three days I

will raise it up again."

It was His Intention to publicly die and then raise His Body from the grave, transfigure it, make it Immortal and Glorious and Ascend into Heaven, proving we can trust Jesus Christ in life and in death, proving He is the Way to Heaven; proving He is the One True God!

He ever lives to answer any and all with enough sense to humbly obey Him.

The Great Commission
…15And He said to them, "Go into all the world and preach the gospel to every creature. 16Whoever believes and is baptized will be saved, but whoever does not believe will be condemned. https://biblehub.com/mark/16-16.htm

"Brothers, what shall we do?" 38 Peter replied, "Repent and be baptized, every one of you, in the name of Jesus Christ for the forgiveness of your sins, and you will receive the gift of the Holy Spirit. 39This promise belongs to you and your children and to all who are far off—to all whom the Lord our God will call to Himself."…

https://biblehub.com/acts/2-38.htm

Peter and John Before the Council
...11This Jesus is 'the stone you builders rejected, which has become the cornerstone.' 12 Salvation exists in no one else, for there is no other name under heaven given to men by which we must be saved."
https://biblehub.com/acts/4-12.htm

John 14:20-26
20 In that day you will know that I am in my Father, and you in me, and I in you. 21 Whoever has my commandments and keeps them, he it is who loves me. And he who loves me will be loved by my Father, and I will love him and manifest myself to him." 22 Judas (not Iscariot) said to him, "Lord, how is it that you will manifest yourself to us, and not to the world?" 23 Jesus answered him, "If anyone loves me, he will keep my word, and my Father will love him, and we will come to him and make our home with him. 24 Whoever does not love me does not keep my words. And the word that you hear is not mine but the Father's who sent me.25 "These things I have spoken to you while I am still with you. 26 But the Helper, the Holy Spirit, whom the Father will send in my name, he will teach you all things and bring to your remembrance all that I have said to you.

People ripping words out of context these days, try and make Jesus Christ in the Old Testament, somehow different than He was in the New Testament. When God flooded this world because the hearts and thoughts of all men were deliberately evil, He wasn't kidding! What would have been cruel is to let innocent babes grow up in that kind of world! When He ordered the extermination of various tribe that attacked His People Israel, He order them as a matter of life and death! You have to place yourself in the distant past in which they were deliberately trying to annihilate the Children of Israel. Only then will you understand the One who said to Love Him and each other meant it! If people who imagine they came from monkeys and pond scum through evolution despite all evidence to the contrary, have their way they are DELIBERATELY turning people into that kind of evil! Just look at how television programming has changed in our lifetime! It is totally filthy from just shows like Leave it to Beaver and Andy Griffith.

If mankind doesn't learn from the flood, God tells us that if mankind becomes that evil again, HE WILL RESERVE THE WORLD FOR FLAME! So, it isn't a matter of the LGBTQ group at all parading the banner of God not sending against them the flood, THE RAINBOW, instead they are marching to their DOOM BY FIRE! And all of us need to rouse them out of their depravity or we are headed there as well! Whenever your sexual proclivities became what you march over, you are at death's door! Mankind just doesn't understand that the base desires of our flesh, LUST, is contrary to the Virtues of LOVE, that is our lasting Spirit. The lusts of the flesh are TEMPORAL and so God commands against sexually immorality of all kinds, because the flesh DIES, while His Virtues of Love, Peace and Joy last FOREVER! So, God has forever established until He perfects us all, sexual unions to be between one man and one woman! All other sexual relationships are banned with eternal suffering. (Rev 21:8) This is the real reason why they want to believe they came from monkeys and pond scum, instead of God! If you are someone who is not in a God condoning relationship, you must pray that He changes you in that regard. YOU MUST REPENT OF ANY AND ALL SEXUAL IMMORALITY! (Rev 21:8)

https://www.youtube.com/results?search_query=ashen+remains+of+sodom+and+gomorrah - the ashen remains of Sodom and Gomorrah and the other cities that were destroyed for such wicked sexual immorality still exist as a warning to us all.

God explains that ALL His Commandments are dependent on Loving Him and each other, so if you're interpreting anything in His Words, the Holy Bible, as anything but Loving Him and each other, YOU'RE INTERPRETATION IS WRONG!

    We have tens of thousands of ancient manuscripts, dating all the way back in history; commensurately with the Lord Jesus Christ and His Apostles; like no one else in ancient history! So, any modern translations of the Holy Bible can be researched with those ancient manuscripts for accuracy. We have historic records from His earliest disciple onward!
https://www.youtube.com/watch?v=ay_Db4RwZ_M and https://carm.org/about-the-bible/manuscript-evidence-for-superior-new-testament-reliability/ so every copy can be compared for its historicity. Bottom line, you can trust what the Holy Bible states and any and all questions you can bring up to our Eternal Creator. There is simply no way one can read all of the examination of Holy Writ in one lifetime. If you must read them start with the early church fathers. (Clement of Rome, Mathetes, Polycarp, Ignatius, Barnabas, Papias, Justin Martyr, Irenaeus... etc.)

    Never set aside the VERIFIED HISTORY of the Holy Bible for imaginary nonsense from anyone! Even nonsense proposed by scientists! Their imaginations of how the universe came to be, and how life evolved ARE NONSENSE, the verified history of the Holy Bible has been confirmed by the Nobel Prize winning scientists, and by GOD

HIMSELF! TRUST FOREVER IN GOD AND HIS WORDS! Know that our ancestors passed them down to us through physical and spiritual wars, so study those Words of God all your days!

When I tried to get off the beaten path God corrected me by showing me in a dream a smorgasbord full of delicious food. He loaded up a plate with all my favorite things and then He stirred it together and said, "Take heed; lest in your much eating, you fail to savor the best part." He knew that I didn't like what He was doing to the food by mixing it altogether, so I couldn't savor what each particular portion is good for, and He was telling me that I was ever learning and not applying what I had learned. We can get caught up in ever learning! What I'm trying to teach you is that it's fine and dandy to learn many things from God, BUT DON'T EVER FAIL TO SEEK AND SAVE THE LOST! When you have more that your share from His Gospel trove here on earth, you must not fail to do your part in saving others!

IT'S TRUE just as your most memorable and joyous event was when Jesus Christ saved your soul, you have to value that for everyone else! So, tell others how to KNOW Him! until everyone does!

God, Jesus Christ, reveals Himself to those who love and obey Him. No one has any excuse.

The Contents of the Holy Bible Explains the Why Things Are Made the Way They Are

The contents explain why God made things the way they are, for example you. The way God designed our physical bodies (Creation), explains His Spiritual Truths (Himself and His Words, the Holy Bible) to us. Each and every cell of your body receives life inspiration. This inspiration is in the form of blood enriched with oxygen from your lungs. As the blood goes to every part of your body, it removes the waste, and gives that inspiration to each and every cell. So, with each and every breath (Spirit) the blood carries nutrients (Food, the Bread of Life) to every single cell and gives that cell what it needs to live, and cleanses each cell regularly. Thus, the way our bodies are designed by our Eternal Creator show that we all need Him. His Life's Blood, that is Pure and Holy, to be applied to each and every one of our lives for INSPIRATION and NECESSARY CLEANSING from all our sins. Just as the blood He made for our bodies brings inspiration, nutrition, and cleanses each cell in our bodies, so His Blood must be Spiritually applied by Him for our Spiritual lives and for cleansing us spiritually from our sins. Acts 4:12; 10:34-43, 1Jn 1:7   The Holy Blood shed for us all in the Name of our Lord Jesus Christ is what we all NEED to live! He cleanses us all from every sin and provides for us all true inspiration from above! The Lord has designed everyone to NEED His

Holy Blood. This is why He tells us plainly that the life of flesh is in its blood. Lev 17:11 As He stated, HE IS THE ONE WHO HAS ETERNAL LIFE, THE ONE WE ALL MUST COME TO IN ORDER TO HAVE THAT LIFE. (Jn 5:39-40)

It's also why the scriptures recorded that we overcame by HIS BLOOD and the Word of our testimonies.

<u>*The War in Heaven*</u>
...**10**And I heard a loud voice in heaven saying: "Now have come the salvation and the power and the kingdom of our God, and the authority of His Christ. For the accuser of our brothers has been thrown down—he who accuses them day and night before our God. **11** <u>They</u> <u>have</u> <u>conquered</u> <u>him</u> <u>by</u> <u>the</u> <u>blood</u> <u>of</u> <u>the</u> <u>Lamb</u> <u>and</u> <u>by</u> <u>the</u> <u>word</u> <u>of</u> <u>their</u> <u>testimony.</u> <u>And</u> <u>they</u> <u>did</u> <u>not</u> <u>love</u> <u>their</u> <u>lives</u> <u>so as to shy away</u> <u>from</u> <u>death.</u>   https://biblehub.com/revelation/12-11.htm

The Holy Bible explains that mankind was created and made from God IN THE BEGINNING IN HIS LIKENESS so we never were anything but HIS LIKENESS. Look at how many ways God makes us in His Likeness. WE ARE MADE IN THE IMAGE OF GOD! (not any "evolved" lesser kinds of creatures) There is no doubt we are intelligently designed by our Eternal Creator.

1Tim 2:5 ...the Man Christ Jesus... and 1John 5:20 ...the One True God...

Man expressed as:	Good Connotations:	Bad Connotations:
Gods (gods) - Jesus Christ has the Supremacy in All Things 1Cor 14-19 - we are created in His Image	John 10:33-38, 1 Jn 3:1, 2Cor 4:4, Phil 2:6, Gen 1:27, Jn 1:14	Ps 86:6-7, 2Th 2:4, Rom 1:18-25, Rev 13:14,15, Rev 14:9-11, Rev 16:13,14, Lk 10:20 and 11:26
Spirit (spirits)	Jn 4:24, Ps 104:4, Heb 1:7,13,14, Rev 3:1, Heb 12:9, 1Jn 4:1, Jn 14-16	1Jn 4:3; 2:18,20, Rev 16:13,14, Lk 11:26, 2Jn 2:7, 1Tim 4:1, Acts 19:12-13
Angel (angels)	Ex 32:34, Ps 104:4, Heb 1:7, 13,14, (Mt 13:39 + Jn 4:35-38), (Rev 12:7,11,17 + Rom 1:20), (Mt 25:31 + Lk 20:36)	Mt 25:41, (Rev 12:7 + Rom 1:20), (Jude 4, **6**, 13 + 2Th 2:3), 1 Cor 6:3
Soul (souls)	Ps 16:10, 30:3, Jn 12:27, Mk	2Pet 2:14, Rev 18:13,14, Acts

	8:36-37, Mk 12:30, Rev 20:4, 1Pet 4:19, Jas 1:21, Mt 12:18	15:24, Mt 24:28, Eze 18:4, 20, 1Jn 3:8
Star (stars)	Gen 39:9,10, Rev 12:1, 1:20, (Rev 2:28 + 22:16), Job 38:7, 1Pet 1:19, Num 24:17, 1Cor 15:41, Mal 4:2, Dan 12:3, Ps 148:3, 136:9, Mt 13:43, Gen 1:16; 22:17, Deut 1:10	Jude 4-13, Rev 12:4, 8:12, Mt 24:9
Light (lights)	Jas 1:17, Jn 3:15-21; 5:35; 8:12; 12:35,36, Eph 5:8, 1Th 5:5, 1Pet 2:9, 1Jn 1:5,7, 2:8-10, Acts 26:18; Mt 5:14, Gen 1:14-16, Lk 12:35, Phil 2:15	

Darkness (night)		Mt 6:23, Lk 11:35,36, Jn 3:19, 35-46, Jn 11:9-10, 2Cor 6:14, Prov 4:19
Lightning (lightnings)	Job 37:3, 38:35, Ps 144:6, Eze 1:13,14, Dan 10:6, Ps 18:14; 77:18; 97:4; 135:7, Zech 9:14; Mt 24:27; 28:3, Lk 17:24, Rev 4:5, 8:5; 11:19; 16:18, Nah 2:4	Lk 10:18
Fire (flames)	Heb 12:29, Ps 104:4, Is 24:14,**15**, Ps 29:7, Is 66:15,16, 10:17, Rev 2:18,19; 12:4,5, Lk 12:35; Dan 7:9-11, Lk 12:49, Acts 2:3	Is 13:8, Eze 28:18, Jas 3:6, (Rev 13:13 + 12:4), Rev 17:16
Lamp (lamps, candles)	Prov 20:27, Lk 11:33-36, Zeph	Job 18:6; 21:17, Prov 24:20;

	1:12, Rev 1:20; 2:1; 11:4, Mt 5:15, Ps 18:28, Prov 31:18, Job 29:3; 41:19, Mt 25:1-8, Eze 1:13, Dan 10:6, Zech 4:2, Num 8:2,3, Gen 15:17, 1Sam 3:3, 2Sam 22:29, Ps 132:17, Rev 4:5	13:19; 20:20, Rev 8:10; Job 12:7
House (houses, cages)	Jn 14:2, (Job 4:17-19 + Gen 2:7), Lk 19:46; 6:48, 1Pet 2:5, Heb 3:2-6, (Ex 12 + Heb 7-10)	Zech 12:4; 7:26,27, Mt 10:25; 12:29-44, Prov 7:27; 2:18; 3:33; 14:11; 17:13, Rev 18:2; Jer 5:27
Tent (tents)	Song 1:5,8, Jer 30:18, Ex 40, Ps 78:55	Hab 3:7, Ps 84:10; 69:25
Tabernacle (tabernacles)	Ps 84:1; 118:15; 46:4, (Zech 14:16-19 + Lev 23:34-44 + 2Cor 5:1-17 + Hos	Job 11:14; 12:6; 15:34, (Hos 9:6 + 2Cor 12:7), Ps 78:51; 83:6, Mal 2:11,12, Dan

	12:9), Prov 14:11, 2Pet 1:13,14, Rev 21:3, Num 24:5, Heb 8:2; 9:21	11:45, Zech 14:16-19
Eye (eyes)	Mt 6:22, Lk 6:41,42, (Eze 1:18-20 + Rev 4:6-8), (Rev 1:14; 2:18; 3:18, 5:6, 19:12 + Ps 104:4), Eph 1:18 (1Pet 3:12 + Ps 91:11), Job 42:5, Prov 5:21; 15:3, 30, 22:12; 29:13; 7:2; 22:9, Ps 92:11; 33:18; 88:9; 54:7; 32:8; 94:9; Zech 4:10	Mt 6:23, (Mt 7:3-5 + Lam 5:17 + Job 17:7), (Zech 11:17 + Mt 5:29), Mt 20:15, Mk 7:22, 2Pet 2:14, Prov 30:12; 23:6; 28:22; 30:17, Job 24:15, Eccl 1:8; 4:8
Cloud (clouds, vapors)	Lk 21:27, Heb 12:1, (1Cor 10:1,2 + Ps 99:7 + Ex 33:9,10), Mt. 24:30; 26:64, 1Th 4:17, Rev 1:7; 14:14-16, (Prov 16:15	Jude 4-**12**, Jas 4:14, 2Pet 2:2:17, Zeph 1:15, Joel 2:2, Prov 25:14, Eze 34:12

	+ 1Cor 3:7-9), Job 37:15, Eze I:4, Hos 6:4; 13:3, Zech 10:1, (Dan 7:13 + Jude 14), Mt 17:5, Ps 68:34; 104:3, Prav 8:28	
Water (waters)	Gen 1:1, (Gen 2:21-23 + Jn 19:34,35 + Jn 7:37,38 + Phil 1:12), Eze 26:3, Ps 69:30-**34**-36, Job 7:12; 9:8, Is 11:9, Rev 4:6; 15:2, Prov 8:29	Rev 17:15; 8:8, Jude 13, Jas 1:6, Lk 21:25, 2Sa 22:5, Zech 10:11, Is 57:20, Jer 51:55, Ps 124:2-5; 46:3, Eze 28:8, Hab 3:8, Rev 7:1-3; 13:1; 16:3, Prov 23:33-35
River (rivers)	(Eze 47 + Rev 22:1,2 + Jn7:38,39), Jer 31:9; Prov 21:1, Ps 89:25, Is 43:19,20; 66:12, Eccl 1:7	Is 18:2,7, Hab 3:8,9, Eze 29:3-5; 32:2, (Rev 8:10 + Amos 5:7), Rev 16:4

Coals of Fire (firebrands, stones of fire)	2Sam 4:17; 22:9,13, Is 6:6; Hab 3:5, Eze 1:13, (Eze 10:2 + Rev 1:20 + Jn 10:28-30 + Ps 140:10 + Rev 16:21), Eze 28:14	Lam 4:8, Prov 6:26-**28**-34; 26:18-21, Amos 4:11, Is 7:4, Rev 8:7,8
Rain (Snow, Hail, Whirlwind, Storm)	(Hos 6:3 + Joel 12:23 + Zech 10:1; 14:17,18 + Gen 2:5), (Ps 18:8,12,13 + Eze 10:2; 13:11-13 + Rev 8:7; 11:19; 16:21; 6:13), Prov 1:24-33, 2Kings 2:1,11, Job 38:1; 40:6, Ps 58:9; 148:8, Is 66:15, Jer 4:13; 23:19; 30:23; (Ps 77:16-19 + Eze 1:4-14), Nah 1:3	(Rev 8:7-11 + 12:4), Prov 10:25, Eze 38:1-9-23, (Lk 17:29 + Rev 16:21 + Mt 7:26,27 + Rev 7:1 + 14:10), (Ps 77:16-19 + Eze 1:4-14)

Fountain (fountains, springs, wells)	Jer 17:13; 2:3, (Rev 21:6 + Jn 4:20-26), Lev 11:36, Deut 33:28, Ps 36:9; 68:26, Jas 3:11,12, Prov 13:14; 14:27, Song 4:12-16, Rev 7:17; 14:7, Prov 8:24,28, Is 41:18, Num 21:17, Is 58:11; 35:7; 49:10, Prov 16:22; 18:4, Is 12:3	Prov 25:6, Rev 8:10; 16:4, Hos 13:15, 2Pet 2:17
Horse (horses)	Zech 10:3,5, (Is 66:15 + Zech 6:1-8), (Prov 21:31 + Rev 19)	Jer 12:5; 5:8; 13:27; 8:16; 46:4,9, Rev 9, Eze 23:20, Jer 13:27
Chariot (chariots)	Hab 3:8, Ps 104:3; 39:1; 68:17, Zech 14:20, (Ps 68:4,33 + Is 19:1), Deut 3:26	Jer 46:9, Is 21:7-9; 43:17, Ps 46:9, Eze 39:17-20, Jer 4:13, Nah 2:3,4,13

Tree (trees)	(Mt 17:15-19 (Rev 2:7,22 + Gal 5:22,23), Jer 17:8, Ps 1:3; 52:8; 92:12; 148:9, Hos 14:6,9, Prov 3:18; 11:30; 13:12; 15:4, (Prov 27:18 + 2Tim 2:6 + Rev 6:14 + Is 34:4 + Jn 17:18), Rev 11:4, Is 44:23; 55:12, (Is 61:3 + Gen 2:4-9 + Rev 22:1,2 + Rom 1:20 + Mt 13), Eze 17:24; 47:11	(Mt 7:15-19 + Jude 12 + Rev 8:9), Eze 31, Ps 37:35, (Mt 15:13,14 + Gen 2:5 + Jude 12 + Mt 13:25,38-42 + Rev 20:15), Zech 11:2
Mountain, Hill, Valley (mountains, hills, valleys)	Ps 71, Is 55:12; 40:4,9; Ps 114:4-6, 148:9, Is 49:11-13, Ps 72:3; 68:15,16, 65:12; 98:8; 104, Is 2:2, Hab 3:6, Mic 6:1, Num	Jer 51:25; 17:3-7, Ps 76:4, Eze 6:2-14; 7:7, Is 5:25, Jer 3:23, Is 64:1-3, Eze 36:4-6, Mic 1:4

	24:4-6, Lk 3:5, 1Kings 20:28	
Vessel, Cup, Bowl, Vial, Bottle (vessels, cups, bowls, vials, bottles)	2Tim 2:19-22, 2Cor 4:7, Heb 9:21-23, Rom 9:23-25, Ps 23:5; 116:13	Rev 2:27, Jer 48:11,12, Rom 9:21,22, Ps 2:9, (Is 65:3,**4**,5 + Rev 9:18; 17:1-**4**)
Way, Path (ways, paths)	Jn 14:6, Jer 16:6 (Psalms and Proverbs all), Ps 16:11, Prov 2:9, 5:6, Mt 3:3, Lk 3:5, Is 45:2; Ps 65:11	Prov 2:12-15, Jer 18:11-15 (Psalms and Proverbs all), Is 59:7,9, Prov 4:14, Jer 6:16-19
Flower (flowers) as opposed to weeds	Song 2:1,2, 12; 6:2, Hos 14:5, Ps 103:15, Is 40:6-8, 1Pet 1:24	Mt 25:24-30
Ship (ships)	Jas 3:4, Eze 30:9, Dan 11:30	(1Tim 1:19 + Rev 8:9), Is 23:1,4, Ps 48:7, Eze 27:25
Voice (voices)	Rev 1:15; 14;2,3, Ex 19:19, (Rev 19:1,5,6 + Ps	Lk 4:33, Mk 1:26, (1Pet 5:8 + Zeph 3), Job

	29), (Rev 4:5 + 10:3,4 + 6:1 + 8:2 + 19:4,5,6), Jn 16:13	3:24, (Zech 11:3 + 11:6)
Trumpet (trumpets)	(Ex 19:19 + Is 58:1), (Heb 12:19 + 1Cor 14:8 + Jer 4:9), Job 39:24,25, Rev 1:10; 4:1, (1Th 4:16 + Joshua 6 + Rev 8:2), (Heb 12:19 + Num 10:1 + Rev 19:17)	
Thunders (thunders)	(Rev 10:3,4 + 6:1 + 2Cor 3:2,3 + Eph 1:13), Mk 3:17, Ex 19:16, Rev 6:1; 14:2; 19:6, Ps 18:13; 29:3, Job 37:4,5, 2Sam 22:14, 1Sam 7:10, Jn 12:29	

Roar (roars)	Is 42:13, 1Ch 16:32, Ps 96:11; 98:7; 104:21	Lk 21:25, Zech 11:3, Ps 74:4, Eze 22:25
End (ends)	Rev 22:13; Rom 10:4, Is 40:28; 41:5-9; 45:22; 52:10, Ps 67:7; 98:3; 65:5; 59:13; 22:27, 1Sam 2:10, Deut 33:17, Mic 5:4, Acts 13:47	(Prov 17:24 + Ps 14:1 + Mt 6:23,24 + 20:15)
Beginning (beginnings)	(Jn 1:1,2 + 15:27 + 17:5 + Eze 36:11), Col 1:18, Rev 1:8; 21:6; 22:13	
Word (words)	Jn 1:1, Rev 19:13, 1Jn 5:7; 1:1, Jas 1:18, (Ps 12:6 + 1Pet 4:12 + Lev 12:2 + Jn 16:33), Heb 12:19; (Rom 10:17,18 + Lk 10:1,16), (Lk 21:33 + 1Jn	

	5:20), (Ps 107:20 + Is 9:8), Is 55:11	
Herb, Grass (herbs, grasses)	(Gen 1:11,12 + Mt 7:15,19), (Prov 27:25 + Mt 13:30), 1Pet 1:24, (Is 40:4,5,6 + Rev 8:7 + 1Pet 3:10-12)	(1Pet 1:24 + Rev 8:7), (Is 37:27 + Mt 13:3-26,38-42 + Ps 92:7), Ps 37:2; 90:5-7, Dan 4:14-16
Salt (salts)	Mt 5:13; Eze 47:11	Mk 9:50, Mt 5:13
Mustard (mustards)	(Mt 13:31 + 17:20 + Mk 4:30-32 + Lk 17:21)	
Vine (vines, grapes)	Jn 15, Jer 6:9, Mal 3:11, Hos 14:7	Jer 2:21, Hos 10:1, Joel 1:12, Hos 2:21
Beast (beasts)	Acts 10 the Lord likens us to spiritually clean beasts, and makes even our physical nature clean. You must pray in order to	Unclean beasts are the states of those who refuse to repent and why the scriptures say so. Rev 13:14; 9:11; 15:2; 16:2;

	discern what type of creature you are. Each man or woman of God is likened unto a spiritually clean Creature like a song bird on the back of creature now made clean (your physical self) like a doe. When you know your true self, you stand a much better chance of being mated for life. In all respects, we learn from His Word and from His Creation. You should cherish what is commendable and shun what is deplorable, that	10; 13; 17; 20:10, Jude 10, 2Pet 2:12; 1Cor 15:32

	is the message God sends to us by likening us to clean or unclean creatures.	
Lions (lions)	Rev 5:5, 10:3, Hos 13:7,8, Mic 5:8; Gen 49:9	Nah 2:8-13, Ps 7:2; 17:12; 22:13; 35:17; 57:4; 91:13, 1Pet 5:8, 2Tim 4:17
Lamb (lambs)	Jn 1:29,36, Lk 10:3, Jn 21:15, Rev 5:6-6:16, Eze 46	
Sheep (sheep)	Jn 10; 21:16,17, Mt 18:12,13; 10:6,16, Rom 8:36, Mk 14:27	
Deer (deer)	Gen 49:21, Prov 5:17, Ps 42:1, Is 35:6, Song 2:9,17	
Bullock (bullocks)	Hos 12:11, Jer 46:21; 50:27, Is 34:7, (Jer 52:20	

	+ Rev 21:14 + Mt 16:18)	
grasshoppers, worms	(Is 33:4 + Lev 11:22), Is 40:22, Num 13:33, Job 25:6, Ps 22:6, Is 41:14	
Ram (rams)	Is 60:7, Jn 10, Eze 34:17	
Goat (goats)	Eze 34:17, Jer 50:8, Song 4:1; 6:5, Prov 27:23-27, Eze 43:22-25	Mt 25:32,33-46, Zech 10:3, Is 34:5-8, Jer 51:40, Eze 27:21
Serpent (serpents)	(Num 21:8,9 + Jn 3:14), Mt 10:16	Mt 23:33, Lk 10:19, Rev 12:9, 20:2, Is 14:29; 65:25, Jer 8:17
Dragons (dragons)	Is 43:20, Ps 148:7	Rev 12; 20:2, Jer 51:34, Is 51:9, Rev 16:13, Ps 91:13
pigs		2Pet 2:22, Prov 11:22, Mt 7:6
dogs		Mt 7:6; 15:26,27, 2Pet

		2:22, Phil 13:2, Rev 22:15, Prov 26:11,17, Ps 22:20; 59:6, Is 59:14
bears		Prov 28:15, Lam 3:10, Amos 5:19, Is 59:11, Hos 13:8
wolves		Jn 10:12, Lk 10:3, Jer 5:6, Mt 7:17, Acts 20:29
locusts, worms		Joel 1-2:25, Nah 3:15-19, Mk 9:42-48, (Rev 9:1-11 (has to be about med because of Prov 30:27), Jude 6 + Jn 12:30,31)
Eagle (eagles)	Eze 17, Deut 32:11,12, Jer 48:40, Is 40:31, Ps 103:5, Lk 17:37	Eze 17, Jer 49:16,22, Lam 4:19

All clean and unclean scriptures are to be thus applied. God is getting us to understand WHY He calls some creatures unclean and why He doesn't. All creatures that He has called unclean have a least one detestable trait, that we are to shun. And all clean creatures have at least one applaudable trait that we should honor and uphold. The scriptures are to be spiritually understood and Merely apply your learning and find out why God calls some creatures unclean. Most all unclean creatures do not have one mate for life, that is the reason for them being unclean. Mankind is to have one mate for life. So do not be as unclean animals. There are other unclean traits. Like dogs eating their own vomit. It's not like God didn't make our pets; it's just down here He likens that to an unclean characteristic.

not be kept with carnal thinking. The is nothing your flesh cannot eat in the way of clean and unclean creatures. What you ingest comes into your flesh and it is removed by elimination. The scriptures are meant to be understood in this manner.	In heaven, our pets don't have unclean characteristics any longer. He changes our pets, just like He changes us from unclean sinners, to His Perfect Sons and Daughters, clean in all respects.	
Dove (doves)	Jn 1:32, Song 2:14; 5:2; 6:9, Is 38:14; 60:8	
Horn (horns)	1Sam 2:1,10, Job 16:15, 2Sam 22:3, Ps 18:2; 89:24; 92:10; 112:9; 148:14, (Rev 5:6 + Hab 3:4 + Jn	Ps 75:4,5, Dan 7:1-8, Rev 17:1-16

	10:28,29 + Rev 1:20)	
Rock (rocks)	1Cor 10:4, 1Pet 2:8, Rom 9:33, Mt 16:18, Ps 18:2,31,46; 28:1; 62:2,6,7, (Nah 1:6 + Rev 6:13 + 16:21 + Is 34:4 + 28:2 + 29:6 + Lev 20:2,27 + 24:14,16,23)	
Weapons (weapons, shields, swords, arrows, spears)	Deut 34:29, Ps 127:4; 7:13; 18:14; 77:17, (Ps 64:7 + Zech 9:13,14), Eze 21:1-17, (Ps 47:9; 59:11; 119:114; 18:35; 3:3), Hab 3, Prov 35, (Lk 22:38 + Rev 11:1-6)	Prov 25:18, Jer 9:8, Ps 64:3, Prov 26:18, Eze 21:21-**23**, 21:18-32, Is 7:23-25; 10:17; 33:12, Prov 15:19; 22:5, 2Cor 12:7, Ps 17:13; 57:4

In His Image

King of kings	Rev 19:16; 1:6; 5:10, 1Tim 6:15,16
Lord of lords	Rev 19:16, Jn 13:13,14
Prince of princes	Dan 8:25
Apostle of apostles	Heb 3:1, Rev 18:20
Prophet of prophets	Acts 3:22,23, Rev 18:20; 22:6,9; 19:10, Jn 15:26
Bishop of bishops	1Pet 2:25, 1Tim 3
Shepherds of shepherds (Pastor of pastors)	1Pet 2:25, Jn 10:11, 1Pet 5:4, Eze 34, Jer 23:4
Father of fathers	Lk 11:13, 1Jn 2:13,14, 1Cor 4:15
Priest of priests	Heb 3:1-13:11, Rev 1:6; 5:10; 20:6
Judges of judges	Acts 10:42, Heb 12:23, 1Cor 6:1-5, 1Cor 11:31
Savior of saviors	Is 45:15,21, 2Tim 1:1-10, Obad 21
Master of masters	Mt 23:8,10; 26:18, Jas 3:1, 2Tim 2:5, Prov 25:13, Jn 3:10
Son of sons	1Jn 4:9; 3:1,2, Heb 1:5; 5:5, Lk 3:20-22, Rom 8:14-19, Gal 4:5-22, (Jn 1:12,13 + 3:1-21), 1Pet 1:23, Gal 3:16, Phil 2:15
Teachers of teachers	Jn 14:26; 3:2, 2Tim 1:11
Preacher of preachers	Lk 4:18,19,43; 9:2, Mt 28:18-20, Mk 16:15-18

Deliverer of deliverers	Ps 18:2; 40:17; 71:4; 144:2, Rom 11:26, Lk 4:18
Comforter of comforters	Is 51:12, Jn 14:26, 2Cor 7:6,7,13
Healer of healers (Physician of physicians)	Mt 9:12, 8:16,17, Mk 16:18, Acts (Jesus Christ is our Healer forever!)
Husbandman of husbandmen	Jn 15:1, 2Tim 2:6, 1Cor 3:9
Sower of sowers	Mk 4, Mt 13, 2Cor 9:6, Gal 6:7,8
Provider of providers	Gen 22:14, Heb 11:40, 2Cor 8:21
Master builders of builders	Heb 3:4, 1Cor 3:10,12, Rom 15:20, 1Pet 2:5
Branch of branches	Jer 33:15, Zech 3:8; 6:12, Jn 15:1-6
Ruler of rulers	Mic 5:2, Lk 12:42 + Rom 15:20, 1Pet 2:5
The Anointed One of anointed ones	(Is 61:1 + Lk 4:18), Ps 105:15, 1Jn 2:27, Heb 1:19
The Holy One of holy ones	Is 43:3, 1Pet 1:16
Nobleman of nobles	Lk 19:12, Prov 8:16, Acts 17:11
Commander of soldiers	Is 55:4 + 2Tim 2:3,4, Rev 19:16
Overseer of overseers	Mk 9:7, Acts 20:28, 1Pet 5:2
Leader of leaders	Is 55:4, Ps 23:2,3, Jn 10:3, Ps 80:1

Lover of lovers   Song of Solomon
Musician of musicians   Psalms

    In fact, any and all honorable titles belong to our Lord Jesus Christ, as Col 1:15-19 reminds us all. His disciples have them all through Him, we are as nothing without our God, but with Him we are mighty indeed. We are truly created in His Image, if we have received Him and His Word and been born of God Almighty thereby. You will KNOW you are one of His when He addresses you as His son or His daughter. His Holy Spirit of Truth calls us such and whereby we KNOW GOD is our, "Abba, Father." (Rom 8:15)

    THIS PROVES YOU ARE MADE IN THE IMAGE OF GOD! SO DON'T EVER LET ANYONE LIE TO YOU IN THAT REGARD! Overwhelming evidence we are made in the image of Eternal Creator, our Lord Jesus Christ, Yahoshuah Ha Mashiach.

    You are not some randomly designed creature, or some kind of undirected mutation of imaginary evolution, you were carefully thought of, created and made by Our Eternal Creator, the living Lord Jesus Christ, in all these ways and more. Every person was made with the intention of becoming a Divine Masterpiece, one of God's

Own Loving Sons and Daughters who will spend eternity with Him being Loved by Him and all Creation. So that is the reason He doesn't want anyone to harm themselves, to pierce themselves, brand themselves, put graffiti in the forms of tattoos over our bodies, it's all because God Himself Created You and Intends to Lovingly Perfect You, so Honor Him and His Commandments! Putting tattoos on your perfect selves is worse than if someone painted over the Sistine Chapel with graffiti. Your bodies were Created by God and are meant to Glorify Him, to be a Holy Habitation of the Loving Spirit of our Heavenly Father forever. God will forgive you if you disobeyed Him in your ignorance, but when you realize why He doesn't want us to hurt ourselves or place marks all over ourselves, just don't do it any longer. I still remember a tatted convict who picked me up and hugged me for preaching to prisoners. He said the reason he was covered with tattoos of demons, devils, 666, and the like all over his body was that the devil had held him as his captive, and he couldn't change his past, so now he's just a "stained glass window for the Lord" who had set him free! **WE ARE ALL CREATED IN THE IMAGE OF OUR ETERNAL CREATOR!** You were not made by anything EVOLUTIONARY. Evolution is a bunch of hogwash. This should enable you to seek Him until you find Him! He likens His Kingdom beyond all earthly endeavors you must seek Him and His Kingdom with all your heart and soul! For me it was a matter of living or dying before God let me know beyond all doubt that He exists. I don't say that it will be likewise as hard for you, you have to be ready to listen to and obey Him. It seemed like an epic struggle for me, but now that I let you know that you can know Him, you must seek to know Him until you do! The reason I think God reveals Himself to those who love and obey Him and not to those who don't, is due to the fact He is choosing who will spend eternity with Him and He wants to be certain of His choice. Be certain that knowing our Eternal Creator is worth it! Be KNOWN by God Almighty! He knows you, make sure you are known by Him as one of His Own Dearly Beloved Sons or Daughters! You are carefully designed by our Eternal Creator to be one with him forever and ever.

We all need him to understand things that are true from things that are not. We need His Holy Blood applied to our bodies by His Holy Spirit. Then we understand that we are destined for to be with Him forever. You must repent and be baptized in His Name. Pray to receive His Holy Spirit until you are absolutely certain that you know Him and He is teaching you now and forever!

God is Ruling the Nations According to His Words

https://www.blastthetrumpet.org/PublicLetters/AAAUpdatedPublicAlertsMattersofLifeandDeath/Updates053016/Observable%20Divine%20Judgments.pdf - When you read Deuteronomy Ch. 28 God describes rewards and consequences for the nations that either obey Him or don't. As long as we were teaching the Holy Bible to children in our schools, America was Blessed and became a great nation. But ever since evil-u-shun crept into our schools and replaced the solid teaching of God's Commandments our nation has been in decline. All according to those consequences.

https://www.blastthetrumpet.org/PublicLetters/AAAUpdatedPublicAlertsMattersofLifeandDeath/Updates053016/End%20Times%20Verse%20By%20Verse.pdf - God is Ruling and Reigning over Creation and so it is prudent for everyone to know what He expects of us and lives accordingly. Prophecies in the scriptures most definitely apply to every generation right up until the time of His Glorious Return, so everyone read and learn from them accordingly. One of those consequences is having enemies creep into our nation, people that hate America and Americans, and blame us for the evil they've experienced in this world. Resenting our freedoms and prosperity that we had as long as we we're faithful to the One True God and honored Him and His Words as a nation, but now that children are turning away from God, being lied to in our public schools, consequences are happening to us as a nation, and more and more Americans are feeling those consequences. I hope it doesn't result in the destruction of our cities, our civilization, law and order, our nation as a whole, because Americans truly repent of deliberately deceiving our children and turning them into sexually immoral people (in our public education/schools) and return to God and His Commandments given us all in the Holy Bible. **TEACH THE CHILDREN THE TRUTH! We have the WORDS of ALMIGHTY GOD! The Holy Bible MUST be put back into our public schools and taught as the absolute TRUTH (FACTS ABOUT OUR CREATOR, CREATION, REALITY PAST, PRESENT and FUTURE) that it is!**

https://www.blastthetrumpet.org/PublicLetters/AAAUpdatedPublicAlertsMattersofLifeandDeath/Updates053016/CHRIST%20IS%20THE%20FULFILLMENT%20OF%20THE%20LAW.pdf - Christ fulfills His Law and Prophecies exactly, so you need to meditate on His Words and Look Forward to the time WE ASCEND to meet Him in the air when He Returns!

https://www.blastthetrumpet.org/PublicLetters/AAAUpdatedPublicAlertsMattersofLifeandDeath/Updates053016/The%20Climax%20of%20the%20Age%20Christ%20the%20End.pdf - Now God tells us that the wicked will go on being deceived and become worse but He also tells us there is a harvest of the Righteous that I believe still has not occurred. So, HE TELLS US TO LABOR in this earth until He Returns! Tell EVERYONE that they can KNOW HIM! WE WILL TRIUMPH OPENLY WHEN HE RETURNS!

https://www.blastthetrumpet.org/PublicLetters/AAAUpdatedPublicAlertsMattersofLifeandDeath/Updates053016/The%20Road%20to%20Eternal%20Life%20has%20been%20Paved%20with%20the%20Blood%20of%20the%20Saints.pdf - No matter what we face in the future, ask God to make you faithful and true. We join others who had a Holy Zeal for Him no matter the cost.

https://tile.loc.gov/storage-services/public/gdcmassbookdig/foxesbookofmart00fo/foxesbookofmart00fo.pdf - Many have gone before us who gave their all! Love and Serve our Lord Jesus Christ, with all your heart, mind, soul and strength. Knowing that your labors in Him are not in vain.

https://www.ccel.org/ccel/v/vanbraght/mirror/cache/mirror.pdf - Our Brothers and Sisters down through the generations loved God and us all enough to pay the ultimate price. EVERYONE SHOULD REVERENCE GOD AND HIS WORDS IN THE HOLY BIBLE! Too much honorable blood has been shed to give us His Words!

https://www.blastthetrumpet.org/PublicLetters/AAAUpdatedPublicAlertsMattersofLifeandDeath/Prophecies%20Show%20Divine%20Inspiration%20of%20the%20Holy%20Bibl2.pdf - GOD HAS ACCURATELY FORETOLD THE FUTURE; DECLARING THE END FROM THE BEGINNING IN THE HOLY BIBLE! You need to know Him and His Words and Counsel to us for your own good!

http://biblehub.com/2_peter/1-19.htm - "We also have the prophetic message as something completely reliable, and you will do well to pay attention to it, as to a light shining in a dark place, until the day dawns and the morning star rises in your hearts."

Yahoshuah the Messiah, aka Jesus the Christ, fulfills the Law and the Prophets; not just these many prophecies concerning His Incarnation http://christianity.about.com/od/biblefactsandlists/a/Prophecies-Jesus.htm; but even events before and after! HE IS THE TOTAL FULFILLMENT of the Law and Prophets!!!!!!!!!!!!! http://biblehub.com/matthew/5-17.htm and http://www.project.nsearch.com/profiles/blogs/the-blood-of-jesus-found-on-the-ark-of-the-covenant or http://www.youtube.com/watch?feature=player_embedded&v=3i0RBDRnwAo

    Even though just that study alone (prophecies fulfilled by Yahoshuah the Messiah's Incarnation; Jesus the Christ; Immanuel; GOD who took on a body of flesh to walk among us) is enough to convince a rational mind of the Divine Inspiration of the Holy Bible; the Holy Bible is filled with hundreds of accurate prophecies that have for the most part all been fulfilled and what hasn't appears to be rapidly occurring in front of our eyes just by paying attention to current events.

http://biblehub.com/mark/13-37.htm

1- ICBMs were so clearly prophesied that even their modern dimensions were given.

"2012, WWIII, nuclear war, Uranium warheads, ICBMs, SLBMs, and mushroom clouds all detailed over 2,500 years ago in the Bible? No way! You would have heard about it, right? WRONG! See this brutal "end of the world" prophecy explained in a clear and concise manner for the first time ever!..." - https://www.youtube.com/watch?v=lRCh54zN7hc

This interpretation of Zechariah 5 was originally expounded upon by Michael Rood (A Rood Awakening). However, this particular video is Tiborasauus Rex's commentary on this interpretation of Zechariah 5 based on his different perspectives of some of the details and thus some of the views in this interpretation may differ slightly from Michael Rood's original interpretation. For more on this topic: listen to Zechariah's Thermonuclear War CD by Michael Rood.

I have seen Michael Rood's presentation on this topic and believe it is worth purchasing from His website; if you have the means. http://store.aroodawakening.tv/zechariah-s-thermonuclear-war.html

2- automobiles/armored vehicles- http://biblehub.com/nahum/2-4.htm for all who do not have a Strong's Concordance and who have the means; get one. http://www.biblestudytools.com/concordances/strongs-exhaustive-concordance/ http://www.tgm.org/bible.htm and http://www.amazon.com/Strongs-Expanded-Exhaustive-Concordance-Supersaver/dp/1418542377

http://biblehub.com/2_timothy/2-15.htm Get every tool, skill and talent our Creator makes available to you and get a Holy Bible https://www.christianbook.com/interlinear-hebrew-english-bible-volume-edition/9781565639775/pd/639774 that has the original text with Strong's Numeric Reference above each word http://biblehub.com/interlinear/ ; will more easily enable you to more clearly see the true meaning of the Author. By doing that you will understand that our Creator often refers to this ungodly world, by all the ungodly empires, and even the names of their capital cities, in such a way as to mean all the world that still is in darkness; deceived by satanil to this day. A prime example of this http://www.kingjamesbibleonline.org/Revelation-11-8/

  Anything that happened in the past; such as the days of the Old Covenant, was like seeds planted in the garden of this earth (both for good and evil); such that if there was one Moses; there are some who have by God's Grace become the body of Moses (all who attempt to practice the Law from a carnal perspective; but have yet to enter the Promised Land because they have yet to cross over the Jordan (spiritually speaking) and follow Yahoshuah/Yeshua into it; they are STILL in the wilderness; and have yet to taste of the Goodness of God! And the same with the Prophets; and conversely the evil empires of this world and the names of their dark cities of old are speaking prophetically about this present time concerning all who still oppose our Creator in thought, word and deed and is why scriptures state http://biblehub.com/revelation/17-11.htm because all along in the children of disobedience it has been this same spirit of error deceiving them, causing them to hate God, to hate God's people, to be greedy, ambitious, murderous, to desire to conquer the world, rape, pillage, plunder until their own vices bring about their end or until the Creator intervenes and sends judgment and wrath; destroying them and their wicked ways. This pattern has been seen in all of history; every time the spirit of anti-christ incarnates and moves upon the masses under control by the spirit of error to do wickedly and it is no different today. The same spirit of anti-christ always hordes weapons of war, always greedily tries to conquer the world and destroy anything godly in it anywhere, always is greedy, ambitious, arrogant, proud, deceptive, and as such the Creator in visions to the prophets, and revelations refers to the wickedness of this whole dark world by terms such as Babylon, Nineveh, Egypt, Persia, Rome, Greece or any other dark empire who abused and mistreated His Children, His People, and so such persons also are references to satanil like Caesar, Hitler, Alexander, Pharaoh, etc. etc. Once you understand that any populations mentioned in the prophets are not just talking about literal, specific, physical, carnal, interpretation, but are simultaneously describing the ethereal, general, invisible, spiritual, then you will understand that when God speaks or inspires to be written such words; He is referring to ALL His Creation; visible and invisible; and is why scholars constantly argue and debate because our Lord tells us http://biblehub.com/2_peter/1-20.htm and is why it is imperative to have the Spirit of our Creator in your life teaching you what His Words actually mean; so no one can deceive you. http://biblehub.com/1_john/2-27.htm, http://biblehub.com/john/16-13.htm so when I tell you the prophet was shown something like this https://www.youtube.com/watch?v=05pdi-MzvAI when he wrote this http://biblehub.com/nahum/2-4.htm you will more easily see the correlations and truth. It is also why I expounded on topics such as the fact Ezekiel and John were shown the whole earth from outer space in http://www.godempowersyou.com/documentation/HistoricalTestimonyandMinistry/MansChronologicalExistenceExplained.pdf just read the descriptions and look for yourself https://www.youtube.com/watch?v=3hdyRh60R-Q and now sapphire and jasper stones https://twitter.com/geologytime/status/1030083544025104384 - see how these stones look like the earth does from space?

      Just imagine if you were alive a couple millenniums ago and the Creator had suddenly lifted you into outer space (the heavens as they called it) and were looking at the earth; long before rocketry, space flight, telescopes, etc. And the Creator had given you a time lapse revelation like He did with Ezekiel of spirits/eyes that the Creator would send into the earth over the coming years; that those souls would follow His leading from above, speak His Words, do His Works (more on this in http://www.godempowersyou.com/documentation/HistoricalTestimonyandMinistry/MansChronologicalExistenceExplained.pdf) I'd say they described what they saw as accurately as possible.

3- The Gulf War - http://www.biblestudytools.com/jeremiah/50-9-compare.html , http://www.islamicity.com/forum/printer_friendly_posts.asp?TID=4694 , https://www.youtube.com/watch?v=O5_v_uxAwR0, so we can see that the prophetic scriptures in the Holy Bible concerning Babylon; geographically speaking, we are talking in modern terms about Iraq. https://www.ancient.eu/uploads/images/75.png?v=1569518174 We read in verse http://biblehub.com/jeremiah/50-12.htm that a geographical region in context referred to as http://biblehub.com/jeremiah/50-8.htm the land of the Chaldeans is a location that broke away from its "mother" http://z14.invisionfree.com/Cold_War/ar/t429.htm , http://wiki.answers.com/Q/Why_did_Iraq_think_that_Kuwait_should_belong_to_them.

As anyone who can read and comprehend history it is easy to see that the biblical text in Jer. 50 and 51 when talking of Babylon is speaking to us of modern-day Iraq (geographically speaking; all in darkness by the spirit of anti-christ spiritually speaking) and when mentioning the Chaldeans is talking about the geographical region of modern-day Kuwait. So, as you can read God is counseling those in that region to leave; when a coalition of nations is raised against Iraq http://biblehub.com/jeremiah/50-9.htm and warning that Kuwait will be plundered. http://www.nytimes.com/2003/05/01/world/aftereffects-plunder-2000-treasures-stolen-gulf-war-1991-only-12-have-been.html?pagewanted=all&src=pm , http://sites.estvideo.net/impasse/kuwait.htm, (I know scholars point out historical fulfillment of these texts and all I am pointing out is that God's Word is so powerful cyclical events occur until all is exhaustively fulfilled! (often, we observe an ancient city is destroyed, rebuilt, destroyed again, rebuilt again, destroyed again, etc.); as our Creator tells us when we repent and return to Him building and life occurs and when we depart from Him destruction and death occurs. And that no matter how many times mankind thinks to defy the Creator and rebuild; while yet still doing wickedly (warning about 911 https://www.youtube.com/watch?v=mOHJKrxhBME); He will see that their confidence and pride falls into rubble and ruin; until they actually do repent or until they are all no more. Just because the entire region hasn't been decimated yet, does not mean God is slack concerning His promises; it just means He desires all souls to repent; rather than to continue to do so wickedly that they destroy one another and are all completely destroyed; ultimately. Who recalls seeing this? http://www.csmonitor.com/2002/1119/p02s01-woam.html The Creator told us that they'd lay down their arms quickly by this prophecy. http://biblehub.com/jeremiah/51-30.htm Or how many saw newscasts of the smart weapons hitting the targets exactly?

https://www.youtube.com/watch?v=1HaDE9KCk2o our Creator told us of these smart weapons over two thousand five hundred years ago by the prophet Jeremiah. "Indeed, I'm going to stir up and bring against Babylon a great company of nations from the land of the north. They'll deploy for battle against her, and from there she will be captured. Their arrows will be like a skilled warrior; they won't miss their targets. "

http://biblehub.com/jeremiah/50-9.htm As the Lord in me advised you to seek out the original text. http://biblehub.com/text/jeremiah/50-9.htm when you click on the word for "arrows" it comes from a root word that means to pierce; I'd say those smart weapons fit the context perfectly. The Creator further tells us that He would http://biblehub.com/jeremiah/50-25.htm for those who would think other weapons are not mentioned. Try to keep in mind 2500 years ago they didn't have laser guided smart bombs so they used the closest words in their language for something that would pierce accurately ("arrow") but the reason we know that the prophet could not be talking literally about bows and arrows; is that in context the prophet describes massive decimation of the land and region. I know people; even "scholars" will argue with me about Jer 50. and 51 having anything to do with the Gulf War; but when I know I have been given a revelation straight from our Creator; anyone's else opinion contrary to direct Divine Revelation is meaningless to me. If it was just how I interpret the text, I would say so and listen intently to other opinions on the matter; but when our Creator teaches me personally concerning anything as Truth; I become immovable on that topic. As I was reading these texts to my unbelieving roommate; on the news simultaneously, the fulfillment was being shown him exactly as I read and without any prior knowledge of a live newscast that would come on; as confirmation by our Creator and a clear sign to a soul who still did not know Him. While these chapters obviously cover more than just the Gulf War to say that they had no part in it whatsoever is a lie or a statement of ignorance.

4 - the Book of Revelation - Please understand that the Book of Revelation was NOT depicting future events exclusively! http://biblehub.com/revelation/1-19.htm but are visions of PAST, PRESENT AND FUTURE http://biblehub.com/revelation/17-8.htm (by the way; that is the verse that shows at the time of John; satanil had been bound ("is not") proves he was in the bottomless pit; and is NOT a future event like those preaching the false doctrine of the pre-tribulation rapture encourage people to believe) events from the moment the revelations were given to John. People don't understand that God is in Heaven but His Holy Spirit of Truth is in all His Disciples, Christians, and yet the devil also has a spirit of error, the scriptures teach that bind his body of believers by that spirit of deception. So even though the devil incarnate doesn't stand on the earth until the end right before Christ returns, his spirit of deception is still

deceiving people away from Christ. His body of believers down through the ages is called the Beast in the scriptures.

Anyway, my point in emphasizing that these visions are about past, present and future events; is that people I meet virtually everywhere; especially in churches are constantly preaching and thinking the events are yet to come because they fail to comprehend the true meaning of the visions and how the Creator fulfills them. To understand what I'm trying to pass on as I was taught by our Eternal Creator; one needs to go back to Genesis. http://biblehub.com/genesis/2-5.htm; why? because He tells us He manifests all things He has Created/Imagined/Imaged/Designed in due season (over what we think of as the passage of time) That FIRST He Created/Imagined all things BEFORE THEY ARE MANIFEST http://biblehub.com/genesis/1-11.htm; BEFORE they are made visible earth. This is the real reason why the scripture states both "created and made". One is describing the visualization process and the other is describing the particulars involved in actually making the designs have substance. From an eternal perspective that is how He is able to accurately describe what we think of as the future or what we think of as prophetic. He has already thought of all things BEFORE they are MADE visible and He describes such in the contents of the Holy Bible. The Book of Revelation is no different. In other words, when you read such things as "a third of the trees burned with fire" people are constantly looking at some future event rather than looking at the entire history of the world and all combined forest fires and headlines like http://earthobservatory.nasa.gov/GlobalMaps/view.php?d1=MOD14A1_M_FIRE , http://www.wunderground.com/blog/weatherhistorian/the-worst-wild-fires-in-world-history, people are short-sighted in general but our Creator is not. He is showing John the history of the age; how things will unfold worldwide over what we think of as time. That is not to deny end-time catastrophic events; I am only pointing out another way our Creator fulfills His Word. All plants in the "storehouses of heaven" all snow, all horses, all men, women and children, all fires, all plagues, etc. it all appears in due season, at the time appointed, each are MADE manifest; visible; until ALL is fulfilled. http://biblehub.com/ecclesiastes/3-1.htm So while people; even "Christians" ever look to the future; the Book of Revelation has been getting fulfilled like rain drops from heaven each hitting the ground moment by moment. Seven Messengers have come already! Seven Trumpets have ALREADY SOUNDED! SEVEN SCROLLS HAVE ALREADY BEEN OPENED!!!!!!!

http://www.williambranhamstorehouse.com/thecollection.htm

As this Messenger aptly points out in His Book, "Revelation of the Seven Church Ages". I have NOT received direct Divine Revelation as to who the Seven Messengers were and as such, I am not about to criticize what this Brother has written on the topic. I am firmly convinced by the fact that Paul is responsible for such a significant part of the compiled books of the New Testament that He absolutely was the First of the Seven. I believe He even tells us this http://biblehub.com/1_corinthians/7-40.htm Paul KNEW he was full of the Holy Ghost; he went about laying hands on others in the book of acts to receive such! but here in the Holy Bible we have a sentence that has an unusual use of the uppercase "Spirit of God" and in a way that is peculiar of Paul "thinking" he has such. Now I know it wasn't compiled (the Book of Revelation) when Paul was inspired to write those words; but the Author has been doing things such as that to show us the way to Truth all along. So when Paul appeared, a trumpet sounded as he went about preaching http://biblehub.com/isaiah/58-1.htm, and a scroll was opened as He wrote Divinely Inspired words http://biblehub.com/2_corinthians/3-2.htm, and a cup/vial/vessel was poured out http://www.biblegateway.com/passage/?search=2+Timothy+2%3A20-22&version=NKJV, and having been sealed/marked by the Holy Ghost http://biblehub.com/ephesians/1-13.htm those scrolls, letters, books, are made manifest when we write God's words under Divine Inspiration. http://biblehub.com/psalms/45-1.htm the seal is broken by God Himself when He places His Angels, His Messengers, His Spirit, Incarnate upon the earth and instructs them to speak and write His Words at that moment! So, the Book of Revelation is God showing us like a great amphitheatre of events that will and have

transpired all over the world; throughout all His Creation; in what we think of as visible space over what we conceive of as the passage of time. While we can easily see end time events exactly as prophesied are currently before our very eyes:
https://www.youtube.com/watch?v=If9yzHwOeUc,
https://www.youtube.com/watch?v=XM1g9lQJkWU,
https://www.youtube.com/results?search_query=blood+seas&oq=blood+seas&gs_l=youtube.12..0l7j0i5l3.17536.20302.0.22320.10.10.0.0.0.0.118.1034.2j8.10.0...0.0...1ac.1.11.youtube.h_7ChgN5q_I,
https://www.youtube.com/watch?v=8J4d2P68C8c,
https://www.youtube.com/watch?v=X2mDYM-DeZg,
http://biblehub.com/revelation/8-9.htm,
http://www.biblegateway.com/passage/?search=Revelation%208:8-18&version=NIV,
https://www.youtube.com/watch?v=acUfQ8jbR6w,
https://www.youtube.com/watch?v=JBotWk5t3pQ,
https://www.youtube.com/watch?v=3l8TT1dv-PM,
https://www.youtube.com/watch?v=jHoFSXh9Ejk,
https://www.youtube.com/watch?v=6PrhG5gmVb8,
http://biblehub.com/jeremiah/23-15.htm

Yes, while the whole world is witnessing thousands/millions of individual events linked directly to prophecies in the Holy Bible; it does not negate the fact; that in the past waters have been poisoned, in the past waters have turned blood red, in the past there have been wars, dead people, dead fish, burned forests, etc. While these end time concentrations of prophetic events should be causing every soul on the planet to repent and call upon the Living God zealously for mercy and to bring them into His Presence in a good way (because they were grateful for the sacrifice of our Lord and Savior, Yahoshuah the Messiah, aka Jesus Christ); these current events; COMBINED with all past and future events; are the actual complete and total fulfillment of the scriptures. This is one of the reasons our Creator told us; http://biblehub.com/luke/16-17.htm. And is why the Gulf War was just partial fulfillment of the events described by our Creator concerning that region.

Another example of the vision covering an extended period of time and regions of heavens and earth is the prophecy about the dragon's tail. http://biblehub.com/revelation/12-4.htm; we know the tail represents false prophets, http://biblehub.com/isaiah/9-15.htm; so this vision of the dragon is all persons past, present and future, filled with the spirit of error, who have manifested as dark, greedy, bloody, world empires, wicked, who basically tell lies to one another constantly and through their deceptions (like the theory of evolution and atheism - https://www.youtube.com/watch?v=4mxXICZ9mXo&list=PL7F9B57EBDCCEECF8) they lead souls astray. All who have ever existed and who ever will exist came from our

Creator, Lord and Maker, and were meant to shine like the stars forever. http://biblehub.com/matthew/5-16.htm, http://biblehub.com/daniel/12-3.htm but people who heed such deceptions and ignore the many times the Creator calls out to them; end up falling; end up with their light extinguished; becoming dark. http://biblehub.com/2_thessalonians/2-3.htm, http://biblehub.com/ecclesiastes/12-6.htm, " 5"Indeed, the light of the wicked goes out, And the flame of his fire gives no light. 6"The light in his tent is darkened, And his lamp goes out above him." http://biblehub.com/job/18-6.htm Instead, it is my hope that everyone who reads this by God's Grace will https://www.youtube.com/watch?v=DtIIFJIxdUw ! http://biblehub.com/acts/1-8.htm, http://www.biblegateway.com/passage/?search=Acts+2%3A38-39&version=KJV, https://www.youtube.com/watch?v=wN5SILxm55Q

When you find the definitions of terms in the Holy Scriptures inspired by the same Author as that Being that gave John the revelations; then you too can get a better understanding of what they mean and as I expound a little in http://www.godempowersyou.com/documentation/HistoricalTestimonyandMinistry/MansChronologicalExistenceExplained.pdf I am not herein going to write an exposition on the Book of Revelation; it is only my desire to point out factually prophecies have been, and are being fulfilled in front of the whole world with every passing second in so many ways; it would be virtually impossible to document them all. But the most obvious should be sufficient to convince even the most skeptical of their need to repent and call upon our Living Lord and Savior, Yahoshuah the Messiah, aka Jesus the Christ.

https://www.youtube.com/watch?v=uKm9G4zUP_Q, http://biblehub.com/revelation/16-8.htm

5 - http://www.biblegateway.com/passage/?search=Jude+1&version=NIV, http://biblehub.com/luke/17-28.htm, http://biblehub.com/2_timothy/3-1.htm, http://www.biblegateway.com/passage/?search=2+Timothy+3%3A1-8&version=NIV, our American culture (and other cultures around the world) have become so wicked and so perverse; whole new terms have come into existence just to describe the level of depravity. (LGBTQ) and people so completely insane and wicked they actually march in the streets demanding their "right" to abuse children https://www.youtube.com/results?search_query=LGTB+marching+in+the+streets&oq=LGTB+marching+in+the+streets&gs_l=youtube.3...30587.37370.0.37794.19.19.0.0.0.0.106.1733.17j2.19.0...0.0...1ac.1.11.youtube.2ecULSa6-Jo, and http://americansfortruth.com/issues/the-agenda-glbtq-activist-groups/national-glbtq-activist-groups/nambla/page/2/ This level of perversion is

absolute fulfillment of the scriptures indicating that unless these people, cities, and perhaps whole nations repent they are about to be destroyed in many ways and perhaps even be left in desolate ruins like http://www.youtube.com/watch?v=3Qi8MnzgT3E While those who have chosen to become so wicked they are fulfilling scriptures that tell them they are headed toward insanity, depravity and devastation http://www.biblegateway.com/passage/?search=Romans%201:28-32&version=NIV, they actually think those who are trying with all their heart, mind, soul and strength to prevent it; hate them; and so the wicked slander, libel, hate and attack those who actually love them enough to risk their own welfare to tell them the truth and plead with them to repent before they are destroyed terribly and worse find themselves in the flames of damnation http://biblehub.com/revelation/20-15.htm . It has sadly come to pass therefore, that I am instructed by our Creator, to tell His People plainly, leave all such wicked cities full of such persons who no longer endure sound doctrine; who refuse to hear and heed the Word of God. http://www.biblegateway.com/passage/?search=2+Timothy+4%3A3-4&version=NIV (modern sodomites religiously defend anything that counters the Holy Bible, Truth, and the need to Repent of their wicked ways; hence they are some of the most ardent defenders of the fiction called the theory of evolution. https://www.blastthetrumpet.org/PublicLetters/AAAUpdatedPublicAlertsMattersofLifeandDeath/Updates053016/NO%20MORE%20BRAINWASHING%20p1.pdf

I said hundreds of prophecies fulfilled but it is actually millions; every such soul that fulfills such texts is a sign (a very ominous harbinger) but is of themselves fulfillment of the prophecy; but when you see whole crowds of such wicked persons marching in streets demanding their perversions and even screaming for their "rights" to slaughter babies; then know that the total destruction of all such persons is close at hand. This level of wickedness only remains at the moment because God's people have yet to heed His Instruction: http://biblehub.com/mark/6-11.htm God is calling all Christians to depart from such wicked cities as are so ripe for destruction. Pray, pray fervently, and He will show you in dreams and visions where He wishes you to go!!!!!!!! God will make the way; God will Provide!!!!!!!! I am concerned for those calling themselves Christians who have become too materialistic; that if you ignore leaving the wicked places that you might face consequences not only of being destroyed with them; but perhaps abused by the wicked; perhaps rounded up into concentrations camps; so, when I exhort you all to pray now and to pray fervently; DO IT!!!!!!!! Make absolutely certain you are where God wants you to be in these end times!!! Being out of place can have dreadful consequences!!!!!!!!

6 - There are so many signs and prophetic scriptures being fulfilled that you can spend every day just reviewing world

news and if you know the Bible well; then you can see it happening in daily news what our Creator told us would happen two millenniums ago (and some prophecies even prior to that)
https://www.youtube.com/watch?v=y9sxvf1aQKI&list=PLhgltHNBzIs0aq-n9h4WkHxISC0TsW1Vi&index=2 and while all of the messengers of Christ do not agree on everything (because we are all imperfect until our Creator finishes transforming us) we agree that end time events are now occurring. It is time for all souls everywhere to Repent and Call upon the Living Lord Yahoshuah the Messiah, Jesus the Christ!!!!!!!!

You NEED to KNOW GOD and HIS WORDS in the HOLY BIBLE so you KNOW WHAT is happening and why! And can shout with all believers, "COME, LORD JESUS, COME! WE NEED YOU!"

7 - WWIII -
https://www.youtube.com/watch?v=wLnszvv9J7s,
http://beforeitsnews.com/war-and-conflict/2013/08/its-on-russia-china-walk-out-of-un-security-council-meeting-on-syria-2447920.html,
https://www.youtube.com/watch?v=-OPIc5jY2T0,
https://www.youtube.com/watch?v=JE3VStqF7N8,
https://www.youtube.com/watch?v=Ah5rbMxzQAY,
https://www.youtube.com/watch?v=sw4zynAR8wI,

http://www.biblegateway.com/passage/?search=Joel+3&version=NIV, http://www.harvestthehungry.com/#!syria-will-attack-israel/clt7, (I am NOT promoting Islam by including this reference; it's just that much of mainstream Christianity has their eschatology so messed up by the false doctrine of the pre-tribulation rapture; they have incorrectly interpreted these vital chapters of prophecy regarding WWIII http://www.discoveringislam.org/china_gog_magog.htm; I want people to accurately note nations that exist today had other names when written millenniums ago and one must be an astute student of history to identify them properly. When one does so, then the prophecies play out before their eyes in current events exactly.

The King Who Exalts Himself (Daniel Ch. 11)

36 "The king will do as he pleases. He will exalt and magnify himself above every god and will say unheard-of things against the God of gods. He will be successful until the time of wrath is completed, for what has been determined must take place. 37 He will show no regard for the gods of his ancestors or for the one desired by women, nor will he regard any god, but will exalt himself above them all. 38 Instead of them, he will honor a god of fortresses; a god unknown to his ancestors he will honor with gold and silver, with precious stones and costly gifts. 39 He will attack the mightiest fortresses with the help of a foreign god and will greatly honor those who acknowledge

him. He will make them rulers over many people and will distribute the land at a price.[d]

40 "At the time of the end the king of the South will engage him in battle, and the king of the North will storm out against him with chariots and cavalry and a great fleet of ships. He will invade many countries and sweep through them like a flood. 41 He will also invade the Beautiful Land. Many countries will fall, but Edom, Moab and the leaders of Ammon will be delivered from his hand. 42 He will extend his power over many countries; Egypt will not escape.43 He will gain control of the treasures of gold and silver and all the riches of Egypt, with the Libyans and Cushites[e] in submission.44 But reports from the east and the north will alarm him, and he will set out in a great rage to destroy and annihilate many. 45 He will pitch his royal tents between the seas at[f] the beautiful holy mountain. Yet he will come to his end, and no one will help him.

http://www.isaiah18.com/Cush.html, the prophecy tells us that at the time of the end some leader who honors the military, who is greedy (gold, silver, treasures, idols, etc.), who possesses land and naval forces, who has power over many nations, including specifically control over such nations as Libya, Egypt, Saudi Arabia, Iraq. hmmm what recent current events are mentioning such things? http://www.globalissues.org/article/75/world-military-spending, especially note who honors the god of forces most (military)

http://cdn1.globalissues.org/i/military/13/country-distribution-2012.png

then note Libya:
http://www.thedailybeast.com/articles/2011/08/30/america-s-secret-libya-war-u-s-spent-1-billion-on-covert-ops-helping-nato.html,
http://edition.cnn.com/2011/OPINION/08/26/ellison.libya.obama/index.html,

of course we are familiar with USA involvement in Iraq but also note Saudi Arabia:
http://www.youtube.com/watch?v=PxVWckPZX0A,
http://www.youtube.com/watch?v=LoRHLrXmqbc,

and of course USA recent involvement in also controlling Egypt:
http://worldnews.nbcnews.com/_news/2013/08/15/20033815-obama-condemns-egypt-over-violence-cancels-joint-military-exercise?lite,
http://atlasshrugs2000.typepad.com/atlas_shrugs/2013/07/egypts-muslim-brotherhood-morsi-says-he-is-counting-on-obama.html,
http://www.foxnews.com/opinion/2013/07/09/what-egyptians-think-obama-after-morsi-disaster/ ,
http://therightscoop.com/report-obama-to-meet-with-muslim-brotherhood-turkish-diplomats-all-pushing-for-morsis-reinstatement/

To explain the satanic NWO involvement in all of this one just has to do a little research online; it's all there and not difficult to uncover. But the obvious is what the Lord tells us about the spirit of anti-christ and the manifest heads of the beast. It is always some nation, leader, who with militant might seeks to rule the world, is greedy, ambitious, full of vices, oppressive, destroyer, who hates God and God's people and sows death and destruction in that greedy ambition. When the GNP of America these days, is primarily the military industrial complex, big Pharma, and entertainment; all you have to do is look at the effects of these and how they all serve the satanic NWO obviously. So, while manufacturing WMDs more so than any nation on earth and more than many nations combined; these same warmongers bent on reducing the global population, infiltrate nations, and start riots, revolutions, that lead to war. They use the media, to get races to hate each other, factions, anyway they can to sow violence and get the poor to kill themselves off; while they luxuriate in the blood-soaked bills of their greedy profits off the deaths they've intentionally caused worldwide. It's not about winning or losing necessarily it is about killing off the masses and getting rich in the process. https://www.youtube.com/watch?v=1Sip9PDKB9o, so then you start to look at the ties between big Pharma and the poisons in our food, water, and air that make you sick, and that make you go to the drug prescribing doctors and nurses, that give you more poisons (virtually all man-made drugs have harmful side effects) until you die. (They make you sick and get rich off of your suffering and death in the process; all while pretending to help you; (on your way to an early grave)). It's not that they do it intentionally, they just don't have any medicines that are only helpful with NO HARMFUL SIDE EFFECTS, so WHY DO MEDICINES HAVE HARMFUL SIDE EFFECTS, can't mankind create medicines that are ONLY BENEFICIAL?!

And if you know anything about Hollywood, record productions these days, and media control, you have of course noted the satanic/illuminati presence brainwashing the masses with lies and deception; to keep the poor "dumbed-down" from uniting against the murderers and oppressors enslaving them all. https://www.youtube.com/results?search_query=satanic+nwo+in+hollywood&oq=satanic+nwo+in+hollywood&gs_l=youtube.3...285090.290831.0.291047.24.24.0.0.0.0.207.3377.2j20j2.24.0...0.0...1ac.1.11.youtube.3HBpaQ8vnhc, and https://www.youtube.com/results?search_query=satanic+nwo+in+music&oq=satanic+nwo+in+music&gs_l=youtube.12...32609.34392.0.36250.5.5.0.0.0.0.182.742.0j5.5.0...0.0...1ac.1.11.youtube._tCKpPa51IQ, and https://www.youtube.com/results?search_query=satanic+nwo+in+big+pharma&oq=satanic+nwo+in+big+pharma&gs_l=youtube.12...39315.42240.0.44443.10.10.0.0.0.0.204.1437.0j9j1.10.0...0.0...1ac.1.11.youtube.CG4U2zrUsl4

And of course, our Creator told us plainly that the anti-christ would do these things exactly. For the purpose of deceiving the world, controlling the world, with a desire to be worshipped in God's stead, and to the destruction of all souls who remain deceived and die in their sins; still having rejected Yahoshuah the Messiah, Jesus Christ as their personal Lord and Savior. Where did God tell us satanil would use media to deceive and control people? http://biblehub.com/ephesians/2-2.htm, where did He tells us drugs would be used to deceive the world? https://www.blastthetrumpet.org/PublicLetters/AAAUpdatedPublicAlertsMattersofLifeandDeath/Updates053016/Our%20Creator%20Told%20us%20in%20the%20Holy%20Bible%20Truth%20About%20Drugs.pdf, and one just has to know world history to see that all world empires used militant might to go forth conquering and to conquer. hmmm how many nations have US military bases? http://en.wikipedia.org/wiki/List_of_United_States_military_bases, http://en.wikipedia.org/wiki/United_States_military_deployments, http://www.politifact.com/truth-o-meter/statements/2011/sep/14/ron-paul/ron-paul-says-us-has-military-personnel-130-nation/

So if you're still in doubt as to who or what nation is currently leading the way as the 8th and final head of the beast and in forging the NWO which is planned to be divided thusly (all also according to biblical prophecy) https://www.youtube.com/watch?v=YWOgfK2_o3w, perhaps this presentation might help you: https://www.youtube.com/watch?v=mOHJKrxhBME or maybe this: https://www.youtube.com/watch?v=9bFVUZ-PYsM,

     (The 8th Head shows us that the 7 heads of the beast were part of its so it's not just one nation, but it's the entire world arrayed against God, practicing murder, sexual immorality, and so on that are against God and His People.) So, Christians need to make certain, their nations SIDE WITH JESUS CHRIST! As long as Americans all side with our Lord Jesus Christ, then our government and nation remains a force that is used for good on earth, but we need to be very concerned when our leaders are corrupted to the point of allowing enemies into our nation, people who hold completely different values from our American Christian heritage. The snake in this world, the devil, the antichrist, would seek to slither in and take control, of any nation that has the militant might of our nation. It has already been happening, by raising children to turn from our God and patriotic heritage of a nation blessed by our Eternal Creator, into people that rebel against Him because they were deceived from a young age in our public schools and media. Such that now, Christians, have difficultly even telling the truth to those deceived persons, and imagine we don't know what we're talking about, because those deceived persons were never taught the truth in all their years of public education. When deceived persons, take control of our nation, that is when the antichrist, by his spirit of error, has usurped authority in our nation, over God Almighty. And is when the superpowers instead of being a force of good, can become a very evil force in this world under the devil. **WE, AS AMERICANS, IF WE ARE TO REMAIN FREE, MUST RETURN WITH ALL HASTE TO OUR ETERNAL CREATOR AND HIS COMMANDMENTS GIVEN US ALL IN THE HOLY BIBLE!** "Whoever is an avowed enemy to God, I scruple not to call him an enemy to his country." - https://www.goodreads.com/quotes/6435724-nothing-is-more-certain-than-that-a-general-profligacy-and

https://www.youtube.com/watch?v=3GpUW0CVGKA That is overt idolatry shown in that video; here is the first part: https://www.youtube.com/watch?v=NdUkLtwI_hI It is part of the tactics of the satanic NWO to use cloaks of seeming righteousness to disguise their actual wickedness; so they use media, education, manmade religions, to brainwash the masses while they infiltrate to control world powers of monetary systems, political, militant and police powers. So, when I point out that mainstream Christianity is always pointing the finger at other nations and worldviews, religions, and at least televised rarely if ever looks in the mirror so to speak to see just how the USA has also been infiltrated by the NWO; it is to get everyone to do so!!! And to realize, I am NOT saying the USA is exclusively the satanic NWO at all! I am saying that currently it is being used by the snakes who have infiltrated our nation to forge the way; but they are also using all world superpowers to do the same! All over the world the satanic NWO infiltrates just like the Nazis who were brought into our own government via project paperclip and other methods. And then immediately began indoctrination in our public education system of children with the fiction called the theory of evolution https://www.youtube.com/watch?v=4mxXICZ9mXo&list=PL7F9B57EBDCCEECF8. The reason they like indoctrination of children with anything other than knowing the One True God http://biblehub.com/1_john/4-5.htm ; is that the spirit of error in them; then makes them easier to control https://www.youtube.com/watch?v=7gwcQjDhZtI via their other methods of global imperialism. Methods such as controlling monetary systems; natural resources; even food and water http://www.businessinsider.com/worlds-biggest-landowners-2011-3?op=1, http://www.naturalnews.com/035603_water_monopoly_privatization.html, http://www.thedailybeast.com/newsweek/2010/10/08/the-race-to-buy-up-the-world-s-water.html, https://www.google.com/#q=buying+up+aquifers, http://www.democraticunderground.com/10022473474 ; such that; by design; poor, oppressed masses fill their mercenary ranks of national military and police powers which they use to fight over those natural resources. The real goal of wars is simply population reduction and control over resources and people www.beyondtreason.com and so the satanic NWO https://www.youtube.com/results?search_query=satanic+nwo+linked+to+abortion%2C+euthanization%2C+depopulation&oq=satanic+n&gs_l=youtube.1.1.35i39l2j0l8.2401.5695.0.7892.11.10.1.0.0.0.110.985.5j5.10.0...0.0...1ac.1.11.youtube.j7IxJ4TtP00 , already in control of currencies and global resources, oppresses the masses; brainwashes them through public education and media; fills them with false sense of duty and patriotism to go get them to kill each other; while they luxuriate in their blood-soaked bills of ill-gotten gains and laugh at how simple it is to manipulate the poor masses of the world to do their will and even kill each other in these planned ways. So, the wealthy leaders of the world under the control of the satanic NWO; get together and stage media presentations; to convince people everywhere that the superpowers of the world are going to war against one another when really; all those wealthy persons we see in the media are in no way part of the bloodshed on the battlefield. So, millions suffer and die at their bequest and for their profit. When they get together in their meetings for global rule and dominion what they don't realize is just how greedy and ambitious each one of them are and so like all other world empires in history they fall by their own greed, pride, ambition and corruption as they will internally end up actually fighting one another because of their personal vices in their hearts and souls regardless of their outspoken allegiance to the NWO one world government - http://biblehub.com/matthew/12-25.htm besides this time of ultimately being destroyed altogether never to rise again by the Almighty Himself.

What is my message here? It is that I wish all people of the world would Repent and call upon the Living GOD and stop letting wealthy, evil, warmongers manipulate you! It is to Israel; not to trust in any superpowers of this world as they will only be a broken crutch!!! http://www.biblestudytools.com/isaiah/36-6-compare.html, https://www.youtube.com/watch?v=UTsxARCpTLw, http://biblehub.com/revelation/13-5.htm, https://www.youtube.com/watch?v=Hi-V_ilJu0w The superpowers of this world are not to be trusted; currently they (all combined) are the manifestation of the eighth head of the beast and are being gathered all according to prophecy http://biblehub.com/joel/3-2.htm, http://biblehub.com/zechariah/14-2.htm, http://biblehub.com/revelation/16-16.htm ; by the Power of our Creator. We get people who see great prophecies of the Holy Bible happening in front of their very eyes that still have the audacity to say there is no evidence for even the existence of GOD (if they truly believe that then God has indeed turned them over to a state of depravity - http://biblehub.com/romans/1-28.htm) So the real meaning of the Battle of Armageddon, is the satanic NWO, ultimately is facing GOD and His People! In fact, Armageddon means "the place of Megiddo"; and Megiddo means "the place of troops". So what our Creator is telling us in the scriptures http://biblehub.com/1_corinthians/15-25.htm, is that satanil and the fallen angles http://www.biblegateway.com/passage/?search=Jude+1&version=NIV, will be made visible (earth) http://biblehub.com/2_thessalonians/2-3.htm "under His Feet" = the earth is my footstool http://biblehub.com/isaiah/66-1.htm, http://biblehub.com/acts/7-49.htm. Our Creator is telling us all plainly that at the end times the world will be filled with incarnate devils and demons (for such purpose as our Creator has made them weak; to be gathered together and destroyed by fire - http://biblehub.com/2_thessalonians/2-8.htm) He tells us that at those end times Michael and Angels of God will also be incarnate fighting against satanil and the incarnate fallen angels (devils and demons) http://www.biblegateway.com/passage/?search=Revelation+12%3A7-11&version=ESV, http://www.biblegateway.com/passage/?search=Daniel+12%3A1-3&version=KJV note that all who are faithful to God; overcome by testifying of Yahoshuah the Messiah; their sins washed away by His Holy Blood (just like blood removes impurities from every cell in our body- Rev. 12:11). And when all those deceived by the incarnate satanil actually realize it; they will look upon that fallen liar in disgust saying, "Is this the man..." http://biblehub.com/isaiah/14-16.htm If you read the book of Jude carefully you will see the fallen angels, (demons, devils) were put in the abyss, where also satanil was bound until these end times, notice that they are released to incarnate in the last days as the book of revelation tells us http://www.biblegateway.com/passage/?search=Revelation+9%3A1-11&version=KJV When Christ first came He defeated satanil and bound him; and thereafter gave power to His followers to cast out demons and devils wherever they encountered them http://biblehub.com/matthew/12-29.htm, http://www.biblegateway.com/passage/?search=Luke+10%3A19&version=KJV, http://biblehub.com/mark/16-17.htm, and so we know satanil was bound at the Beginning of Christ's Reign (see http://www.godempowersyou.com/documentation/HistoricalTestimonyandMinistry/TheFirstResurrection.pdf, and http://www.godempowersyou.com/documentation/HistoricalTestimonyandMinistry/MansChronologicalExistenceExplained.pdf for more details on this topic) just like Jude tells us " And the angels who did not keep their positions of authority but abandoned their proper dwelling—these he has kept in darkness, bound with everlasting chains for judgment on the great Day" and that we read that he bound them in darkness in the abyss with satanil http://biblehub.com/revelation/20-3.htm and what happens when that seal has been broken:

"9 And when he had opened the fifth seal, I saw under the altar the souls of them that were slain for the word of God, and for the testimony which they held:

10 And they cried with a loud voice, saying, How long, O Lord, holy and true, dost thou not judge and avenge our blood on them that dwell on the earth?

11 And white robes were given unto every one of them; and it was said unto them, that they should rest yet for a little season, until their fellow servants also and their brethren, that should be killed as they were, should be fulfilled."

fifth seal; fifth angel = http://biblehub.com/revelation/9-1.htm the release of satanil and the demons in the abyss for the purpose of gathering the nations to make war with God and the saints (as is presently occurring); http://biblehub.com/revelation/12-17.htm and it's of short duration and is why all the saints previously slain by satanic evil on earth were told to wait for a little season (season of darkness under satanic NWO) and persecution of the saints; those who have the testimony of Jesus Christ - Rev 12; notice the angels need the Blood of the Lamb and notice they also have the testimony of Jesus Christ, Yahoshuah the Messiah.

http://www.biblegateway.com/verse/en/Revelation%2019%3A10, the reason for this is (contrary to current popular belief in mainstream religions; both angels and demons (the falling away) incarnate just like GOD did in the person of Yahoshuah the Messiah, aka Jesus the Christ. As He tells us http://biblehub.com/psalms/104-4.htm, the breath of life God gives us (spirit) is also set on fire by Him or extinguished depending upon whether or not during the trial of our incarnation we are found faithful by receiving the Salvation offered in Yahoshuah the Messiah, aka Jesus the Christ, or if we choose all our days to do evil and despise our Creator. That is the manifestation of sorting the sheep from the goats, men from snakes, wheat from tares, heavens from earth, angels from devils, and is ultimately what our Creator is telling us in so many ways that one third of His Creation ultimately chooses to rebel and becomes darkened and destroyed choosing to cling to wickedness and lies rather than repent and obtain the Grace offered of Mercy and Salvation for all who are Grateful for the Sacrifice of the Messiah crucified in our place; in our behalf!!!!!!!! (that's why it's a third of the stars, third of the creatures in the sea, third of the ships, third of the trees, etc. it is all ways of saying the same thing that ultimately a third of the created beings brought into existence choose to hate and war against their own Creator) and will ultimately be destroyed in that foolishness of battling the Lord of Hosts with two thirds of brilliant shining immortal; invincible beings with Him!!! (http://www.kingjamesbibleonline.org/Revelation-Chapter-8/) Not that the Almighty needs any help at all; I just want to point out that while it is sad that ultimately a third of all humanity will be thrown into the lake of fire; two-thirds will NOT! but will shine like the sun and stars forever!!!!!!! Knowing the scriptures tell us that plainly; I am expecting to see massive revivals in these end times and millions perhaps tens of millions running for water asking God Himself to baptize them and fill them with His Holy Spirit!!!!!!!!

But we also now know that satanil and devils are incarnate among us. In other words, not everyone you meet in flesh and blood is some lost sinner, lost brother or sister, just waiting to hear the Gospel. Christians need to understand that the serpents, devils, demons, think nothing at all like they do. They are in no way sorrowful on account of their sins; they feel no remorse whatsoever like a sinner destined to be forgiven by God does. Instead these people delight to do evil; they are without repentance, have no desire to repent now or ever, they enjoy their sins and encourage everyone they meet to participate in sin and evil and wallow in it; the more wicked they become; the more they swell with pride and arrogance in defiance against God and His Instructions for life contained in the Holy Bible and are making every effort toward the day when they can rid the world of God, the Holy Bible, and His messengers: burning churches, Bibles, and murdering, persecuting the saints in all the world. Christians need to note such persons; not with fear, but hopefully with the ability to arrest them because demons in the flesh commit many crimes and if in positions of public trust and authority; war crimes leading to genocides and other atrocities. It takes the gift of discernment to be able to behold demons, devils and angels (in other words, to look at a person and see if they are possessed or are themselves an incarnate devil or angel)

There is a difference between demonic possession and an incarnate snake. A possessed person is tormented by the devils; an incarnate demon relishes tormenting others; not realizing that they will reap what they sow in their own person as they burn in the lake of fire. Anyone, who steadfastly resists the name and power of God, if you are full of the Holy Ghost and attempt to cast out unclean spirits; and instead find them mocking or laughing in return; make note of such wicked persons and in so doing document their crimes and seek their arrests. (they and all like them comprise the image of the beast, the satanic NWO) Just like the Spirit of Truth unites believers in Christ and represent His Image, His Body, on earth, the spirit of error enters into them and unites them (how people like Hitler suddenly come to power and have so many followers hailing them (as unfortunately occurred with Obama here in the USA) and that is what the image of the beast is. It is all who worship self in pride (just like satanil), who worship creatures/creation, fallible mankind, like you hear people boast of their faith in fallible science and such, it is that spirit of error in them, deceiving them keeping them from knowing the One True God and from wisely worshipping the Creator.

http://www.bibleexplained.com/revelation/r-seg15-16/r1613-3frogs.htm and http://www.godempowersyou.com/documentation/HistoricalTestimonyandMinistry/MansChronologicalExistenceExplained.pdf for more details on this topic. So it is not just one false religion or one person who is a false prophet it is ALL false manmade religions (including evolution and atheism - https://www.blastthetrumpet.org/PublicLetters/AAAUpdatedPublicAlertsMattersofLifeandDeath/Updates053016/Evolution%20and%20Atheism%20Intertwined%20Cults%20of%20the%20Insane.pdf) that by the spirit of error http://www.biblestudytools.com/1-john/4.html causes them to teach lies/false doctrines/false prophesy.

There are figureheads in all of them; but all I am pointing out is that the Battle of Armageddon is not just the physical manifestation of WWIII that will occur before our eyes; but is in fact the whole world (ANY SINGLE PERSON, ANY ENTITY, BUSINESS, ORGANIZATION AND ANY NATION) that is against God our Creator!!! and the real BATTLE OF ARMAGEDDON, is the entire satanic NWO, all it involves, all it's devious plots and ploys, and it's ultimate goal is to murder anyone and everyone who does not bow to them and their insanity in choosing to war against our Creator and all who are faithful to Him; despising His Instructions for Life as contained in the Holy Bible. When the veil is lifted and you can finally see their methods clearly; it will enable sane citizens to identify who the enemies of God and all mankind really are and make

arrests as necessary all over the world. So, let's go over their methods of infiltration and control.
http://biblehub.com/2_corinthians/2-11.htm

As aforementioned, the satanic NWO targets any methodology used to control the masses, government, education, military, police, manmade religions, philosophies, worldviews, media, drugs, mind control technologies, etc. But what specific methods do they utilize to gain decisions like http://en.wikipedia.org/wiki/Scopes_Trial and http://en.wikipedia.org/wiki/Roe_v._Wade First they use all the methods listed to gain popular opinions and coordinate their satanic followers (whether or not those doing so realize it). Then they simply spy on the judge/jury and find dirty laundry/sins/crimes on the person(s) involved. They then coerce decisions in their interests through blackmail of exposure of those sins/crimes, bribes and threats. This happens all the time all over the world but should especially be suspect when such decisions overturn the standard historical legal definitions of decades to centuries prior (like these decisions did) and violate common sense, rational thought and result in lives lost (like these decisions have). That is all evidence of the stench of the satanic NWO. They use that method on professors and teachers, on politicians, on corporate CEOs, on generals, on police chiefs, on religious leaders, and anyone they can't control by blackmail (exposure of personal sins and crimes), threats (to their own life and that of loved ones) or bribes; they systematically attack in the following ways. Usually they get one of their controlled minions (see oaths of skull and bonesmen - http://www.theforbiddenknowledge.com/hardtruth/more_skull_and_bones.htm) ; in other words call in a favor (like the mafia); to get someone they already control by threats, bribes, blackmail, to do some dirty work for them; like seduce someone; poison someone; assassinate someone; etc. That is what happened to persons like JFK https://www.youtube.com/watch?v=zdMbmdFOvTs who try to warn the controlled masses of the satanic NWO and their methods. Anyone, who works against them and their efforts to create death and destruction on earth (racism is just one of those methods) is targeted like Martin Luther King Jr. https://www.youtube.com/watch?v=NoO1sLYHHxM It is obvious that satanists have infiltrated our government in all these ways http://www.whale.to/c/sataniccrime.pdf, http://www.youtube.com/watch?v=dTLUg-ThADg, http://www.youtube.com/watch?v=mtstlx96s8M (as you can see not just politicians, but lifers in the CIA, FBI and other government organizations are covering for sins and crimes; even as great as child trafficking, pornography and horrific abuses; and is also why they are adamantly for continuing and funding organizations like Planned Slaughterhood responsible for the deaths of millions of innocent babes to date). So through personal corruption the satanists infiltrate and take control of the entities that control the masses like they did with education http://en.wikipedia.org/wiki/General_Education_Board; who is one of the larger contributors and promoters of the satanic NWO depopulation agenda (and of course is responsible for the continued brainwashing/indoctrination of the fiction known as the theory of evolution) http://www.infowars.com/for-the-record-rockefeller-soft-kill-depopulation-plans-exposed/ and http://www.whale.to/b/rockefeller_q.html. Their control of music and other media is obvious as well. https://www.youtube.com/watch?v=JwsDyqZzCrs, https://www.youtube.com/watch?v=FIeQSYLHXO0, https://www.youtube.com/watch?v=F-8G9PbMZaI, https://www.youtube.com/results?search_query=satanic+nwo+in+media&oq=satanic+nwo+in+media&gs_l=youtube.12...28578.29943.0.32856.4.4.0.0.0.0.90.355.4.4.0...0.0...1ac.1.11.youtube.LbDQ_HtOce8 These are people who actually worship satanil and many die early over it. https://www.youtube.com/watch?v=8jLo_r8Az7w, http://bossip.com/559101/amy-winehouse-death-illuminati-satanic-sacrifice-for-quitting-illuminati-video69691/ , http://mediaexposed.tumblr.com/post/7984782005/amy-winehouse-joins-the-notorious-27-club Anyone, that gets too close to information that they wish to silence can become such a target and many die suspiciously as a result. http://vigilantcitizen.com/vigilantreport/the-hidden-life-of-marilyn-monroe-the-original-hollywood-mind-control-slave-part-i/ . Until people (especially Christians) stop ignoring the obvious; in psychological denial, satanists will continue to use these methods of blackmail, bribing, threats, and murder of those who get in their way. We MUST FACE them! We MUST EXPOSE them! We MUST ARREST them!!!!!!!! or in the near future these wicked persons might be breaking our doors down to haul innocent people away into concentration camps. (FEMA camps are being staffed - https://www.youtube.com/watch?v=3esrlNnwT-c) So ungodly people through their means can influence whole nations, if the people allow them to. It is the duty of people, not to submit to any ungodly agendas of their governments. WE HAVE TO SIDE WITH OUR LORD JESUS CHRIST AND HIS RIGHTEOUS COMMANDMENTS ALWAYS!

Influential ministries be on your guard!!!!!!!! the satanic NWO infiltrates by sending a man or woman to seduce husbands and/or wives that have powerful ministries (especially televised ones), in that way they create scandals, (like all the homosexuals and pedophiles that were busted in the Catholic church) and destroy effective Christian ministries. Christians everywhere pray for such powerful ministries they are being targeted by the satanic NWO and is why laws are being made to pillage, plunder and destroy them (the IRS is an armed force of satanic NWO retribution, illegally operating here in the USA - https://www.youtube.com/watch?v=XLwHrxjPT5E, https://www.youtube.com/watch?v=7gwcQjDhZtI. Our nation was founded as a free nation, but has become increasingly enslaved by the corruption and wealthiest people on earth we fought to be free from. So, beware of anyone who shows up in your organization and is suddenly so sweet on the persons in power within that organization. It could be someone who just "sleeps their way to the top" but in these days it could be infiltration for the purpose of control through blackmail (exposure of scandal) and of course this is how they control media personalities. http://www.huffingtonpost.com/2013/01/06/david-letterman-sex-scandal-divorce_n_2405129.html So anyone who is an activist beware, be on your guard, it could mean not just your career; but your life!!!!!!!!

By writing this, if I or any other whistleblowers or Truth seekers end up dead; should not be cause of other people to fear these satanists. They are just people, greedy, deceptive, arrogant, bloodthirsty people, but they are just people! Criminals, crimes and atrocities against humanity; for all the above reasons and should be arrested at once!!!!!!!! *crimes against humanity = brainwashing children, mind control on the masses through media, music, inciting wars, using internationally banned methods and weapons on people, poisoning food, water, air, medication, using drugs and technology on citizens for mind control and more!!!!!!!!

What I say to you; I say to all, "REPENT! for the Kingdom of God is at hand!!!!!!!! The Day of His Judgment and Wrath is near!!!!!!!! Only those who know, love, and obey the Living God, the One True God, will remain!!!!!!!!" http://biblehub.com/1_john/5-20.htm

http://www.biblegateway.com/passage/?search=Matthew+7%3A21-23&version=NKJV - religion will not save you! You MUST KNOW the LORD, the One True God, and be led by His Holy Spirit!!!!!!!! http://biblehub.com/romans/8-14.htm If you are doing your own thing; even while calling yourself a "Christian"; if you are not listening to the Holy Ghost and obeying Christ thereby; then you need to fulfill what is written in http://www.biblegateway.com/passage/?search=Acts+2%3A38-39&version=KJV and pray according to http://biblehub.com/luke/11-13.htm! Because if you do not KNOW the LORD; are not FILLED WITH HIS SPIRIT; are not LED BY HIS SPIRIT; then you are yet in rebellion! You are yet in your sins! You are in a religion; carnal will worship, that has nothing to do with http://biblehub.com/john/14-15.htm; for the carnal mind cannot understand the things of God! http://biblehub.com/romans/8-7.htm so you MUST Repent! You MUST be baptized in the Holy Name of Yahoshuah the Messiah, aka Jesus the Christ! You MUST pray to receive the Holy Ghost until you know and communicate with the One True God, Creator of the Universe and He with You! That is the only way you can know GOD be "led by His Spirit"; by uniting with His Holy

Spirit and also thereby enabling you to hear His Voice! http://biblehub.com/romans/8-7.htm

Jn 16:13 And that brings me to:

8 - http://biblehub.com/revelation/19-10.htm that if you will break away right now from false doctrines, false traditions, false worldviews, the lies that you have been told all your life and believed in and hear the Voice of the Lord your God calling you, to humble yourself right now wherever you may be; stop doing whatever you are doing and drop down and pray. Pray like you never have before to KNOW the One True God! Call upon Yahoshuah/Yeshua the Messiah out loud to answer you! to let you KNOW Him! to fill You with His Holy Spirit! For in the moment, you are filled with the Spirit that Created the Universe; will be the moment you know TRUTH! The moment you know EVERYTHING WONDERFUL! The moment you KNOW the ONE TRUE GOD, CREATOR OF THE UNIVERSE. And Having His Holy Spirit, you will begin having revelations from the Lord God Almighty also! You will understand how He showed the prophets what is to come; because He will be showing the future to you also!!!!!!!!
http://biblehub.com/john/16-13.htm, http://biblehub.com/acts/2-17.htm, http://biblehub.com/joel/2-28.htm

In that moment you will understand how it is that millions while facing death, threats of death still testified boldly of the life, death and resurrection of the Living Lord Jesus Christ. The reason you will understand; is because the Lord of the Universe will be living in and upon you!!!!!!!! (as He prayed http://biblehub.com/john/14-20.htm, http://www.biblegateway.com/passage/?search=John+17&version=NIV

  When that happens, you will KNOW the One True Living God http://biblehub.com/1_john/5-20.htm and He will KNOW you! Because He will be teaching you thereafter; http://biblehub.com/1_john/2-27.htm personally; you won't be just be reading His Words in the Holy Bible, you will be hearing the Words He will speak to you: http://biblehub.com/matthew/7-23.htm

  If there is one thing I could do; it would be to persuade all souls to cry out to the Living God, Creator of the Universe, Lord Yahoshuah/Yeshua, (English) Jesus the Christ, until they all knew beyond all doubt the One True God! That is the only legitimate government under God Almighty, the Creator of the Universe and all therein; are those who KNOW Him! Thus any power on earth, leadership that proclaims Yahoshuah the Messiah, aka Jesus the Christ, is their personal Lord and Savior, lets the Gospel be proclaimed freely to all citizens in their tribe, city, business, state, nation, etc. is a legitimate authority as defined in http://www.biblegateway.com/passage/?search=Romans+13%3A1-7&version=NIV, these leaders serve public interests by calling the people to national days of prayer as our founders in the USA did, they develop social services based on Christian ideals, such as taking care of widows, orphans, feeding the hungry, clothing the naked, relieving oppression; not adding to it. By their profession of Christ and by what they do; will you and all know who has true authority granted by the Living and Reigning King of kings! and all who oppress their people, rob their people, develop excessive taxation rather than alleviating poverty and creating national programs that develop jobs with living wages, all who oppose the Gospel of Jesus Christ, censor freedom of speech (knowledge) and religion (to be able to choose or reject the Living God and Reigning Lord of lords), all who do wickedly no matter what they profess are IMPOSTERS, they are the infiltrating snakes, that should be arrested at once for their many crimes against humanity and the Living God! All who deliberately choose not to profess Christ, do wickedly, and fail to exhort the people to righteousness or right living are NOT of God; these are the manifest satanic NWO persons who have infiltrated positions reserved only for God's Messengers, those who demonstrate having the most integrity among us and a love for the people that alleviates their burdens during the days of their incarnation; by calling everyone to repentance and right living so that they can be blessed, prosperous, instead of cursed and suffering. We, as followers of Christ, have a duty to observe and respect all legitimate authorities, and we have a duty to arrest the imposters who are now destroying the world and all life on the planet, who are "the beast".

People who watch prophecy coming to pass before our eyes, should be looking at Israel.

The Destroyers of Jerusalem Destroyed
1Behold, a day of the LORD is coming when your plunder will be divided in your presence. **2**For I will gather all the nations for battle against Jerusalem, and the city will be captured, the houses looted, and the women ravished. Half of the city will go into exile, but the rest of the people will not be removed from the city. **3**Then the LORD will go out to fight against those nations, as He fights in the day of battle. **4**On that day His feet will stand on the Mount of Olives, east of Jerusalem, and the Mount of Olives will be split in two from east to west, forming a great valley, with half the mountain moving to the north and half to the south.…
https://biblehub.com/zechariah/14-2.htm

Zechariah 14

New International Version

The Lord Comes and Reigns

14 A day of the Lord is coming, Jerusalem, when your possessions will be plundered and divided up within your very walls.

2 I will gather all the nations to Jerusalem to fight against it; the city will be captured, the houses ransacked, and the women raped. Half of the city will go into exile, but the rest of the people will not be taken from the city. **3** Then the Lord will go out and fight against those nations, as he fights on a day of battle. **4** On that day his feet will stand on the Mount of Olives, east of Jerusalem, and the Mount of Olives will be split in two from east to west, forming a great valley, with half of the mountain moving north and half moving south. **5** You will flee by my mountain valley, for it will extend to Azel. You will flee as you fled from the earthquake[a] in the days of Uzziah king of Judah. Then the Lord my God will come, and all the holy ones with him.

6 On that day there will be neither sunlight nor cold, frosty darkness. **7** It will be a unique day—a day known only to the Lord—with no distinction between day and night. When evening comes, there will be light.

8 On that day living water will flow out from Jerusalem, half of it east to the Dead Sea and half of it west to the Mediterranean Sea, in summer and in winter.

9 The Lord will be king over the whole earth. On that day there will be one Lord, and his name the only name.

10 The whole land, from Geba to Rimmon, south of Jerusalem, will become like the Arabah. But Jerusalem will be raised up high from the Benjamin Gate to the site of the First Gate, to the Corner Gate, and from the Tower of Hananel to the royal winepresses, and will remain in its place. **11** It will be inhabited; never again will it be destroyed. Jerusalem will be secure.

12 This is the plague with which the Lord will strike all the nations that fought against Jerusalem: Their flesh will rot while they are still standing on their feet, their eyes will rot in their sockets, and their tongues will rot in their mouths. **13** On that day people will be stricken by the Lord with great panic. They will seize each other by the hand and attack one another. **14** Judah too will fight at Jerusalem. The wealth of all the surrounding nations will be collected—great quantities of gold and silver and clothing. **15** A similar plague will strike the horses and mules, the camels and donkeys, and all the animals in those camps.

16 Then the survivors from all the nations that have attacked Jerusalem will go up year after year to worship the King, the Lord Almighty, and to celebrate the Festival of Tabernacles. **17** If any of the peoples of the earth do not go up to Jerusalem to worship the King, the Lord Almighty, they will have no rain. **18** If the Egyptian people do not go up and take part, they will have no rain. The Lord[b] will bring on them the plague he inflicts on the nations that do not go up to celebrate the Festival of Tabernacles. **19** This will be the punishment of Egypt and the punishment of all the nations that do not go up to celebrate the Festival of Tabernacles.

20 On that day holy to the Lord will be inscribed on the bells of the horses, and the cooking pots in the Lord's house will be like the sacred bowls in front of the altar. **21** Every pot in Jerusalem and Judah will be holy to the Lord Almighty, and all who come to sacrifice will take some of the pots and cook in them. And on that day there will no longer be a Canaanite[c] in the house of the Lord Almighty.

So, this present day where people are actually siding with the rapists, robbers and murderers AGAINST Israel is duly noted as potentially leading up to the final conflict with GOD ALMIGHTY and the ungodly nations attacking His People and attempting to destroy His creation, this world and life on earth.

While I look at Jerusalem, I remember:

Hagar and Sarah
…**25**Now Hagar stands for Mount Sinai in Arabia and corresponds to the present-day Jerusalem, because she is in slavery with her children. **26**But the Jerusalem above is free, and she is our mother. **27**For it is written: "Rejoice, O barren woman, who bears no children; break forth and cry aloud, you who have never travailed; because more are the children of the desolate woman than of her who has a husband."… https://biblehub.com/galatians/4-26.htm

And is why I caution believers to make sure their nation serves Jesus Christ! because otherwise persecution could arise. Believers need to remain faithful unto death! Ask the Good Lord, just as He tells us, DAILY to deliver you from evil!

Matthew 6:9-13

King James Version

⁹ After this manner therefore pray ye: Our Father which art in heaven, Hallowed be thy name.

¹⁰ Thy kingdom come, Thy will be done in earth, as it is in heaven.

¹¹ Give us this day our daily bread.

¹² And forgive us our debts, as we forgive our debtors.

¹³ And lead us not into temptation, but deliver us from evil: For thine is the kingdom, and the power, and the glory, for ever. Amen.

The Holy Bible is the Most Thoroughly Researched Book on Earth

It Contains Well Verified Facts of History from Genesis to Revelation

The Holy Bible, as mentioned in the previous section, has accurately told us the history of mankind even before it happened! So, when science has been WRONG for CENTURIES, the Holy Bible has been RIGHT and it is STILL RIGHT today and forever, BECAUSE it factually contains the Words of God Almighty given to mankind and He doesn't lie!

Anyone believing the opinions from anyone, even so-called scientists, over the Words of God in the Holy Bible is committing idolatry and is making a most serious mistake. NEVER trust the opinions of ANYONE over GOD! NEVER!

The Holy Bible has been researched down to every letter it contains for centuries. It is by far the most studied literature on the planet. If you did not have the Holy Bible throughout all your years of education, you are at best lacking a proper education and more than likely had your head crammed full of lies, deceptions and self-delusions.

Never, ever set aside the well verified FACTS OF HISTORY for fairy tales about so-called prehistory! The well verified facts of history need to be taught EVERYONE WORLDWIDE so that they all understand and learn about our Intelligent Creator and are not so easily led astray by anyone.

I am outraged at just how many innocent children have been deceived in our public education system http://www.facebook.com/notes/michael-swenson/teach-the-children-truth-teach-them-well/515687638510200 and I hope this will serve to help deprogram all of them and prevent any further brainwashing to continue on earth anywhere. It might seem as if I have chosen poorly to be so aggressive in my writing and what some might find critical; but my anger stems not from those who were so deceived by the theory of evolution, and atheism, they thought it acceptable and even pleasurable to murder me by incompatible blood transfusion and when that failed by suffocation; (and all the evil I have suffered intensely from because of such widespread corruption these worldviews have caused www.blastthetrumpet.org – I'm telling people about my suffering, the crimes I have experienced even though I think it shameful to talk about such things, because I want people to recognize these crimes and prevent them in the future from continuing. I've had to include the true names of the criminals, not because I haven't forgiven them all, just because the world needs to recognize my testimony is true. Hospital homicides and covering them up by governing authorities, is some of the worst betrayal in this world. Trusting people with our lives and safety that are preying upon us, is tragic and threatens the collapse of law and order, even civilization if such sin and crimes remain and are not halted by repentance of all involved. I have learned that taking matters into our own hands, acting even with an eye toward Justice for all, or worse acting vengefully only creates even more evil in this world, we have to learn from God and His Followers, who were still praying, "Father, forgive them." While those murdering them were still in the evil act. To esteem Mercy for everyone, not just ourselves, because that is the only way for people to choose to repent and learn to love God and everyone enough, not to sin against anyone any longer; it's the only way to end evil, with ourselves as an example. God tells us if people ignore Him and His Children, our Love, His Commandments, He is bringing all those maltreated souls with Him, in the Day of Vengeance for all persons who refused to get His Message and did not repent of their murders, their sexual immorality breaking people's hearts, marriages and families, and all their many lies and chose not to repent of any and all wicked sins. I am telling the world about what God has taught me, so you should be for keeping this website active until the Lord Jesus Christ comes again, because it tells humanity about the future until that Glorious Day and how to deal with waste, and create structures that can give electricity to the world, terraforming the desertified regions of the earth, and much more by returning to God and not embracing deceptive worldviews); so my passion in preaching is not only from the great suffering I've endured (when God tells us to pray "deliver us from evil" how many know to pray that He delivers us from our OWN evil thoughts, words, ways and deeds, to never commit sin after coming to know Him (1Jn 3:9 we have to have that intense desire, that passionate longing constantly with us in our thoughts and hearts to be Perfect like He is Perfect, to be Righteous as He is Righteous, to be Loving as He is Loving. Even though we all make mistakes no matter how hard we try, when we strive for that High Calling to be Holy as He is Holy, we know that God is working in our lives, actually Saving us), so we pray that He works in and upon us such that even if we are tempted, He prevents us from falling. When we know the heartache of what adultery causes, the broken vows, the separation of marriages, the harmed children and broken families, we become angry inside that we would ever even be tempted to commit such evil, and have the understanding why God tells us not to do evil things, and to even run from it. That He makes us to be faithful and true like Himself.) So everyone is being harmed by not recognizing God and His Commands to us in the Holy Bible and is why I am adamantly against lying to innocent little children; they are being brainwashed with that garbage (into becoming God-denying atheists with the lie of the theory of evolution in our schools) in the first place; and that if somehow the Lord doesn't shine into their lives; they will remain in the miserable existence of the darkness of ignorance that leads to the everlasting flames of damnation. You see, when mankind deliberately ignores God and His Commandments, thinking they know better, that is sin and even crimes against creation, humanity as a whole. For example, God tells us specifically how he wants us to steward/garden the earth, so when mankind ignores Him and His Instructions for life, that causes the curses/Divine Consequences of weeds, plagues and pestilences. But mankind rather than repent and return to God and His Commandments, poisons the world with herbicides and pesticides, and is causing extinction events, and sickness and death not only to other creatures, but to ourselves in the process! (Why I wrote Population Management) I want people to recognize that God tells us what to do and what not to do, because HE LOVES US, and when we sin, commit crimes, it causes us ALL to suffer, sometimes it appears that only God and His Martyrs, Prophets and Apostles, even innocent Children are suffering the most, not the sinners themselves. Because we are focusing only on this life (actually blaming God for death and suffering of his saints and innocent children), instead of realizing that God takes such people who have learned to obey Him, straight to Heaven, delivering them from even more suffering due to the evil in this world. But we are all suffering even unto death by disobeying our Creator, by sinning in any way. So my passion, whether it comes through by giving those so arrogant they disdain all who testify of our Eternal Creator, a taste of their own medicine http://biblehub.com/psalms/18-26.htm, or when I am so truly motivated toward the Salvation of all souls that I beseech everyone to seek to KNOW THE CREATOR here and now and forever, in such a way that it seems to be practically begging; it is all because http://biblehub.com/1_corinthians/9-22.htm that I will do anything honorable, God allows, to try my best to persuade all souls to call upon the Resurrected Messiah, Yahoshuah, aka the LORD JESUS CHRIST, right now everywhere, until they KNOW beyond all doubt, He has answered them to their present and Everlasting Joy!

The scientific, legal, factual ubiquitous evidence overwhelmingly supports the reality we exist in by observation in the following ways: (In this list I am not claiming it to be exhaustive; only partial and yet I still hope it is sufficient to persuade all souls to come into their right minds and true understanding of the Universe and the Power that Created It All)

1) epistemology (ɪˌpɪstɪˈmɒlədʒɪ) — n

the theory of knowledge, esp the critical study of its validity, methods, and scope

[C19: from Greek epistēmē knowledge]

A) The Law of Cause and Effect
- http://www.icr.org/cause-effect/ By this one scientific principle we know with absolute certainty that something caused the Universe to come into existence.

B) The Law of Non-contradiction
- http://en.wikipedia.org/wiki/Law_of_noncontradiction - and by this scientific precept we also know the Universe did NOT cause itself to come into existence; for it would have had to existed before it actually did in order to bring about causal force upon itself.

To paraphrase something MUST exist to act upon anything else.

"Aristotle on Non-contradiction

First published Fri Feb 2, 2007; substantive revision Wed Jan 26, 2011

      According to Aristotle, first philosophy, or metaphysics, deals with ontology and first principles, of which the principle (or law) of non-contradiction is the firmest. Aristotle says that **without the principle of non-contradiction we could not know anything that we do know.** Presumably, we could not demarcate the subject matter of any of the special sciences, for example, biology or mathematics, and we would not be able to distinguish between what something is, for example a human being or a rabbit, and what it is like, for example pale or white. Aristotle's own distinction between essence and accident would be impossible to draw, and the inability to draw distinctions in general would make rational discussion impossible. According to Aristotle, the principle of non-contradiction is a principle of scientific inquiry, reasoning and communication that we cannot do without." - http://plato.stanford.edu/entries/aristotle-noncontradiction/

Scientific FACT: The Universe did NOT Create Itself

http://www.facebook.com/notes/michael-swenson/acknowledging-the-eternal-creator-takes-no-faith-it-is-scientific-fact/491948024217495

?So what did bring the Universe into existence?

2) 2nd Law of Thermodynamics (Entropy Aspect)

http://hyperphysics.phy-astr.gsu.edu/hbase/thermo/seclaw.html "Since entropy gives information about the evolution of an isolated system with time, it is said to give us the direction of "time's arrow". If snapshots of a system at two different times shows one state which is more disordered, then it could be implied that this state came later in time. For an isolated system, the natural course of events takes the system to a more disordered (higher entropy) state." The visible universe is slowing down, disintegrating, cooling off, reaching a state of equilibrium. (This confirms what God has told us in the Holy Bible about Creation since the beginning when His Creation fell due to sin - Genesis and Rom 8:20)

3) Newton's Third Law

http://www.physicsclassroom.com/class/newtlaws/u2l4a.cfm "For every action, there is an equal and opposite reaction." By the above scientific laws, we know the universe was brought into existence by a Power equal to or greater than all the combined power in the universe. That Power must be invisible, must be eternal, and of such a magnitude to create all the visible and invisible contents of the universe.

    This is what the Holy Bible states about God, the Creator. http://biblehub.com/1_timothy/1-17.htm "Now to the King eternal, immortal, invisible, the only God, be honor and glory forever and ever.
Amen." http://biblehub.com/john/1-3.htm All things were made by him; and without him was not anything made that was made. http://biblehub.com/colossians/1-16.htm "For by Him all things were created, both in the heavens and on earth, visible and invisible, whether

thrones or dominions or rulers or authorities-- all things have been created through Him and for Him."

It even states what the sciences have observed with the advent of optics through microscopes that visible objects are made up of things that are not seen. http://biblehub.com/hebrews/11-3.htm - "By faith we understand that the universe was formed at God's command, so that what is seen was not made out of what was visible"

Instead, the Creator through the Divinely Inspired Holy Bible tells us that it is Him, that invisible Power that brought everything into existence is also what is that invisible energy holding it together. http://biblehub.com/colossians/1-17.htm "He existed before anything else, and he holds all creation together."

However, as aforementioned He tells us that all things visible are passing away (and is how we know for Him to be Eternal, He must be invisible). http://biblehub.com/2_corinthians/4-18.htm "So we fix our eyes not on what is seen, but on what is unseen, since what is seen is temporary, but what is unseen is eternal."

This present creation is subjected to death and decay because we have sinned, so these truths are speaking of this present fallen creation.

Science has confirmed these biblical statements as true in the aforementioned.

(Understand that when God perfects us, creation will no longer be subjected to decay and death, that is when visible creation also becomes an expression of the Eternal Creator and is what He tells us that in the End the Creator and His Creation will exist Harmoniously and be as One in Holy Matrimony Rev Ch 21-Ch 22, 1Cor 15)

4) archeology- and just plain visible discovery anyone who is able to travel to these locations can make http://www.youtube.com/watch?v=3PSZNYdfawQ&list=PLBD9B9FDCB6D5F4AA I provide controversial links; even links that some "Christians" might criticize for the sole purpose that by providing them; some claiming that there is absolutely no evidence for God the Creator (despite the existence of the Universe), and the accuracy of the Biblical accounts, might see that in fact there is an abundance of evidence; however, controversial it may be. In addition, if any of it is factually proven fraudulent I want the world to know that my knowledge of our Creator is not based on physical artifacts, buried cities, ruins and remains of lost civilizations, monuments or anything that could be construed as only possessing knowledge about a concept or topic; but that my personal knowledge of our Creator; comes from personally knowing our Creator, communicating with our Creator, learning directly from our Creator and that the reason I am showing such

physical evidence of the validity of the Divinely Inspired Scriptures is for the sole purpose that I want everyone else to personally know and learn directly from our Creator as well. I recognize that until the last of the liars are thrown into the Lake of Fire there will always be fools denying all the evidence presented herein; but I am attempting to enlighten those who through no fault of their own were indoctrinated with garbage in the name of science; with the hope that they will be so enraged when they realize it that they will never again allow such nonsense to be taught to innocent little children all over the world, but that people everywhere will have Joy in communing with our Creator forever. Some of us, Christians included, are concerned about sharing such things, artifacts and such, because they are afraid that if someone claims to be able to prove it false that it will somehow hurt the weak in faith; but my point is that once a soul is actually filled with the Holy Spirit of God Almighty; they will no longer believe; or no longer have an intellectual construct of our Creator; they will no longer rest upon an artifact here or there in all the world; but they will know with their entire being the One True God. If in that effort, we are unable to humble ourselves, to risk ridicule, mockery, the chance to be proven wrong concerning a single aspect of our efforts to lead souls to the Eternal God, the Eternal Truth; then, in my opinion, for personal pride we risk a soul suffering now and perhaps forevermore. I am therefore willing to present knowledge that is in fact controversial; including such persons as believe in ancient astronauts, extraterrestrials and the like; because how can I claim to love our Creator and truth, and sweep under the carpet such things as might challenge preconceived notions that we have already comfortably embraced when in fact that is exactly what I am adamantly against in that so many evolutionists and atheists I have met are so religious they refuse to even look at any evidence contrary to their chosen worldview that in my opinion is causing grave damage and peril to the planet and all life on it (And as I have stated has been directly responsible for my own severe suffering and apart from a miracle(s) from, God an early demise www.blastthetrumpet.org). That stated, having seen the risen Christ numerous times, and having had death experiences, I personally testify that I have experienced that the Holy Bible is Divinely Inspired and so much so that it is accurate about existence after "death" of our incarnate bodies; to such a degree that I ended up in a place I had never even heard of or read about and didn't even know what it was called until years after it happened to me. I read about the place I went to when I temporarily died as a young man (a then professing agnostic) and was then resuscitated; only years later I read about that place in the Holy Bible. As such, it doesn't matter what people talk about; what they show me; how many might talk of demons, devils, extra-terrestrials, UFOs, ancient astronauts, billions of years, etc. because I know beyond all doubt that whatever exists, wherever it exists, was all made by the One True God; the Creator of the Universe, our Creator, Lord, Maker, Redeemer, Provider, Healer and Savior who has the Pre-eminence in All Things; anything Honorable, Glorious, Virtuous, He

Holds the Highest Titles of All; Ineffably Amazing and Astounding; whom I personally know and is so Truly Wonderful I want everyone else to know as well.

A) Noah's Flood- (this link has a map of the approximate region of "the mountains of Ararat" http://creationrevolution.com/2010/10/does-noahs-ark-still-exist/ and is why Arch Bonnema ended up not in the traditional location lower down of a large sea going petrified vessel; but found one at over 13,000 feet! Amazingly, another find has apparently been discovered at similar elevation on Mt. Ararat! http://stevenmcollins.com/WordPress/?p=2185)

1. I wish these finds were not so hidden from the eyes of the world but that honest scientific analyses would be done thoroughly on any and all candidates for Noah's Ark that perhaps one might shine forth above them all! https://www.youtube.com/watch?v=o6G2_2gSY3o Evolutionists ask us to believe animations and drawings as science because there is factually no observable evidence for macro-evolution of one kind to another (plants becoming animals, animals becoming plants, fish becoming horses, trees becoming tadpoles and the likes of which trash they brainwash children to believe until they become completely insane enough to deny; (turn their eyes, ears, and all perceptive abilities including rational

thought away from becoming aware of reality so they can go on living in their fantasy world of animations and drawings); what we can actually observe such as all the scientific evidence validating the accuracy of the Holy Bible); but when OBSERVABLE EVIDENCE IS PRESENTED TO THEM THEY HAVE THE AUDAUCITY TO CALL ALL WHO ACKNOWLEDGE THE CREATOR "religious" IN DEROGARTORY FASHION AND WHILE STILL CLINGING TO A WORLDVIEW THAT HAS NO SUPPORTABLE EVIDENCE ANYWHERE IN THE UNIVERSE arrogantly CLAIM that they're "scientific". A very large ancient sea going vessel is found on a mountain top in the location the Holy Bible states Noah's Ark came to rest, the boards the vessel was made of date commensurately with the account in the Holy Scriptures; there are still people who claim there is no scientific evidence. All who are making such claims are choosing to remain willfully ignorant. All who are interested in truth, continue to view all the overwhelming scientific evidence proving the historical accuracy of the scriptures.

Multiple finds (I have not personally visited the sites but have examined enough media evidence of those who have and listened to their testimonies to be sure that something in fact of their claims actually exists in those locations; but let's say the real one was found; it would be just like the NWO agenda to disseminate false data of additional finds; such that people when looking for such evidence; finding none or something obviously not true would possibly conclude that all other evidence is not worth examining); as I was saying... Multiple finds of very large sea going craft in the region of the mountains of Ararat; might leave some pondering which is the real Noah's Ark and some claiming none of them, etc. Some might claim it could not have become petrified; but we know petrification can occur rapidly as these many examples prove. https://www.google.com/search?q=petrified+pickle&tbm=isch&tbo=u&source=univ&sa=X&ei=ktMVUpSOAY2ujALIh4HQBA&ved=0CDsQsAQ&biw=1067&bih=702 Others might ask me why would I present more than one large sea going craft https://www.youtube.com/watch?v=iCyOVGBnNp8&list=PLedgj2YVsQTy1QGYuPrgDb21GV6pXRSqT found near the top of mountains of the Ararat region. It is this very fact large sea going vessels, dating prior to modern oceanic crossings by Magellan, Ericson, Columbus, etc. and so much prior as to exist around the historic flood account that clearly counters all those claiming it is impossible or complete myth. Perhaps one of the candidates for Noah's Ark will outshine all the rest if scientific analyses is allowed of them extensively. But the fact that these large vessels dating appropriately exist in the biblically described region at all is sufficient physical evidence to share with the world. I have encountered these brainwashed religious fanatics who; while denying such sea craft exist at all and especially at over 13,000 ft. near mountain tops just like the biblical account states; then claim the fossil record has transitional forms by pointing to illustrations, and fossil reconstructions already scientifically proven fraudulent, as the basis for their faith in the name of so-called science. I am linking such finds not with 100% certainty that Noah's Ark has been found; but just showing that it is not only possible; such craft dating appropriately exist in the geographical region the actual Ark Noah built is stated to have come to rest and that what we read in the Holy Bible has actual verifiable physical evidence; while what evolutionists and atheists believe does not and yet they constantly insult and make zealous efforts to discredit us even to the point of blatantly lying; arrogantly. It is as ridiculous to claim a living creature having four appendages, called legs, is transitionally related to one having four appendages called fins as to claim that because the sky, and water, and many sapphire stones are all blue (false premise intentionally given to prove just how far from the mark these people have fallen, citing false premises constantly themselves and most definitely then coming to their insane, completely irrational false conclusions; for which the only reason they actually believe such ludicrous notions is the fact they were shown the same animations over and over again in public education in proven brainwashing fashion until they believe something that is such obvious fiction is actually factual) they must have all evolved from a common blue ancestor like "O look something shiny!" perhaps that blue star up there somewhere "billions of years ago..." ("Once upon a time..."). There is a common SCIENTIFIC, OBSERVABLE factor in all the universe and that is: it was

CREATED by the CREATOR who has declared Himself plainly in all creation and in the written compilation of Divinely Inspired Books called the Holy Bible.

https://www.youtube.com/watch?v=loTkguzRaCU - Ron Wyatt certainly thinks he discovered Noah's ark.

It has obviously happened to these religious adherents of evolution and atheism just as our Creator tells us, http://biblehub.com/romans/1-28.htm "Furthermore, just as they did not think it worthwhile to retain the knowledge of God, so God gave them over to a depraved mind, so that they do what ought not to be done."
and http://www.biblegateway.com/passage/?search=Romans+1%3A22&version=KJV "Professing themselves to be wise, they became fools,"

http://www.facebook.com/notes/michael-swenson/evolution-and-atheism-intertwined-religions-of-the-insane/492209810857983

2. After the Flood - http://www.creationism.org/books/CooperAfterFlood/CooperAFEndnotes.htm I hope to include the scientific category of genetics and the human genome later on

which has proven what they call the human bottleneck of the fact all modern persons alive today have come from one mother and some of the "secular" (I find the term "secular" misleading perhaps I should refer to them as non-Christians; because I have yet to meet a person in all the world who could not be factually described as religious (there is no doubt the ardor of devotion of adherents to unsubstantiated atheism and the theory of evolution constantly show forth zeal that fits the description of religious worship when attempting to defend their irrational worldview); it seems to be a characteristic our Creator has imbued us with; otherwise, if you claim to be irreligious you are telling the world you lack a worldview, a set of beliefs and convictions that you can rationally and reasonably defend; in other words, admitting ignorance. Now ignorance isn't a crime, but willfully ignoring the knowledge imparted to us from our Eternal Creator in the Holy Bible condemns your own soul.

https://biblehub.com/acts/3-23.htm, Jn 3:36 This is also one of the reasons I argue separation of church and state is as impossible as separating the Creator from Creation. It is easy to observe by ubiquitous evidence that everyone is subjective to a greater or lesser extent and in that observation therefore, one religion or another prevails according to the dictates of those in power and authority; it is why I point out that of all the world's religions; including atheism and evolution, that the time has come to acknowledge the One True God and the Truth of His Words, His Laws, and the Reality of His Creation; such that we may all live and be blessed; instead of suffer and die;

being cursed) scientists state one and some state two fathers; just as the scriptures state. It is reasonable to conclude that a POSSIBLE reason that there is a flood account, anthropologically speaking, worldwide is that the descendants of Noah told their children; who told their children; etc. who filled all the world. http://www.apologeticspress.org/apcontent.aspx?category=9&article=64, and http://creation.com/many-flood-legends

3. The Global Flood Layer - (Geology) - http://www.answersingenesis.org/get-answers/features/worldwide-flood-evidence, https://www.youtube.com/watch?v=KGeULHIjDn8, https://www.youtube.com/watch?v=jwGgSNDPhO0, https://www.youtube.com/watch?v=5v7TQAEfAC4&list=PLv1rbD886yCbjUM3d1XVCEN9GTOclZNXD, https://www.youtube.com/watch?v=gt8J38vtzHA, http://dictionary.reference.com/browse/sedimentary+rock, The same sedimentary layer found in North America has been found in Eurasia! I hope people understand that just the very existence of the sedimentary layers worldwide; is evidence that at some point in time the world was covered by water. Some might then argue that only regional floods happened at various times in the history of the world but to do so, once again, they must deny the evidence that the same geologic flood layers has been found all over the world indicating irrefutably a simultaneous global flood. I

also hope people noticed that the professor of fluid dynamics was pointing out that these particular sedimentary flood layers we observe could not have been formed by a world covered with water deeply over a long period of time; but rather in order for such formations required rapid moving catastrophic deluge of large waves close to surface particulates; otherwise, the waves at the surface would have little to no effect at the sediments deep down. Also note that worldwide they have found fossilized footprints of creatures running from rapidly rising water https://www.youtube.com/watch?v=QOx7yMDbt_Y and even fossils where many creatures were obviously gasping in their final death throes. https://www.youtube.com/watch?v=2iUpKepDuJc
  In various locations; fossils are all found heaped together as if by rushing flood swept them at once to their deaths heaped against existing hillsides or mountain sides and yet so fast unable to prevent their drowning.
http://www.s8int.com/boneyard5.html

4. The Springs of the Deep
- http://biblehub.com/genesis/8-2.htm, and https://www.youtube.com/watch?v=2FFnrW_SUdM, and https://www.youtube.com/watch?v=WQ4UE63tJNI, significant scientific advancements had to occur in order to confirm that "springs of the deep" even existed; as our Creator told us millenniums ago. (Oceanography,

Photography, Computer Sciences, Marine Biology, 20th and 21st century submersibles, metallurgy, tempered glass, hydrodynamics, fields of engineering in designing the submersibles and equipment necessary and MANY more scientific advancements just to prove to mankind the evidence that fountains of the deep actually exist just like our Creator has told us all for millenniums. But you go on claiming your unsubstantiated worldview is scientific and those who acknowledge the Eternal Creator aren't; but all the rest of us know you are ignoring reality and the sciences in the process.) And for those who wonder where all the water went that we know flooded the world they are ignoring reality yet again of just how much water is present on the surface of the earth; how much is frozen in ice, how much is present in the atmosphere, and those huge deep oceanic ridges that those same modern scientific advancements have just shown us.
https://www.youtube.com/watch?v=d0td79QuxpA, and https://www.youtube.com/watch?v=NkAHEPXaw4M, keep in mind that the very deep sea where these fountains of the deep have been found is some of the most hostile environment to mankind on the planet; we need all kinds of special equipment to even see it for a short duration; but God told us of these things in such a way that it has been recorded in writing for thousands of years (and handed down verbally even longer) for us all to plainly read. With 75% of the surface of the earth presently covered by water of various depths and volume; and with mankind only knowing about 1 or 2 percent of what is in that portion of the earth (the oceans and the depths);

perhaps; just perhaps, that's where all that water is spewing forth from these fountains/vents means that somewhere down below them there is also perhaps even more water. And since we still have not explored the very deepest chasms in the floor of oceans; perhaps just perhaps those chasms opened up just like sink holes all over the world and drained the water that once covered the world as shown by the sedimentary layers on every continent. I know to people who have been taught since they were very young that it takes extremely long lengths of time for mountains to form and for life to appear but once again, they deny reality in thinking such things. https://www.youtube.com/watch?v=1q29FjphM1g, https://www.youtube.com/watch?v=k5yVgxXXDZ0&list=PL0122A1D15ED58683, https://www.youtube.com/watch?v=O3wClN2mmUs, https://www.youtube.com/watch?v=TkAG2avvRI4&list=PLeIzbbAejmLEcGg6lck1qfKrAUNBI-Z9z What if geologic sites like canyons were actually not just washouts from the flood; but what if they were huge earthquakes that caused gaps that significant or brought about the rapid and massive washout that removed all the sediment/delta that we don't find at the base of the Colorado River (as should be there if those who believe the canyon was carved over "millions of years" was the true explanation for its existence). Just like the people claiming such are obviously wrong; perhaps they are wrong also about the time it took to form mountains. What if catastrophic events caused the formation of mountain ranges, simultaneously with the chasms, earthquakes, that drained the flood? (In what some today call plate tectonics) I can still remember in grade school seeing a film where they showed us the evidence for plate tectonics and that Africa and South America were once connected. The clinching evidence they showed us in the film was a tree that was split in half; according to the film half of it was on the continent of South America while the other half was on the continent of Africa. I remember it clearly because the same film was claiming that it took "millions of years" and as soon as they showed the split tree as proof the land masses were once joined, I immediately asked the teacher, "Are they saying that tree is millions of years old?" I wish I could find that film to find out if it was just complete fiction (like so much they taught us in public education) or if that tree actually did exist. My point is, anyone, anyone at all, that talks about "millions or billions or trillions of years ago", is immediately talking about imagination and fantasy; pure fiction. In fact, people who discuss prehistoric topics (beyond documented recorded history) are beginning to enter the fictional, imaginary realm by definition. When a person digs up anything; without a recorded explanation from a person that was there when the discovered item was buried; without such explanation being found with the item being dug up (as in the case of some time capsules), the excavator automatically engages their imagination in order to explain the find. So, when people claim the big bang theory is scientific; please call them a liar. You and I know they were not there and they really do not have a clue therefore about "billions of years ago". I have shown you videos of reality, floods, earthquakes, sink holes, volcanoes, mountains, can all happen quite suddenly! And I have also shown that life soon recovers the ashen cover all over the ground from a volcanic eruption; that it only took a few decades; not "millions of years". So please stop calling your theories of evolution and origins "scientific". The only scientific evidence that actually exists proves Intelligent Design by the same Creator who Inspired the contents of the Holy Bible.

B) The Ashen Remains of Sodom and Gomorrah-

http://www.pinkoski.com/sodom-a-gomorrah.html - the cities in the Bible that were destroyed by fire and brimstone have been found and the visible remains can be seen by travelers to this day. https://www.youtube.com/watch?v=oG3QsisQrkc&list=PL86F56C259B75C886

2. http://www.biblearchaeology.org/post/2008/04/the-discovery-of-the-sin-cities-of-sodom-and-gomorrah.aspx#Article

God, Our Creator tells us why He has given us this example of His Power and Righteousness in the Book of Jude in the Holy Bible:

"7 Even as Sodom and Gomorrah, and the cities about them in like manner, giving themselves over to fornication, and going after strange flesh, are set forth for an example, suffering the vengeance of eternal fire.

8 Likewise also these filthy dreamers defile the flesh, despise dominion, and speak evil of dignities.

9 Yet Michael the archangel, when contending with the devil he disputed about the body of Moses, durst not bring against him a railing accusation, but said, The Lord rebuke thee.

10 But these speak evil of those things which they know not: but what they know naturally, as brute beasts, in those things they corrupt themselves.

11 Woe unto them! for they have gone in the way of Cain, and ran greedily after the error of Balaam for reward, and perished in the gainsaying of Core."

These ashen remains serve as a warning to all the modern wicked persons who are taking every opportunity to blaspheme, denigrate, our Creator, His Instructions for Life in the Holy Bible, and His Messengers, Followers, in all the world. (LGBTQ) We warn you all to repent swiftly; if you do not want to experience consequences great and small for your wickedness; if you do not want to be on the receiving end of Divine Wrath and similar annihilation as what was done to these wicked persons; the remains of which still testify to this day of the need for us all to call upon our Creator for mercy and to change us into beings that thirst and hunger after righteousness instead of wickedness!

"Satanil, the LORD Rebuke you!"

C) The Exodus Account-

The Holy Bible records Divine deliverance for the Israelites from the Egyptians and describes geophysical specific details that have been confirmed and documented in history even with erected monuments still visible for anyone to see as this video points out. http://www.youtube.com/watch?v=-mB5Aw14e4M this video shows the evidence in step-by-step fashion proving the biblical account as accurate. If anyone watches this video and still claims that it is not Mt. Sinai confirming the biblical record as factual history; there is no doubt they are in a state of psychological denial and willful ignorance. http://www.youtube.com/watch?v=XU25s2xrxfc in addition they found chariot wheels http://www.100goodmen.com.au/other/redseacrossing/img20.html and even a wheel claimed to belong to the Pharaoh's chariot at the bottom of the crossing location in the Red Sea. http://www.youtube.com/watch?v=tD7hL3kKrRw and the pillars of Solomon still mark the crossing site. http://www.100goodmen.com.au/other/redseacrossing/img25.htmlhttp://www.100goodmen.com.au/other/redseacrossing/img14.html

http://www.100goodmen.com.au/other/redseacrossing/img9.html

D. Goliath's skull
- http://iamisatthedoors.wordpress.com/2012/06/20/2011-goliaths-skull-found-in-holy-land/ Even if we're so inundated with information and misinformation these days that we immediately are tempted to disregard anything we perceive based on assumptions made about the source of the data; especially if such information/misinformation is in anyway contrary to our present chosen worldview; atheists and evolutionists have been denying the existence of giants altogether; claiming that as absolute reason to deny the biblical accounts; including the fight between David and Goliath. That is why they (evolutionists) have to claim that none of these are real and why NWO money interests try and cover up such discoveries and keep them from public knowledge by not covering them in major media or using major media to discredit such finds if they become publicly known (https://www.youtube.com/watch?v=E1RD49XG12Y&list=PLB4AA57115499DE65) So, let's say one takes the position that this image of a giant skull with an embedded stone in it is a complete fabrication of digital technology or even 3d modeling. I have been using software and graphics software for many years and computers since they were monochrome monitors with "basic" programming as the language of the day, I watched them when they were still

using punch cards for operations and huge tape reels for memory and data storage; as such, I would personally acknowledge that if that image is only digitally created, whoever did it, did an amazing job! It would be one of the best imaginary digital creations I have ever seen; better than most Hollywood productions! (and you know they're highly paid professionals) Likewise, if it's only a 3d model; whoever constructed it would easily be on par with such professionals in Hollywood who are deemed some of the best in the world. So just like those who argue the ancient ship found at over 13,000 ft isn't Noah's Ark, and the ashen remains of Sodom and Gomorrah with brimstone still in the ruins are just some kind of elaborate hoax, and the burnt Mountain in Saudi Arabia isn't the real Mt. Sinai despite all the surrounding detailed evidence and its own unique properties unlike any other in the entire world, they also would here be left with a giant skull with a stone in it; while claiming consistently that even though all these artifacts, locations, city remnants etc. were found exactly where the accounts in the Holy Bible state they would be; that it is all still only myth and legend. The rest of us know that in order to hold such a position any longer you are in a state of psychological denial; and in refusing to acknowledge your own perceptive abilities choosing to remain in a state of irrational insanity; a land of make believe, a snow globe world of fantasy; irrespective of the reality in which we all actually exist. Let us take a moment and say okay, suppose, just suppose, that even though we have original codices dating over centuries and even millenniums, manuscripts of the Holy Bible; that has preserved details all these unbelievers were systematically brainwashed into believing were complete myths; and yet even though the actual physical remains of these so called myths have been found and are available for people to visit and see for themselves; (provided the satanic NWO hasn't somehow covered up or destroyed the evidence); if they can afford to do so; despite that even though every detail leading up to the discovery of Mt. Sinai http://www.arkdiscovery.com/mt_sinai_found.htm , like the bitter springs, the palms and the twelve springs, the chariot wheels at the bottom of the Red Sea at the crossing site marked by the Pillars of Solomon; the split rock http://www.paradisecafediscussions.net/showthread.php?tid=7750 where God provided by the faith of Moses; who struck that stone with his staff; water in the desert of such abundance that significant erosion is there for all to see the scientific proof clearly visible to this day; but let's just agree to ignore all that detailed information provided in the Holy Bible and visible in reality so you can go on in your comfortable state of insane denial of overwhelming observable evidence; thinking there is no God and that the Holy Bible is only stories and myths rather than historical fact. And under those false assumptions and premises, you tell me and the whole world; if you can, just how all these things came about that just happen to coincidentally match the scriptural accounts in detail. You tell me just why you disbelieve objective physical evidence; reality, in favor of illustrations, animations and fantasies (supporting your imaginary scientific evidence for your so called scientific theory; that has been proven to be pure fiction; by actual science and observable facts about anything real, time and again; known as the theory of evolution); yes, please tell us why you choose to believe fallible people who dream-like talk about billions of years ago as if they were there over clearly observable facts. You have the right to choose to ignore the real scientific evidence that supports the biblical account throughout and that science is actually still catching up with in understanding the Divinely Inspired and Revealed Knowledge therein and to go on living in your self-deluded fantasy world of evolution and atheism; for which there is no scientific support of any kind and never will be; as the sciences have already disproven the theory you were brainwashed to believe in by government controlled public education and propaganda; funded by the satanic NWO. **You have the absolute right to firmly hold onto your religions of atheism and evolution; but understand that all sane, rational minds the world over will never acknowledge that your beliefs in such foolish, irrational and insane notions are in any way scientific.** (but satanil is just another being they brainwashed you so thoroughly into denying his existence that you deny the observable reality in which we exist in order to remain in such a state of willful, deceived and self-deluded ignorance). Since satanil means adversary of God, by stating such a being does not exist is once again ignoring the obvious that unfortunately it is easy to encounter people that claim to hate God, especially the God of the Holy Bible, and so much so they ignore reality and the use of their own senses to adamantly deny He even exists. The progenies of our NWO public education have been taught; despite easily observable facts about reality, that neither God, our Creator, or satanil exist; in that way those who know better can control you, manipulate you, as in self-pride, everyone then thinks no one else can tell them what behavior is right or wrong, but that everyone can do whatever they want; (regardless of who or what is hurt or even killed in the process). The NWO satanists that brainwashed you into believing that complete load of crap knows it results in bloodshed and chaos (that is the result of everyone thinking no one else (not even the actual God and Creator of the Universe) has the right to tell them what to do and that they alone are their own moral judge of right and wrong behavior). It is one of the most destructive worldviews ever to manifest on planet earth and has resulted in an increase of racism, wars, infanticide by the tens of millions worldwide as abortion is the number one killer of innocent babes now; more slaughtered in recent history under the religions of atheism and evolutionary thought than in all the ages past! Many aptly link the insanity of these religions to communism, marxism, that have resulted in the deaths and oppression of mass millions, and such other philosophies and worldviews devaluing human life, creating slavery and even leading to euthanization and the NWO global practices of genocide https://archive.org/details/DarwinsDeadlyLegacy and https://www.youtube.com/watch?v=UHNck5UnP_Y currently underway in all their poisoning of our food https://www.youtube.com/watch?v=g4Op1_LFys8, https://www.youtube.com/watch?v=KNCGkprGW_o, water https://www.youtube.com/watch?v=dbj4zdYZnJc, air https://www.youtube.com/watch?v=gR6KVYJ73AU, medications https://www.youtube.com/results?search_query=medications+with+lethal+side+effects&oq=medications+with+lethal+side+effects&gs_l=youtube.3...108294.116052.0.116372.36.36.0.0.0.0.121.3412.26j10.36.0...0.0...1ac.1.11.youtube.ZIPEPelb6oU and destruction of the environment greedily to such an extent mass extinctions are underway around the world https://www.youtube.com/watch?v=XM1g9lQJkWU. As a personal victim/survivor of what I have found has been going on worldwide of local hospital homicides http://chriskresser.com/medical-care-is-the-3rd-leading-cause-of-death-in-the-us; in which millions of innocent citizens have been murdered and hacked up for their organs http://www.infowars.com/horror-as-patient-wakes-up-in-ny-hospital-with-doctors-trying-to-harvest-her-organs-for-transplant-profits/ (yes, right here in the USA, Great Britain and European block countries; not just China, and other Asian nations, http://www.blastthetrumpet.org, I am earnestly motivated to see these destructive worldviews of atheism and evolutionary thought come to a permanent end! So, if I sound upset, enraged, throwing their arrogant sarcasm back in their faces; you better believe it; because as I see it; their worldview of atheism and evolutionary thought is by far the greatest danger to the survival of humanity and all life on the planet the world has ever witnessed! Dr.

James Kennedy and many others in agreement. https://www.youtube.com/watch?v=_sBcLiy4N8U&list=PLC5FDA68518EABE1E And since it is the NWO satanic agenda and openly espoused belief https://www.youtube.com/results?search_query=nwo+depopulation+agenda&oq=NWO+depopulation&gs_l=youtube.1.3.0l4j0i5.35654.211271.0.215091.17.17.0.0.0.0.127.1602.15j2.17.0...0.0...1ac.1.11.youtube.AH9WDL3lHCQ and practice (again poisons in food, water, air, medication, environment causing deaths to millions prematurely as ubiquitous evidence; there is no way any can claim the people in charge don't know what they are doing when they scientifically study how to manufacture these things and purposely add poisons to feed https://www.youtube.com/watch?v=mKj6fWEWaMI of not only what we end up eating but directly into processed foods and beverages; not to mention toxic GMOs; so it is obvious the so called rulers of the world are openly practicing genocide upon the populace; as they openly have stated is their intent and belief to depopulate the planet https://www.youtube.com/watch?v=9wMMJkk6feY, and https://www.youtube.com/watch?v=kVeA07d2F_I, and https://www.youtube.com/watch?v=IPBotpbZ1v8, and https://www.youtube.com/watch?v=S48Qq-6WaNE, and https://www.youtube.com/watch?v=UHNck5UnP_Y, and https://www.youtube.com/results?search_query=agenda+21&oq=agenda&gs_l=youtube.1.0.0l10.2760.3745.0.6980.6.5.0.1.1.0.119.516.2j3.5.0...0.0...1ac.1.11.youtube.UZz0uX7dpYY (why not counter carbon dioxide with planting trees, hunger by fruit and nut trees, etc. in suburbs and city blocks, instead of killing people?) to murder citizens in genocidal fashions, to reduce the global population and rid the world of all they consider inferior, like everyone they are brainwashing with the crap of evolution and the insanity called atheism, https://www.youtube.com/watch?v=xg2SsVGbJkA (it's not just arrogant or prideful persons in the Jewish faith but in any and all faiths all over the world the wealthy have been murdering poor people in hospitals for their organs www.blastthetrumpet.org), the satanic NWO consists of persons all over the world who consider themselves superior to everyone else (just like the pride of lucifer/satanil in them moves them to be http://www.biblegateway.com/passage/?search=Isaiah%2014&version=NIV; while they ignore the fact we all piss, shit and bleed the same and especially ignore these verses: **16Those who see you stare at you, they ponder your fate: "Is this the man who shook the earth and made kingdoms tremble, 17 the man who made the world a wilderness, who overthrew its cities and would not let his captives go home?"**

That aptly point out that even though these wealthy oppressors think of themselves like gods and goddesses superior to everyone else; that they look upon like cattle, sheep to be slaughtered; that they are in fact just human beings like all the rest they so disdain), they are usually ultra-wealthy (by that I mean those who own the mints; that print the money; that they force all the rest of us to work/slave for on seemingly lower and lower slave wages day by day until we drop dead from their depopulation methods. I am NOT opposed to honest work, proper education (instead of brainwashing); teaching children the value of stewarding the earth and life on the planet by giving children a small garden patch each year for each of them to plant and lovingly care for; speaking over their gardens in faith and having the joy of eating the harvest thankfully; by having them visit elders as part of their education and glean the wisdom and knowledge of the previous generation into huge databases that would exponentially increase innovations, inventions and quality of life on the planet I cover other solutions for what I think should be done; as opposed to what the satanic NWO is doing to destroy children and life on the planet here: http://www.godempowersyou.com/documentation/Ideas.pdf, and http://www.facebook.com/notes/michael-swenson/solutions/516489485096682 etc; I am opposed to treating anyone like a slave and when they clearly have the means; instead pay wages so low people have to work multiple jobs just to pay the same ultra-wealthy people for their greedy hold on commodities and energy) they are the same persons who are so ambitious for power they systematically murder anyone that threatens their idolatry of self-worship in prideful arrogance, and is why even the Messiah, Yahoshuah, aka Jesus Christ, was murdered by their efforts and influence on the general populace and those who they pay as mercenaries to enforce their will), you are only openly showing them and their brainwashing to be successful by ignoring physical evidence proving the Divinely Inspired scriptures; that leads you and all mankind to the One True God http://biblehub.com/1_john/5-20.htm , our Creator; Salvation and to be free of the genocidal maniacs of the NWO now and forever! Because they know this, they practice dissemination of misinformation (lies) to keep you from knowing the One True God and thereby dethroning their stranglehold on the people of this world once and for all!

E. The Shroud of Turin - I have encountered people on and offline that actually argue that none of the biblical figures, places, etc. ever even existed; so much so they claim to sincerely believe that the Holy Bible is a compilation of nothing more than fairy tales. When pointing out that people have been using those so-called fairy tales to find long buried cities and artifacts; they of course have to completely ignore the evidence to remain in their self-deluded willful ignorance. For two millenniums people acknowledge the modern age and the Lordship of Yahoshuah the Messiah every time they wrote the date A.D.; http://en.wikipedia.org/wiki/Anno_Domini. In the year of our Lord; only with the modern advent of satanic brainwashing in our public education have fools arisen who deny such obvious acknowledgement of truth. I, for one, will continue to use A.D. when referring to present dates; for His Reign is

Forever! http://biblehub.com/luke/1-33.htm,http://biblehub.com/isaiah/9-7.htm,

http://www.biblestudytools.com/parallel-bible/passage.aspx?q=daniel+2:39-49&t=rsv&t2=niv . But to keep their chosen worldview they work as hard as possible not only to deny the overwhelming evidence themselves but to encourage everyone else including children in public education to do the same. Evidence like

http://www.shroud.com/

F. The Titulus
- http://en.wikipedia.org/wiki/Titulus_Crucis - I am well aware of people who readily dismiss relics by thinking modern dating methods are inerrant but to them I point out that in fact modern methods have been shown repeatedly to have large variations of error in their practice, such as errors caused by bio-plastic coating http://www.historian.net/shroud.htm; and http://www.angelfire.com/mi/dinosaurs/carbondating.html . Not to mention human error in general; so, do I believe a relic that was on display in the Middle Ages could have accumulated dust, debris, and biological agents that could skew modern dating methods; absolutely.

G. The Top 10 Relics
- http://listverse.com/2012/10/17/top-10-relics-of-jesus-

christ/ While I place no faith in relics; but in the Creator only; to deny the relics even exist is ludicrous. It is one thing to assume a skeptical position regarding authenticity; but quite another to ignore the reality of their existence. Even more preposterous to deny Christ; when a person of such magnitude as the Messiah and the resulting spread of the Gospel http://www.svherald.com/content/lifestyle/2012/12/24/343929 (small tribes/nations have been given Holy Bibles that never even had a written language!) worldwide http://www.baptisttranslators.com/content/view/53/53/ (We still need to keep up the good work; if you are going to donate to any cause; making the Holy Bible available to all souls is one of the best! By declaring the Gospel to the whole world as our Lord instructed, eventually the prophecy that I am looking forward to more than any other; regarding the souls on planet earth; will be fulfilled:

"No longer will they teach their neighbor, or say to one another, 'Know the LORD,' because they will all know me, from the least of them to the greatest," declares the LORD. "For I will forgive their wickedness and will remember their sins no more. "http://biblehub.com/jeremiah/31-34.htm I am fervently hoping that the fulfillment of this does not come about by unrepentant wicked souls continuing to provoke the Creator until they are all annihilated (as in the days of Noah) leaving only a few wise souls left that all know and worship the One True God; but that I am hoping the fulfillment is rather great Mercy from our Creator as He enlightens billions upon billions of us worldwide by pouring out the Spirit of True Repentance and the Holy Ghost upon us all; so that we KNOW and experience the Spirit of our Creator with all that we are visibly and spiritually; such that every cell of our being rejoices in the presence of our God and we all become transformed glorious beings! The biblehub.com is one of my favorite websites because it has the verses in many versions of the bible so you can see even better the intent/meaning. http://www.biblegateway.com/versions/

you can find the Holy Bible online these days in virtually every major language of the world, however there are still an estimated 2,000-3,000 smaller tribes, and peoples, that still don't have bibles in their own language; please pray our Creator moves powerfully upon all the rest of us who know Him to make sure that everyone soon has a chance to hold the Words of God, the Holy Bible, in their own hands; in their own language; all over the world and that if they can't read that they have a solar powered bible, like a small digital calculator that speaks to them audibly, that they can carry with them in their pockets or purse at all times; not as expensive as a complex smart phone; but rather, at a minimum, just the text to keep expense down and lasting function up; and on up to more expensive digital, hand-carry, solar powered bibles; that include full multi-media presentations and interactive links with information on the Internet in larger databases or servers than the hand-held unit could contain; with a narrator that reads the Word of God to them whenever they want; just by pushing a button!

I have envisioned such a device that has button arrows that scroll left and right through the books and chapters of the Bible that show on a small screen like modern cell phones; such that people can look at the words as the narrator speaks them and perhaps even see pictures or video clips of parables, etc. That way, these digital bibles could actually help people learn to read and write as well! I am aware of course that the Bible is on media that can be played by existing devices http://www.audiotreasure.com/indexKJV.htm but as far as I know to date no dedicated solar powered, hand-held, text display with audio accompaniment, units exist like I would like to see flood the whole world by the billions. I hope Christians everywhere will fund such a project such that so many could be manufactured that costs could be kept very low; like the 1-2$ solar calculators these days; but perhaps might cost more like $5-20 because of the digital content and audio/visual screen with waterproofing technology. But if enough were made (hundreds of millions to billions) the cost for each one would go down substantially. See I know such technology exists but I'm trying to say try your best to make them AFFORDABLE. Since the software already exists (as you can see the links showing the Bible online in many languages and software that reads text aloud - translators like http://imtranslator.net/translate-and-speak/ or http://paralink.com/ which work very well especially since they are free. As you can see the software exists, solar powered calculators exist; so, a solar powered bible in every language that reads to people is possible to make with today's technology and I wish was already everywhere all over the world.) The history in the Holy Bible is presently observable with more historic and current documentation than any other ancient literature in history. http://www.goodreads.com/book/show/1129533.Evidence_That_Demands_a_Verdict (all the volumes http://www.amazon.com/Evidence-Demands-Questions-Challenging-Christians/dp/0785242198 point out such extraordinary aspects regarding the Holy Bible; setting it apart from all other books; that it is an apologetic series that all should become familiar with and peruse at length); to deny the life, death and resurrection of Yahoshuah the Messiah, aka Jesus the Christ, even happened is the height of programming/brainwashing, deception and insanity. http://beginningandend.com/jesus-exist-historical-evidence-jesus-christ/, http://www.angelfire.com/sc3/myredeemer/Evidencep7.html more manuscripts, more documentation acknowledging the life, death and resurrection of the Living Lord Yahoshuah the Messiah, aka Jesus the Christ; exist BY FAR over any other person, place, or thing in antiquity; in all literature; in the entire world.

H. Joseph was in Egypt. There have been recently stele translations support biblical accuracy. Dr. Doug Petrovich. https://www.youtube.com/watch?v=d7kb81AeXX4 There are many external evidence, just research this exciting new discovery.

I. Walls of Jericho - http://christiananswers.net/q-abr/abr-a011.html Once again I mention these things because I have encountered people who like to pose themselves as educated and intelligent (instead of the truth that most anyone who has attended US public education over the past few decades have been victimized by brainwashing to a greater or lesser extent); who actually sincerely believe Jericho http://www.answersingenesis.org/articles/cm/v21/n2/the-walls-of-jericho, Kind David, Solomon, etc. biblical figures, places and things never even existed! And I am pointing out that people actually use the Holy Bible historically and to this day to find such cities http://www.biblearchaeology.org/post/2008/06/the-walls-of-jericho.aspx#Article, relics and artifacts, exactly where the Bible states they are located! (In other words; you have to choose to remain a fool and in denial of your senses to believe such things as these modern atheists so snidely hold in derision; such as, ridiculously claiming that the Holy Bible is nothing more than a book of fables and that none of the biblical characters and sites ever actually existed.) Anyone with eyeballs can see such places exist to this day! https://www.google.com/search?q=jericho+and+its+walls+were+found+exactly+as+the+bible+description&tbm=isc

h&tbo=u&source=univ&sa=X&ei=-QEXUqj8BqOMigLV24HoCw&ved=0CCwQsAQ&biw=1067&bih=702

J. Partial list of biblical cities found - http://carm.org/questions/archaeological-evidence-verifying-biblical-cities and http://sphotos-b-sea.xx.fbcdn.net/hphotos-ash4/1157647_640776525953524_1329795662_n.jpg

K. Partial list of biblical artifacts found- http://en.wikipedia.org/wiki/List_of_artifacts_significant_to_the_Bible

L. More Confirmations of Archeology - http://www.biblestudysite.com/arch.htm

M. Ancient Ur and a Clay Plaque of a Worshipper - http://www.theblaze.com/stories/2013/04/04/archaeologists-uncover-ancient-site-in-biblical-abrahams-hometown/

N. Burial Sites of some biblical figures - http://en.wikipedia.org/wiki/List_of_burial_places_of_biblical_figures Again, whether or not these sites actually house the bones of the departed saints; the fact that such monuments, cathedrals, etc. have been erected in their honor is substantial evidence that persons with means and talent firmly believe the biblical account; so much so, great time, effort and wealth; even wars have been fought over such holy places. I only point this out because of how many people today have been so successfully brainwashed they not only lie; but some of them actually believe there is no evidence supporting the biblical accounts. And I am once again showing the world that to believe such nonsense one has to deny the use of their senses, their perceptive abilities, and their mind; and by doing so such persons are telling the world they have gone insane at worst and are willfully ignorant at best.

O. And Still More Archeological Evidence- http://biblicalstudies.info/top10/schoville.htm many have scoffed that King David even existed but more and more discoveries are showing that the scoffers are once again in a state of mind that denies reality. In fact, scholars have argued over the biblical account of kings and judges, of such figures as rulers of empires and their dates of reign; even lost civilizations; but time and again; the biblical account proves to be accurate. http://www.ucg.org/science/bible-and-archaeology-king-davids-reign%E2%80%94-nation-united/

P. Lost civilizations mentioned biblically and once denied but now more and more are all proven to have existed- http://pleaseconvinceme.com/2012/the-old-testament-has-been-archaeologically-verified/, http://www.youtube.com/watch?v=P0PoG4xoLb8, because some of these lost civilizations included the Nephilim and giants the satanic NWO attempts to suppress it http://www.youtube.com/watch?v=1P42j9Xltyg&list=PLDD19870F568B7818 so that they can continue to brainwash children with the fictional load of crap called the theory of evolution in public education; instead of showing the Truth that science (what we observe on earth and in the universe) supports the accuracy of the biblical account. http://www.youtube.com/watch?v=1zz8_MxcnzY

Q. More sites discovered confirming historicity contained in the Holy Bible - http://www.manavai.com/articles/art1.htm

R. Keep up because finds proving biblical historicity are occurring rapidly - http://www.biblicalarchaeology.org/category/daily/news/

S. Nazareth - people who choose to deny all the above evidence also smugly assert no evidence that this city every existed which again, is a false assertion. http://en.wikipedia.org/wiki/Nazareth

T. Bethlehem
- https://www.google.com/search?q=Bethlehem,+Israel&tbm=isch&tbo=u&source=univ&sa=X&ei=ozAbUsnzOOO7jAKDn4GIDw&ved=0CDkQsAQ&biw=1067&bih=702, In connection with this I want to mention that through advents in astronomy and computer sciences we have such presentations to verify the biblical account of the Bethlehem star that shown when the Messiah was born. http://www.bethlehemstar.net/ I also will include the Zeitgeist presentation because I want people to hear the tangible arrogance, pride used when attempting to denigrate those of us who know and acknowledge the One Truth; God. However, I also include it because while the presenters are attempting to do so; what they are actually showing the whole world was the Creator of the Universe wanted everyone on earth to know the Gospel Account so well, that He placed it in the stars for people to see of various civilizations that He would send His Son to die for us, who would be dead and buried and Resurrected on the Third Day; just as the Holy Bible declares to us in writing. These people; who produced zeitgeist, point out He told it so plainly also in the stars that various civilizations also came to the same

conclusion! https://www.youtube.com/watch?v=guXirzknYYE I rarely see preachers proclaim the scripture http://biblehub.com/malachi/4-2.htm . When I include the link to zeitgeist, I am not in agreement to the viewpoint or bias of it at all; or statements such as claiming Christ was born (incarnated; out of the womb of the virgin Mary) on Dec 25th; which date is not biblical. What I am pointing out is that the stars the Creator made have had the same interpretation by all those civilizations; showing intelligent design created the universe in such fashion that it was recognizable and recorded by people on earth of different cultures; different civilizations; not even possessing the compilation of scriptures we have today of the Divinely Inspired writings called the Holy Bible. Another reason I include the reference is that pagan observances are still in practice today; even by those claiming to follow Christ. (http://www.hope-of-israel.org/hatedf~1.htm) I again prefer Missler's presentation http://www.youtube.com/watch?v=BJ6szvfApNM of the Mazzaroth as opposed to the zeitgeist bias. But God has indeed told us the Gospel story in the heavens; as zeitgeist points out over and over again no matter what civilization the presenter discusses. http://biblehub.com/psalms/19-1.htm The smug presenter disdains the "cartoonist depictions of revelation" and in his arrogance is obviously ignoring https://www.youtube.com/watch?v=If9yzHwOeUc, and https://www.youtube.com/watch?v=XM1g9lQJkWU, and https://www.youtube.com/watch?v=X2mDYM-DeZg, and https://www.youtube.com/watch?v=z1TS9C2bi-0, and https://www.youtube.com/watch?v=8J4d2P68C8c and so many more current events happening exactly as described in the Divinely Inspired Book of Revelation and throughout the Holy Bible; including the advent of WWIII. But again, I used the link to the presentation with the hopes the rest of humanity will not let smug, falsely self-deluded and grandiose, intellectual arrogance and misunderstanding about creation cause them also to ignore reality to their own damnation; as it appears the presenter of zeitgeist wishes to do; amazingly, while ignoring the obvious; that the Gospel Message is in the stars so clearly that the whole world saw it regardless of the Scriptural Account!

U. There are many more discoveries that prove the biblical account http://www.facebook.com/photo.php?fbid=636673253030518&set=a.361018770595969.88428.286013238096523&type=1&relevant_count=1&ref=nf there are more discoveries and posts on the wall of http://www.facebook.com/1mill.creationist?hc_location=stream

R. But people are not only ignoring the physical evidence of the past; they are ignoring prominent evidence that is currently happening in front of the whole world: https://www.youtube.com/watch?v=mOHJKrxhBME; while the pre-tribulation rapture is false doctrine the rest of this presentation is noteworthy. http://ritualabusefree.org/Pre-Trib%20Is%20False.htm

S. https://www.youtube.com/watch?v=7BEjxNL2neY

T. https://www.youtube.com/watch?v=EW3wry_2UsQ

U. https://www.youtube.com/watch?v=YTdKznTA9iY

V. https://www.youtube.com/watch?v=3R2NdIJCUwY

W. https://www.youtube.com/watch?v=kWLIRCvCHuA

X. https://www.youtube.com/watch?v=KeKRZuqEN98&list=PLB3BB6F0F72A5BE5C&index=1

Y. Herodian road
- http://www.israelvideonetwork.com/herodian-road-excavation-at-the-city-of-david

Z. Solomon's Wall
- http://www.israelvideonetwork.com/king-solomons-wall-excavated

Concerning the proof of the existence of Creator God -Yes, I am aware of redundancy; but when modern atheists and evolutionists are the result of intensive repetitive brainwashing in our public education system http://en.wikipedia.org/wiki/General_Education_Board ; and http://www.infowars.com/for-the-record-rockefeller-soft-kill-depopulation-plans-exposed/ and satanic http://theunhivedmind.com/wordpress3/abortion-and-sustainable-development/ NWO http://www.youtube.com/watch?v=0HQnfamp2uY; and http://www.youtube.com/watch?v=sU537f4bnFM controlled media http://www.businessinsider.com/these-6-corporations-control-90-of-the-media-in-america-2012-6; and https://www.youtube.com/watch?v=zOQ1jZOj_ho ; and https://www.youtube.com/watch?v=0hxMaAAmaX0; I find a little redundant deprogramming to be necessary to attempt to bring such persons back to reality and a sound mind.

a) By logic, reason and rational arguments all we observe testifies of the existence of an Intelligent Creator in the following ways:

i) By our powers of observation through our senses given us we behold the universe and by consciousness we perceive that we ourselves exist. In this observation we must come to the following conclusions that we ourselves and all we observe is either:

(1) An illusion

(2) Self-created

(3) Self-existent

(4) Or created by someone or something self-existent

ii) All that we observe in the Universe falls into one of these four explanations for being observed by us and as reasoning rational creatures we then logically consider each of these four possibilities

(1) If everything including the knowledge of our own existence is an illusion then nothing actually exists at all. This notion is ridiculous as an explanation for the Universe

because to have an illusion someone or something must be causing the illusion and someone or something must be having the illusion. So, we come back full circle, that which is causing the illusion or having the illusion must then be self-created, self-existent, or the illusion itself is created by someone or something that is self-existent. Thus, to assume that anyone or anything in all the Universe is an illusion is to lead us to analyze that even that illusion must be scrutinized under the other three possibilities; that of self-creation, self-existence or created by that which is self-existent

(2) So, we consider that which we observe including ourselves (however ludicrous the notion) is that all is self-created.

In the book Classical Apologetics, the authors present the rational arguments against self-creation by stating that two laws of epistemology (the study of knowledge and the nature of its limitations and how it's acquired) must be negotiated: the law of non-contradiction and the law of causality. The idea of self-creation violates the law of causality because by definition the very concept of self-creation claims something came from nothing. Nothing cannot act upon or cause anything by its very definition nothing is the absence of everything. Therefore, if nothing ever was the universe, then nothing exists to this day for something cannot come from nothing by definition. Self-creation as the theory for why each of us and the Universe exists also violates the law of non-contradiction because for something to create itself it implies that something already exists. Something self-created must therefore be before it actually is in order to cause itself to be created by itself which is actually non-existent if self-creation is the explanation of the existence of yourself and the universe. It is easy to see the concept of self-creation is therefore contradictory by its own definition and clearly violates both these laws. So, we know that the existence of ourselves and the Universe are not explained by being an illusion or by being self-created. http://www.facebook.com/notes/michael-swenson/evolution-and-atheism-intertwined-religions-of-the-insane/492209810857983

(3) So, are we and the entire Universe self-existent? Have you and everything in the Universe always existed? By reasoning and logic if something exists now, it exists necessarily. Read the text in Classical Apologetics for why the existence of all things can be summarized under these four rationalizations and that other so-called ideas fall under these four arguments for existence. There are numerous observations and physical laws which show us that every visible thing in the Universe is not self-existent. The second law of thermodynamics for example confirms what we see of the visible universe that it is decaying, slowing down, and deteriorating or otherwise returning to a state of equilibrium of stability (cooling off, losing energy

and becoming motionless). All of us who incarnate grow old and our bodies return to the earth at our deaths. By this law all we see is becoming less complex; not more complex. This law directly contradicts the theory of evolution which was properly renounced by Darwin himself and should have never been propagated among rational beings thereafter. The authors of Classical Apologetics properly argue that if we find anyone or anything in the Universe that is self-existent it is inherently transcendent. They argue if even one molecule or group of molecules possess what all other creatures like ourselves lack, the power of self-existence then that molecule or group of molecules transcends all others ontologically. The Holy Bible confirms the second law of thermo-dynamics in 2Cor4:18 stating what we observe that all things that are seen are temporal. By this law and God's Word confirming the Universe we observe and we ourselves are not self-existent but temporal in nature. It is truly tragic that some people are going around thinking of themselves as God these days. When they can bring even one single atom into existence from absolute void, then I might humor them with an audience as to why they think they are God. The amazing thing someone actually did appear on earth claiming to be God and to be Self-Existent and people tried several times to stone him to death for His apparent blasphemy but eventually they succeeded in crucifying him to death and burying him. This person who claimed to be the visible Self-Existent Creator in order to be such could not be killed and must be alive to this very day. I testify that He is Alive and that I have seen him with my own eyes! This is the One True God as my favorite verse 1John5:20 in the Holy Bible declares http://biblehub.com/1_john/5-20.htm. All rational persons incarnate on earth today readily acknowledge they are not self-existent, eternal God creator of the entire universe and all the rest of us. Which leaves us to the only possible conclusion:

(4) There must be someone or something that IS Self-Existent, Eternal, without beginning and without end, that created all of the rest of the visible Universe which is so obviously and easily observably finite in duration. Whether that self-existent something is wind, vapor, spirit, fire, rock, or anything else visible or invisible, it is still that which created everything else and is therefore far superior to any of us if you know even the tiniest amount about the Universe in which we exist. Therefore, to refer to that self-existent something or someone as the Transcendent and Supreme GOD is reasonable, logical and rational. In fact, this is the only rational conclusion for the existence of the Universe and anyone who doesn't acknowledge this is telling the rest of us that they have lost the use of their five basic senses and their ability to reason. Atheists are therefore one of the greatest threats to global stability and safety. As the Word of God states in Psalm 53:1 "The fool has said in his heart there is no God…"

http://www.facebook.com/notes/michael-swenson/acknowledging-the-eternal-creator-takes-no-faith-it-is-scientific-fact/491948024217495

(5) All that remains for the sane, rational part of humanity is to find out who or what God is and thereby are the questions that really matter to each soul answered. The questions souls ask like, Why do I exist? What is my purpose? Is there Life after death? Why did God make the Universe the way He did? Why is there good and evil? Pleasure and pain? Peace and war? Suffering? Etc. etc. etc.

iii) Concerning the sciences that overwhelmingly support Intelligent Design and that the God of the Holy Bible is that Eternal Intelligent Designer (use the visual aids – read and watch all the citations in this book!) note: any ONE of these scientifically prove beyond all reasonable doubt that not only does God exist, but leads us to know who God is!

(1) Mathematics

(a) Probabilities –

(i) Jesus Christ fulfilled so many prophecies http://christianity.about.com/od/biblefactsandlists/a/Prophecies-Jesus.htm and https://www.youtube.com/watch?v=d9rVoD4Y718 and h ttps://www.youtube.com/watch?v=BrBgF6ag7hA and https://www.youtube.com/watch?v=v_Z7xzdzQ74 Written decades, centuries and even millenniums before He Incarnated that the laws of probability clearly conclude it a mathematical certainty that He was in fact the Incarnation of God as the Holy Bible declares Him to be and that He is now alive as He has ever Self-Existed and as such could not be killed (remain dead and in the grave; cease to exist) http://www.reasonablefaith.org/the-resurrection-of-jesus and http://christianity.about.com/od/biblefactsandlists/a/Prophecies-Jesus.htm

(ii) Prophetic probability of current events described in detail and inerrancy of the prophetic quality of the Holy Bible in General - A great example of how determined you'd have to be to not believe the evidence of probability is by reading Grant Jeffrey's "Armageddon, Appointment with Destiny"; in which he points out how in the sight of the whole world that not only did God bring back the Jews to the state of Israel as prophesied and has occurred nowhere else in all of history, BUT THAT HE DID SO TO THE EXACT DAY!!!!!!!!!!!! Despite years of wars, despite years of persecution and even genocidal events, the descendants of Israel in the sight of the whole world are back in the very location God said they would be and with hardly any ammunition and sometimes only glass bottles won battles that ensured their sovereignty against well-equipped nations that tried to wipe them out like in the six-day war and other earlier wars after their declaration of independent statehood. Yep, in the sight of the whole world; despite overwhelming adversity the prophecy was not only fulfilled but FULFILLED TO THE EXACT DAY (http://www.goodreads.com/book/show/627918.Armageddon; and http://www.1260-1290-days-bible-prophecy.org/bible_prophecy-Israel-nation-1260-years-x2-A-1.htm when Israel became a nation again http://watchmanbiblestudy.com/Articles/1948ProphesiesFulfilled.htm! Only the most rebellious souls would fail to acknowledge the God of the Holy Bible in light of this incredible occurrence in modern history of prophecy fulfilled to the day after thousands of years! And no matter what any of the rest of us in the whole world were doing for, against or in complete ignorance of! I admire much of Grant's work in prophetic study, but again encourage him to seriously pray over his pre-tribulation rapture adherence as well as all the nationally and internationally famous scholars who still do; by doing so you're leaving many innocent citizens unprepared and when open war and persecution arises those poor souls in their isolation will think they were "left behind" and wonder why God hates them or has forsaken them because they were convinced by you into believing in false hope and false doctrine. He has other books in the study of prophecy like, The Signature of God, that just rival those who know how to calculate probability of the random fulfillment of any of these prophecies from being able to consider any longer that atheism is anything but completely irrational and from coming to any other conclusion than that the God of the Holy Bible is the one true Eternal God, Creator of the Universe and Governor of the affairs of mankind.

https://www.accordingtothescriptures.org/prophecy/353prophecies.html

(2) Physics –Law of Entropy –demonstrate by smashing something that works (apply random outside energy to act upon the disintegrated mess) and ask how many billions, trillions, quadrillions of years it will take for natural processes to reassemble it so it works again or better yet before it becomes a living organism(disprove the religion of evolution by visually showing how utterly ridiculous it is to believe
in)   http://www.youtube.com/watch?v=z3FZDysZKFQ; http://www.facebook.com/photo.php?v=216429498436017&set=vb.100002069048072&type=3&theater;http://www.facebook.com/photo.php?v=214886925256941&set=vb.100002069048072&type=3&theater

(3) Optics – proved the earth was round like a polished sapphire/jasper stone like God showed Ezekiel about 700 B.C.

(4) Hydrology- proved the hydro cycle described in the Bible (Job) about 3 millenniums ago

(5) Archeology proved Jericho, Sodom and Gomorrah, Mt. Sinai, Noah's Ark, Egyptians drowning in the Red Sea (Exodus), numerous Biblical historical sites and cities

(6) Cryptology – Bible Code show the software working https://www.youtube.com/watch?v=tDCHeS1ydM; https://www.youtube.com/watch?v=VYlKkIoavnA; The Creator while dictating to scribes that recorded the history contained in the Holy Bible gave them words in such precise order that while recording commandments, instructions, historical accounts, the letters in those words actually encoded messages about future events, these "Bible Codes" revealed events like Timothy McVeigh and Murrah Bldg. Bombing, the Two Towers, assassinations of prominent figures, WWII, nuclear bombs, ICBMs and so much more that over 3 millenniums ago; there is no way they could have known. Some of these encrypted messages include accurate dates; not just current events! There are other forms of encryption in the texts of the Holy Bible; but this took the advent of supercomputers to discover and just this aspect is enough to prove Divine Inspiration of the Scriptures; let alone the reality in which we exist (and all the other sciences that study that reality).

(7) Numerology – give examples of the encoded messages by numerology http://carm.org/what-biblical-numerology, http://asis.com/users/stag/godcount.html, and http://www.hebrew4christians.com/Grammar/Unit_Eight/Letters_as_Numbers/letters_as_numbers.html (by that method dates are placed in the Scriptures of past, present, future events, and other messages by numerology such as Abraham's 318 men and the meaning therein. http://www.studylight.org/ls/ds/index.cgi?a=509 The Creator has messages within messages, encryption within encryptions, and so much so He tells the Gospel story in all these ways, He even inspired people to name their children in such a way as to tell the Gospel as well. https://www.youtube.com/watch?v=fAHR7xrolIQ, the very names of God's chosen, sequentially telling Prophetic Divine Messages that have come to pass in the sight of the whole world!

(8) Microscopy – proof that which is seen is made up of that which is unseen as Bible declares (in other words scientific discovery is constantly proving what God has told us as Truth over millenniums before science finally got around to proving it! God told us millenniums ago http://biblehub.com/hebrews/11-3.htm but it was only confirmed in recent history. http://en.wikipedia.org/wiki/Subatomic_particle

eventually the energy holding it altogether, they are slowly realizing that what our Creator tells us http://biblehub.com/colossians/1-16.htm and http://biblehub.com/colossians/1-17.htm is also true. That the Eternal Creator, the Eternal Power that has Created and Made all things teaches us the Truth; as I am showing you scientific observation confirms.

(9) Hematology – proof "life is in the blood" http://biblehub.com/leviticus/17-11.htm See the aforementioned chapter. You are a carefully designed, in the image of God, destined for to spend all eternity with Him. You need to know him in order to fulfill your Divine Purpose.

(10) Geology –the global flood layers have been discovered https://www.youtube.com/watch?v=dXMwJ3ZyHbo, https://www.youtube.com/watch?v=jwGgSNDPhO0, https://isgenesishistory.com/product/beyond-is-genesis-history-complete-set/

(11) Plate tectonics- Am I the only one who remembers the film in first grade that showed the split tree one half on the coast of South America and the other half on the coast of Africa? (In other words, Pangaea did NOT separate billions of years ago like evolutionists keep trying

to persuade us to believe despite the evidence to the contrary) Some argue that the seven mountains where the whore sits, are the seven continents. That if plate tectonics accounted for the huge expanse of the oceans between the continents, and the mountains, they would be so much higher than they are presently, especially if was over deep time like they claim. Everything beyond RECORDED HISTORY is all just theories, especially regarding the very distant past, ideas that have become popular. **WHAT WE OBSERVE ABOUT REALITY VERIFIES THE CONTENTS OF THE HOLY BIBLE!**

(12) Paleontology- the fossil record clearly shows distinct species with no transitory or missing link varieties necessary to support the religion of evolution. The "Cambrian explosion" more aptly fits the biblical account of many life forms all distinct appearing rapidly; than the nonsense of "evolution" over extended periods of time. What is done to support their religion and the brainwashing of innocent little children is the creation of animated films and artistic drawings based on their religion that have not one shred of solid scientific evidence to support; coupled with the repetitive droning of those attempting to turn our brains into mush by baffling us with their bullshit," billions of years ago...". The theory of evolution is religious fantasy for individuals who don't want to face reality that all things were created by Intelligent Design, by God; so they can assuage their

perverted and guilty consciences for the wicked things they've done rather than repent and so they can pervert little children into becoming "girls and boys gone wild" by brainwashing them into thinking they are only a mammalian animal, descended from a creature like a monkey or ape that was previously all descended from a single celled creature, and that all forms of sexual expression are normal and acceptable (leading evolutionists have even admitted that this is the heart of the reason that despite that science has overwhelmingly disproven evolution and supports Intelligent Design is why they still go on brainwashing innocent children with the lying religion of evolution – get Dr. James Kennedy's sermon on how the Theory of Evolution has detrimentally affected people like no other philosophy in the modern era. Coral Ridge produced "Darwin's Deadly Legacy" DVD https://www.youtube.com/watch?v=4mxXICZ9mXo&list=PL7F9B57EBDCCEECF8 and especially that sermon! He quotes one of the leading evolutionist who actually admits that the real reason evolution is still taught in our public schools is so that it will be easier to exploit boys and girls sexually (as confirmed with their extremely perverse curriculum http://www.youtube.com/watch?v=j7XR9yH2ETk) if they are deceived into not believing in God as they naturally do as small children before being "educated" into the Marxist philosophy into becoming arrogant about how idiotic they became in believing evolution was fact rather than the fantasy it really is. (In other words, through years of repeatedly teaching children in our public schools that they are ignorant if they believe in God and smart if they believe in evolution and instilling the arrogant quotes like religion is the opiate of the masses or a crutch for the weak, etc.); not realizing that evolution is a religion requiring the greatest faith of all! They make up a story out of hoaxes, wishful thinking, a tooth, a broken jaw, etc. and fictionally create this entire animated film of how man evolved from monkeys based on that. If people actually saw the true "scientific" evidence of the so called "missing links" I think some might laugh and others would be justly outraged that people are teaching that load of crap to our children today. Evolutionists, instead of getting defensive about your insupportable religion, it's time to get angry with your educators and all the money and years wasted on being brainwashed and yourselves for allowing it to happen. I was enraged with my teachers when Christ appeared to me for telling me evolution was fact when it clearly is not, but I quickly realized that they weren't just brainwashed in primary and secondary education but in places of higher learning as well and that by the time they went through that many years of being told they spontaneously generated from inorganic material and chaotic explosion it's no wonder they were baffled by such incredible nonsense that had, metaphorically speaking, turned their brains into the pond scum they were deceived into thinking they evolved from despite all evidence to the contrary. The devil is very real, deceiving the people of this world, or everyone would know our Eternal Creator, Jesus the Christ, by now. Don't let another day go by adhering to Unbiblical worldviews that have no basis in reason or logic or reality; so, the rest of your life isn't spent in fruitless

endeavors as well believing lies and becoming liars yourself in the process (all liars will be cast into the lake of fire Rev 21:8). Don't in your deceived ignorance announce to the rest of the world, as so many brainwashed individuals do, that they have lost the use of their senses and ability to reason as they speak with such great authority about billions and billions of years ago...(when their ancestor was just a festering pustule on the butt of some flea bitten, diseased maggot...since we're fantasizing about the religion of evolution and since they're assuming they can actually fly that bullshit by those of us who know better...billions of years ago, what a riot! As if anyone on earth after incarnating for only a few decades can convince the rest of us they truly know anything about imagined "billions of years ago" – they can't even count that high in a lifetime let alone con the rest of us into believing that crap! What they're doing to innocent little children is extremely cruel)!
https://www.youtube.com/watch?v=vvVt4lDSPeY; https://www.youtube.com/watch?v=Q8DDle_2cHM (there is One God- http://biblehub.com/1_john/5-20.htm); https://www.youtube.com/watch?v=ss1K4m89K4o; even though the photo of the ark of the covenant is blurry; the entire story of how it was found and about the earthquake and blood of Christ through the crack in the earth all the way upon the Mercy Seat I find one of the most amazing accounts I've ever heard. How that the Creator knew where Christ would be crucified and that the Blood of the Lamb of God (http://biblehub.com/leviticus/17-11.htm, http://biblehub.com/john/1-29.htm (Christ));

would be sprinkled upon the Mercy Seat of the Ark of the Covenant in keeping with the Law. It is one of those detailed accounts that I don't believe anyone could imagine or make up. I, for one, can see the image in gold even without the enhancement offered; even though the image is blurry. I think this discovery of the cross hole of the crucifixion of Christ; together with a crack in solid rock at the site in which His Blood poured down over 20 feet through the solid rock; to where the stone casing that covered the ark had been cracked and removed to allow that Holy Blood to drip upon the Ark itself perhaps the very greatest and most important find in all of modern history!

(13) Astronomy and aerothermodynamics- with the advent of both optics, photography and rocket propulsion we finally can prove what God showed Ezekiel and John millenniums ago (show the polished stone visual aids and earth images from space; first Ezekiel's with seas and then John's without seas and how from space the earth looks exactly like they both described)

(14) Cosmology – Chuck Missler aptly points out that God even declares to us the Gospel message in the constellations in his "Sings in the Heavens" series https://www.youtube.com/watch?v=BJ6szvfApNM and Frederick A. Larson put together an excellent

presentation on how God's Celestial Clock announced the birth and death of YAHOSHUAH the one and only true Messiah, commonly referred to as JESUS CHRIST in English, and was how the wise men knew to follow the Sign/Star in Heaven to the place of His Incarnation/Birth. A DVD can be ordered at http://www.bethlehemstar.net/ and is recommended viewing. For the very stellar bodies in space to be so obviously and intricately designed to teach us and declares to us such moments in our history, overwhelmingly declares God's existence and who He is! Cosmologists are learning more and more about the galaxies and the Universe and more and more as they discover intricate design, they are concluding that such complexity never could have come from some arbitrary explosion as books like "The collapse of evolution" point out and astrophysicists like Hugh Ross with "The Fingerprint of God" more and more exceptionally intelligent and formerly skeptical atheists as they delve into deeper research not only discover God exists but then boldly declare who He is! Again, I strongly recommend for all those who think sciences don't actually prove who God is to contact Dr. Carl Baugh's ministry "Creation in the 21st Century" who has numerous fossilized remains proving the flood and so many forms of science and scientists that I can't even remember them all each with overwhelming proof that God exists and that He is the God of the Holy Bible

(15) Meteorology-Ecclesiastes 1:6 wind patterns on earth known 3 millennia ago, Job 28:24-26 winds governed by weight recently discovered as true (read pg. 145 signature of God)

(16) Oceanography- psalm8:8 paths of the seas underwater springs Job38:16 polar ice caps Job38:29-30

(17) Dr. Carl Baugh's "Creation in the 21st Century" http://www.creationevidence.org/ addresses that almost all the sciences prove intelligent design and disprove the theory of evolution, Dr. Hugh Ross and Institute of Creation Research http://www.icr.org/ is another source if you want to be overwhelmingly convinced that science proves creation and disproves evolution. http://www.creationsciencetoday.com/

(18) Genetics- DNA research proves we all came from one mother and two fathers just like the Holy Bible declares throughout. Furthermore, DNA, when analyzed is clearly a language; for a language to exist, there must be an Author (visual aid by Perry Marshall http://vimeo.com/16576263) and DNA research has led to the flood and Noah's ark. https://www.youtube.com/watch?v=FWlErubudcE, https://creation.com/en/articles/noah-and-genetics, https://www.youtube.com/watch?v=IfuCdS5DqGs

(19) Some books might interest you that not only does science prove the existence of God and that He is the God of the Holy Bible but that entire fields of science were biblically inspired: The Biblical Basis for Modern Science is one, The Bible and modern science, Many Infallible Proofs, Scientific Creationism, Evidence That Demands a Verdict, The Obvious Proof, The Intellectuals Speak Out About GOD, A Ready Defense, Can I Trust the Bible, Science Speaks, The Collapse of Evolution, The Fingerprint of God and volumes more! Many people have been brainwashed into thinking science contradicts the Holy Bible and all I am attempting to do is show by observable evidence that assumption is false. Any so called science that is CLAIMED to do so falls into that category our Creator tells us about http://biblehub.com/1_timothy/6-20.htm; and soon actual science comes along to properly put that fiction (like the theory of evolution) properly where it belongs (with all of these disproven theories once thought scientific http://en.wikipedia.org/wiki/Superseded_scientific_theories. Many atheists wrongly champion Einstein (because he was not an atheist) as their poster child; and much of the world thinks of him as a scientific genius; but the fact that his theory of relativity (e=mc2) has been disproven https://www.facebook.com/notes/michael-swenson/emc2-is-rubbish/485479484864349; only serves to show all mankind that even those thought to be geniuses are imperfect. Quantum Mechanics, things such

as "spooky action" and "quantum entanglements" are throwing a wrench in much of the previous theoretical physics of yesteryear.

My point in this is so many today go around proudly boasting that they put their faith in science; which is just another way of saying they put their faith in other fallible human beings and yet arrogantly disdain those who put their faith in our Perfect Creator and the Divinely Inspired Scriptures which despite false claims; have stood the test of time and scientific scrutiny for centuries and have yet to be found in error. The Holy Bible's literary accuracy and historicity exceeds all ancient literature in the whole world BY FAR and in fact, is more reliable due to all its careful scrutiny than today's news which often has such bias and subjectivity that retractions have to be printed subsequently. But after millenniums, finds of ancient manuscripts and codices worldwide only serve to verify the accuracy of the Holy Bible and its translations. Any claimed errors in translations from the original meaning are usually do to language differences, limitations, changes of cultures over time (in other words the translation for those people in those days the translation came forth had accurate meaning for them; but in another culture in another time they cannot properly understand those terms; so another translation comes about, etc.) and so on; but the fact the way we know this is by comparison to **original manuscripts, or early copies** is only more evidence that we can trust the Divinely Inspired Scriptures far and away over any

scientific opinion or book from anyone else in the whole world. People need to really consider the opposition the Holy Bible has endured and how many have vainly tried to disprove it and yet it still remains a book like no other in the whole world for verifiable, reliable, true knowledge over millenniums. No other book even remotely compares to the unique aspects of the Holy Bible; as apologist Josh McDowell aptly points out in his volumes of "Evidence that Demands a Verdict".
http://www.angelfire.com/sc3/myredeemer/Evidence.html

(20) Besides all the scientific evidence; including the fact that even many of the fathers of the fields of science were Creationists/Christians http://en.wikipedia.org/wiki/List_of_Christian_thinkers_in_science ; others like Einstein at least acknowledged a Creator http://www.simpletoremember.com/articles/a/einstein/ there is the overwhelming legal evidence (eyewitnesses that sealed their own testimonies often with torture and death - http://www.whitehorsemedia.com/docs/FOXS_BOOK_OF_MARTYRS.pdf) that historians like Josephus and others have recorded http://topdocumentaryfilms.com/the-case-for-christ/ , http://vimeo.com/17960119, http://www.goodreads.com/book/show/73186.The_Case_for_Christ . For example, atheists and evolutionists and all other faiths and ways of life around the world, are you so

certain of your faith that you would go through what Christ, the Apostles and the many disciples through the ages have endured while testifying to the world (read Martyrs Mirror http://www.homecomers.org/mirror/), or how about the numerous testimonies of not only NDEs but Beyond and Back experiences like "A Divine Revelation of Hell" http://spiritlessons.com/mary_k_baxter_a_divine_revelation_of_hell.htm , or "To Hell and Back" by a secular cardiologist https://www.youtube.com/watch?v=vQ8TEGMj-jc (Rawlings; a former atheist; who got saved as a result of his dying patient's emotional outbursts about hell); who documented dying patients and those resuscitated accounts. Will you go on in your arrogance and pride knowing you would never want to suffer like these people did; who are now testifying of the Truth of the Resurrected Christ? I have much to share with humanity but I am putting my own life on the line by exposing the satanic NWO, mass murdering doctors and nurses; sex offending cops because I love the Creator above all and other citizens who should not be treated as I was while trusting doctors with their lives instead face being murdered horribly; and while trusting law enforcement to arrest such criminals; instead find they only are also so corrupt they join in those crimes; letting the criminals go free for sex acts! www.blastthetrumpet.org. I knowingly have chosen such a path also out of respect for the founders of this great nation and every other person who laid down their life to protect our freedoms and our lives from manifest evil on the planet. So, if it means that my blood will water this seed sown to bring forth fruit unto Eternal Life in others; then so be it (besides Paradise is far more wonderful than anything this world offers https://www.facebook.com/photo.php?v=215207041891596&set=vb.100002069048072&type=3&theater) It is the least we can do for Christ and the many slain before us in this common effort to convince all to come to their senses and return wholeheartedly to the LORD our GOD our MAKER. Are you so willing to cling to your vain and now proven false religions and traditions that you will face this (http://www.youtube.com/watch?v=vQ8TEGMj-jc)... when everyone of you could enjoy fellowship with God here and now and forever if you would only choose to do so! https://www.facebook.com/notes/michael-swenson/did-you-know/115636838515284

b) Now that all rational persons on earth know God exists and that He is the God of the Holy Bible if they actually thought about and studied the above references; these other references won't be so shocking:

http://www.abovetopsecret.com/forum/thread163678/pg1 , and
http://www.icr.org/home/resources/resources_tracts_scientificcaseagainstevolution/ ,
and http://christiananswers.net/q-aig/aig-c029.html, and http://scienceagainstevolution.info/v13i8f.htm, and http://www.ucg.org/science/prove-evolution-false-even-

without-bible/ , and http://www.kc-cofc.org/39th/Lectures/2001%20Manuscripts/RichardMasseyMissingLinks.PDF, and https://www.youtube.com/watch?v=7tctDVmaOHc, and https://www.youtube.com/watch?v=UKyyaURZW-o, and https://www.youtube.com/watch?v=onVj4BmfgEs, and https://www.youtube.com/watch?v=b8GgrUposlI, and https://www.youtube.com/watch?v=xA4qfSlPtgI,

Every single "missing link" proposed by evolutionists have scientifically been proven FALSE. Science has overwhelmingly proven evolution to be FALSE. The crap you have learned in public education has scientifically been proven entirely FRAUDULENT http://www.youtube.com/watch?v=0fEGzDEMA9A; regarding the so-called theory of evolution. IT'S A LIE! https://www.youtube.com/watch?v=jMr278CMAIA Adaptation; yes; natural selection; yes; macro-evolution of one kind to another NO! the idea is pure fantasy and any so called "evidence" supporting it pure fiction! https://www.youtube.com/watch?v=atXl6XTwNPA&list=PL550BFBA2981E74F0, and https://www.youtube.com/watch?v=Up-0E4Qetfg

  By adaptation, I mean variations within the kinds. God made everyone unique, not even identical twins are exactly alike, we all have individual spirits that define our characters, who we really are inside, our personalities. We have adaptation/variations to create a different kind of dog, some hairless, some hairy, some small, some big, and so on, but NEVER does a DOG KIND of creature become ANYTHING but a dog kind of creature. There is too much redundancy programmed by each and every kind of creature to prevent them from becoming a different kind of creature like evolutionists imagine! Symbiotic relationships exist also proving Intelligent design and not some rubbish of billions of simultaneous evolutions as these self-deluded and deceived lunatics reach further and further into fantasy; in a vain attempt to hold onto their scientifically disproven worldview. Insects and birds with the means tend flowers appropriate for their beaks and proboscis lengths; that relationship has kept both alive if both did not simultaneously exist from the moment of their existence neither would exist; thus the millions of symbiotic relationships on the planet are incontrovertible evidence against macroscopic evolution; because birds have always remained birds; flowers have always remained flowers; they may change the color of their foliage and petals when hybrid; but they still remain a flower. Only through genetic splicing and genetic modification with the discovery of DNA codes are unique biological abominations being created by less than intelligent humans. They are showing by their ignorant meddling with the language of life (DNA encoding) in order to bring about those kinds of significant changes that the advent of super computers had to come along and the destructive notion to mutate Divine Creation. The evidence is terrifying that having done this it is having catastrophic effects. (More evidence AGAINST evolution and for Intelligent Design by a Being far more intelligent than the fools messing it up) http://eatdrinkbetter.com/2013/03/21/swine-death-catastrophe-in-china-highlights-gm-animal-hazards/ , and http://www.gazettetimes.com/news/local/osu-event-sidesteps-gmo-protest/article_c656183a-c9bf-11e2-88ad-0019bb2963f4.html, and http://www.chicagonow.com/wild-side-chicago/2013/03/are-monsanto-genetically-engineered-seeds-killing-off-honeybees/ , and http://en.wikipedia.org/wiki/Africanized_bee, really all GMOs are just evidence of just how mentally challenged people are and how we absolutely need to KNOW the Creator to stop destroying His Creation; all life on the planet and themselves in their lunacy. http://www.mnn.com/green-tech/research-innovations/photos/12-bizarre-examples-of-genetic-engineering/web-spinning-goats Suppose any of these modifications interbred and destroyed a natural food supply; food even for us! (like goats' milk products) but these idiots don't care what happens to mankind as they continue to destroy life wantonly unabated. http://www.reuters.com/article/2010/12/01/us-monsanto-sugarbeets-ruling-idUSTRE6B00Y520101201, and http://www.naturalproductsinsider.com/articles/2002/07/gmos-could-cause-extinction-scientists-say.aspx, and http://www.relfe.com/GMOs.html, and http://www.gritfish.com/index.php/deep-ecology/life-scientists-view/1696-gmo-caused-extinctions, and http://www.policymic.com/articles/15889/french-gmo-research-finds-monsanto-corn-causes-cancer-america-should-pay-attention

No evidence? billions of souls telling you they KNOW the Creator and no evidence? http://www.facebook.com/notes/michael-swenson/acknowledging-the-eternal-creator-takes-no-faith-it-is-scientific-fact/491948024217495 millions tortured and on pain of death still testifying of the resurrected Christ; no evidence? http://www.homecomers.org/mirror/ prophecies being fulfilled written millenniums ago https://www.youtube.com/watch?v=2uW2uWCZWXY ; no evidence? http://www.facebook.com/notes/michael-swenson/our-creator-told-us-in-the-holy-bible-all-nations-would-be-deceived-by-pharmaceu/511466405598990 seas turning blood red, millions of creatures dropping dead for the whole world to behold as written in http://www.biblegateway.com/passage/?search=Revelation+8&version=NIV,
and https://www.youtube.com/watch?v=If9yzHwOeUc,
and http://video.foxnews.com/v/2574867146001/nasa-spots-giant-dark-hole-in-the-sun/ , and http://www.youtube.com/watch?v=b7hcTwhrKIs,
and https://www.youtube.com/watch?v=z1TS9C2bi-0,
and https://www.youtube.com/watch?v=-N0pLMooeAc,
and https://www.youtube.com/watch?v=8A34mJKVATE hundr

eds of prophecies written millenniums ago coming to pass in front of your eyes... http://www.facebook.com/notes/michael-swenson/prophecies-show-divine-inspiration-of-the-holy-bible/520171808061783; no evidence? http://biblehub.com/luke/21-25.htm

People need to think it through thoroughly and diligently about putting their trust in so called science; which is in effect putting their trust in other fallible human beings http://biblehub.com/romans/1-25.htm; as opposed to trusting the Creator of the Universe. http://en.wikipedia.org/wiki/Superseded_scientific_theories

I find it astounding how much grief some attempt to heap upon Ray Comfort and other people who are desperately trying to keep people from continuing on in their life without knowing the Creator and with all their heart, mind, soul and strength are only trying to make sure they don't end up in the lake of fire http://biblehub.com/revelation/20-15.htm; as worshippers of evolutionary delusional thought http://blog.drwile.com/?p=9851 attempt to denigrate his film http://www.evolutionvsgod.com/ exposing the fact there is no evidence anywhere for macroscopic evolution of one kind of creature to another kind of creature (like a fish becoming a dog or a chimp becoming a banana or vice versa, etc.) Commonalities among kinds exist. Even general commonalities between kinds exist; such as fruit trees produce fruit; but that does NOT mean an orange seed produces a pear tree as macroscopic evolutionists in their strong delusion want people to believe in order to discount and discredit what the Word of God states and what we do observe in reality that each has seed that produces like unto itself exactly as our Creator so plainly tells us. http://biblehub.com/genesis/1-11.htm I hope people around the world throw out fictional theories that have been created in an effort to ignore the Creator and His Wise Instructions for Life; for what we actually scientifically observe; which is that all creation in all the fossilized record and present to perceive to this day all over the world exactly proves the Biblical Account and in NO WAY anywhere; in any imagined time span, gives one shred of evidence to support the fantasy called the theory of evolution.

Subjects once thought of as "scientific" have been systematically discarded in abundance and I am looking forward to the day when people worldwide will do the same with the rubbish called the theory of evolution. http://en.wikipedia.org/wiki/Superseded_scientific_theories

All creation clearly supports the verified history contained in the Holy Bible: https://isgenesishistory.com/product/beyond-is-genesis-history-complete-set/ **NEVER, EVER LEAVE THE PROVEN HISTORY OF GOD AND CREATION PASSED ON TO US FROM THE OUR ETERNAL CREATOR AND OUR ANCESTORS to imagine that** leaving that history behind somehow makes you a scientist. **ANY SCIENTIST THAT LEAVES BEHIND WELL VERIFIED HISTORY OF THE HOLY BIBLE is no scientist at all. HISTORY IS SCIENCE!** Never ignore the WORDS OF GOD in the Holy Bible, it contains the most important facts about the past, present and future!

10) More Evidence - Fulfilled Prophecies

A) The Global Scope of Israel becoming a nation again in the land and geographic location given by God directly to Abraham and Israel, the father of the twelve tribes of Israel; that still exist to this day; despite the fact they were scattered among the nations and persecuted as a people like none other in history, is irrefutable evidence of the Divine Inspiration of the Scriptures. It is absolutely an undeniable event that has taken place in the sight of the whole world and thoroughly documented. But what many are unaware of is that the Creator brought it about to the day! The "illuminate killers" (a Facebook group) have it right; it is ultimately the NWO depopulation agenda run by the ultra-wealthy (Rockefellers, Rothschilds, Bilderberg Group, so called elitists) poisoning our food, water, air, medication, education, propaganda, and turning poor citizens against one another worldwide. And those speaking out against war also are correct that if neither side of a war has poor people willing to kill each other; then those manipulating them to do so have no actual destructive power; if instead of fighting one another, they arrest these real criminals for their crimes against humanity. But for anyone to think Israel as a nation is going away is demonstrating ignorance of the miracle of the reformation of Israel in the exact location they formerly existed after they were scattered as a nation and a people into all the world and that Divine Will that brought them back to the same land and location in the sight of the whole world as evidence of the Awesome Power and Authority of the Creator. Israel became a declared nation again in their rightful land according to prophecy **to the day** our Creator told us of; as Grant Jeffrey aptly points out in his book, Armageddon: Appointment with Destiny, http://www.goodreads.com/book/show/627918.Armageddon . It is declared also by our Creator that regardless of worldwide sentiment Israel will remain even if all the armies of the world gather against the nation. http://www.biblegateway.com/passage/?search=Zechariah+14&version=NIV Since it was the Lord God Almighty that brought back the nation of Israel into existence http://www.biblegateway.com/passage/?search=Jeremiah+23%3A7-8&version=KJV ; I would thoroughly examine their claim; that they are only defending themselves from being exterminated like many of their surviving members warn them of who endured the holocaust of WWII; before arguing that they are the aggressors. In addition, it may be acceptable to hold poor decisions made by others in criticism; but to think the Almighty having performed such an amazing miracle as to bring back Israel as a nation in the sight of the whole world to the day from when they were scattered abroad will overlook thoughts, words, and deeds, against Him and His chosen people; is only self-destructive. Peace will come, only when nations there and all over the world know the One True God and Creator of the Universe. http://www.biblegateway.com/passage/?search=Jeremiah+31%3A31-34&version=AKJV, http://www.biblegateway.com/passage/?search=Jeremiah+23%3A7-8&version=KJV

    The way some willfully ignorant fools http://biblehub.com/psalms/14-1.htm will still argue against reality and overwhelming evidence makes it seem useless to try and rationally persuade such persons who fail to comprehend the Word of God. It is because they cannot understand it; just as He states http://biblehub.com/1_corinthians/2-14.htm. We can only pray that the Creator who knows all souls; will have mercy upon them and reveal Himself to them; to their Salvation. Without knowing the Creator; they simply cannot understand His Words. http://biblehub.com/john/14-17.htm in that day and only when that happens will they Know the Creator and understand what is written in the Holy Bible. http://biblehub.com/john/14-20.htm for He will explain it to them personally. http://biblehub.com/john/14-26.htm and http://biblehub.com/1_john/2-27.htm I write these things more as a defense against the lies and deceptions of satanil and the world of fiction given in the name of science; more as an effort to keep souls from falling away from the Truth of the Creator and His Instructions for Life as contained in the Holy Bible; then of any hope in that I can actually reach those successfully brainwashed by any method; other than that we can reach them by the glorious Gospel http://biblehub.com/1_corinthians/1-18.htm; the Power of God, prayer, and God's Grace (but I will hope and pray nonetheless that not only would souls be strengthened in the faith; and hopefully many more added to it; but also that, even though this is far from exhaustive, it might inspire others to be more comprehensive to build extensive websites that have phrase by phrase links to proven fulfilled prophecies and the sciences verifying the knowledge our Creator has imparted to us all). That is why I have interwoven all that I have written since I came to Know the LORD with those factors. It might seem as if I have chosen poorly to be so aggressive in my writing and what some might find critical; but my anger stems not from those who were so deceived by the theory of evolution, and atheism they thought it acceptable and even pleasurable to murder me by incompatible blood transfusion and when that failed by suffocation (I actually died twice from each of the attempts and was resuscitated both times to the chagrin of the mass murdering doctors and nurses involved; and my now ex-wife www.blastthetrumpet.org); but my rage comes from the fact that innocent little children are being brainwashed with that garbage (called the theory of evolution and atheism) in the first place; and that if somehow the Lord doesn't shine into their lives; they will remain in the miserable existence of the darkness of ignorance that leads to the everlasting flames of damnation. So my passion, whether it comes through by giving those so arrogant they disdain all who testify of the Creator, a taste of their own medicine http://biblehub.com/psalms/18-26.htm, or when I am so truly motivated toward the Salvation of all souls that I beseech everyone to seek to KNOW THE CREATOR here and now and forever, in such a way that it seems to be practically begging; it is all because http://biblehub.com/1_corinthians/9-22.htm that I will do anything honorable http://www.facebook.com/notes/michael-swenson/i-am-deeply-concerned-for-all-souls/511111612301136, God allows, to try my best to persuade all souls to call upon the Resurrected Messiah, Yahoshuah, aka the LORD JESUS CHRIST, right now everywhere until they KNOW beyond all doubt He has answered them to their present and Everlasting Joy!

All of the ancient history is well-verified! The cradle of civilization is exactly where Noah's ark came to rest. It all traces straight down to Jesus Christ who showed Himself to mankind and proved Himself to mankind. We have a GOD! no ifs, ands, or buts! You must repent and receive Him or be lost in realms of delusions. Do not harden your heart toward God! God is fulfilling ever single word of scripture!

Education began with the Church of Jesus Christ! In His Word, He instructs ALL CHILDREN to be made aware of His Existence and His Commandments! Ever since He gave them His Disciples, their numbers grew, and despite opposition they prospered. They mandated Children be taught and their monasteries became universities over time teaching students from the Words of God in the Holy Bible and from studying God's Creation. All the oldest universities were founded by our Creator and to be taught worldwide! They all have mottos that signify His Truth. IT IS A CRYING SHAME THAT THE EDUCATION SYSTEM FOUNDED BY OUR ETERNAL CREATOR HAS BEEN RIPPED ALWAY BY GOD DENYING ANTICHRISTS WHO ARE LYING TO OUR CHILDREN! Demand public education be put back in the hands of God and His People, Christians!

Our scriptures FOUNDED the age of reason and enlightenment! The Holy Bible is the reason other modern books came into existence! The Gutenberg Printing Press for the Gutenberg Bible! Thereafter other books came into existence and founded the age of Reason and Enlightenment!

http://www.blastthetrumpet.org/PublicLetters/AAAUpdatedPublicAlertsMattersofLifeandDeath/Updates053016/Fathers%20of%20the%20Sciences%20and%20Great%20Scientific%20Minds.pdf - This is the reason the founding fathers and the vast majority of Nobel Prize winning scientist were all Biblical monotheists. They knew that the God of Wonders has stored up within Himself all the treasure of Wisdom and Knowledge. (Col 2:3)

In all ways, our nation owes its freedom and rights to God and His Commandments in the Holy Bible! We are founded upon Him and His Commandments and those brave souls fought and died to make our nation free! Number 1 on the Bill of Rights is the right to freedom OF religion and to free speech to declare it. The founders knew that as long as the Gospel of Jesus Christ had free sway to be declared and adhered to, it would prevail. And so, they made certain that should anyone try take away that first amendment on the bill of rights, that the second amendment on the bill of rights ensured everyone had the right to bear arms. The first and second amendments were all about Jesus Christ and His Commandments in the Holy Bible and the responsibility of those who know Him, to keep our nation and its citizens free!

"That he is the best friend to American liberty, who is most sincere and active in promoting true and undefiled religion, and who sets himself with the greatest firmness to bear down profanity and immorality of every kind. Whoever is an avowed enemy to God, I scruple not to call him an enemy to his country." John Witherspoon
https://oll.libertyfund.org/pages/1776-witherspoon-dominion-of-providence-over-the-passions-of-men-sermon

https://christianheritagefellowship.com/christian-quotes-from-the-founding-fathers-2/

It is clear that freedom FROM religion is a subversive and treasonous organization by the quotes from our founding fathers. It is also very clear that we need to put the Holy Bible BACK WHERE IT BELONGS in our public schools!

http://www.blastthetrumpet.org/PublicLetters/AAAUpdatedPublicAlertsMattersofLifeandDeath/Updates053016/Americans%20and%20Citizens%20of%20the%20World%20FREEDOM%20and%20LIFE%20Comes%20from%20GOD.pdf

Ever since we began dummying down children with God denying jargon/lies in our public schools we are suffering! Our nation as a whole is going downhill fast! We MUST return to God and Esteem and Obey His Commandments given us in the Holy Bible or great suffering is due us for deliberately turning our back on him as a nation! (Duet 28)

PUT THE HOLY BIBLE BACK IN OUR PUBLIC SCHOOLS NOW! Everyone NEEDS to KNOW and Learn from our Eternal Creator, Jesus Christ, for our own good! Removing the Truthful Knowledge of God, Jesus Christ, and His Words, only means that lies will be taught children instead, as generations of deceived children now prove.

Toss out all that garbage taught wrongly today, turning students from our Eternal Creator AND PUT THE TRUTH BACK INTO OUR SCHOOLS! God and His Words in the Holy Bible is that Truth!

https://www.youtube.com/playlist?list=PLEVsU6O-XMpGHKna3DpTkYPkn5kZ0MVy5 – scientific documentaries for the history contained in Genesis Vol 1) all creation verifies His Words in the Holy Bible because that is the TRUTH!

https://www.youtube.com/watch?v=ZpM6_luzX-E&list=PLEVsU6O-XMpG_bxzfI68CZhPy9f4TqN2y – Vol 2

https://www.youtube.com/playlist?list=PLEVsU6O-XMpGp3x9qnWu7Ndt4i9psZYMA – Vol 3

Jesus the Christ not only proved Himself as being the One True God FAR ABOVE all other claims in history from anyone else but because He is Eternal; He EVER LIVES to VERIFY His Words to us, His Gospel Message, the HOLY BIBLE. God and God Alone is our Savior; Jesus Christ is the One True God who Forgives us because He Alone Redeemed us by His Own Holy Blood, no one else! Acts 4:12; 10:34-43, 1Pet 1:18-20 You must REPENT of thinking you know better than God on anything. You must all be ready to listen to and obey Him and His Commandments given us all, in the Holy Bible. When you repent and are baptized in His Name, He Gives you His Holy Spirit of Truth! Acts 2:39-39 When God gives you His Holy Spirit of Truth you will know Him as your Father! Rom 8:14-16 The Holy Bible is verifiably true that way by anyone. Jn 14:6-26; 17:17 Tell everyone you can until everyone Knows the Living Lord Jesus Christ! Truly the Holy Bible is PROVABLY and VERIFIABLY Divinely Inspired.

Copyright 2024

www.ingramcontent.com/pod-product-compliance
Lightning Source LLC
Chambersburg PA
CBHW072002150426
43194CB00008B/973